GREGG
College Keyboarding

OBER
JOHNSON
ZIMMERLY

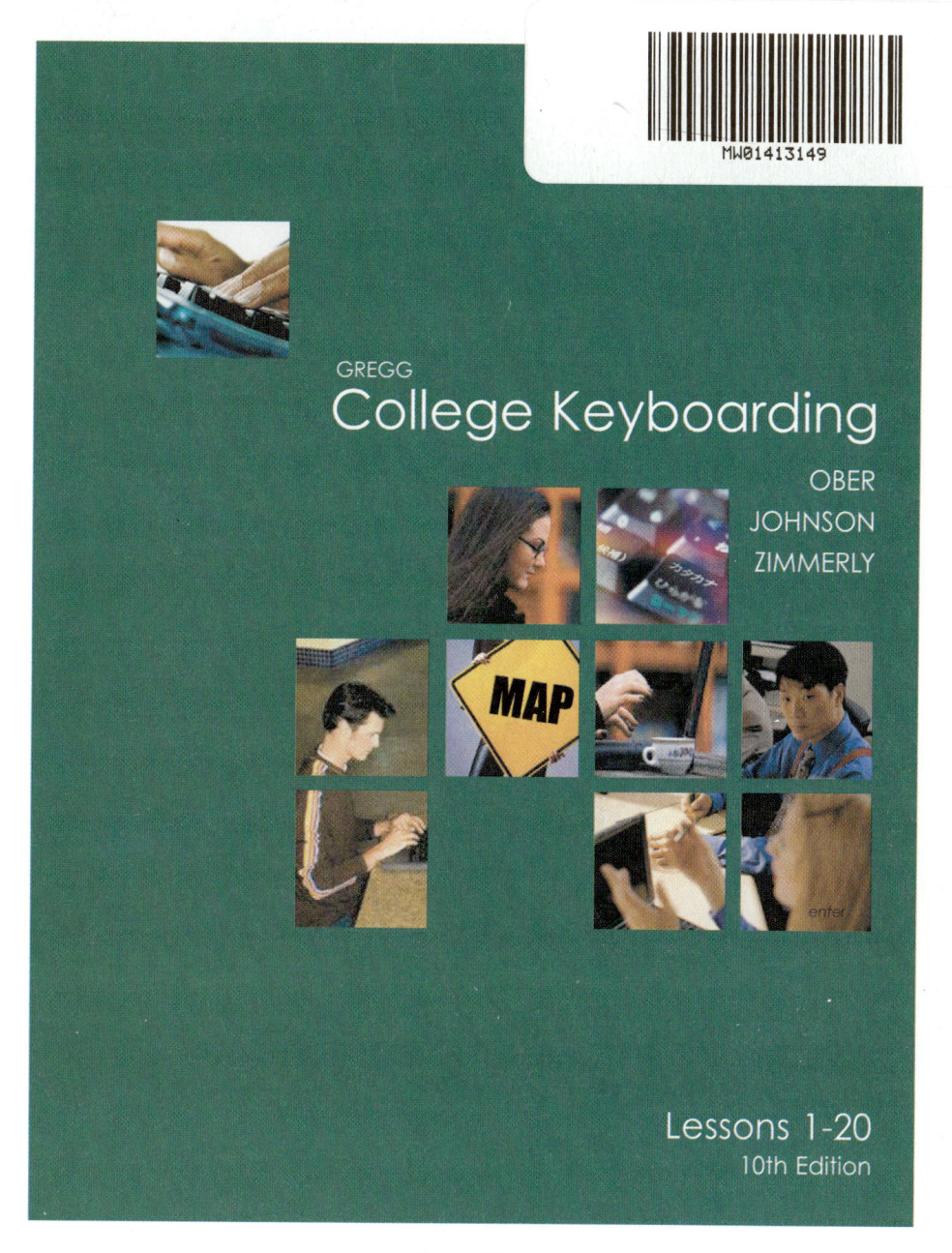

Lessons 1-20
10th Edition

Scot Ober
Ball State University

Jack E. Johnson
State University of West Georgia

Arlene Zimmerly
Los Angeles City College

Visit the *College Keyboarding* Web site at **www.mhhe.com/gdp**

McGraw-Hill Irwin

Boston   Burr Ridge, IL   Dubuque, IA   Madison, WI   New York   San Francisco   St. Louis
Bangkok   Bogotá   Caracas   Kuala Lumpur   Lisbon   London   Madrid   Mexico City
Milan   Montreal   New Delhi   Santiago   Seoul   Singapore   Sydney   Taipei   Toronto

McGraw-Hill Irwin

GREGG COLLEGE KEYBOARDING, LESSONS 1–20
Published by McGraw-Hill/Irwin, a business unit of The McGraw-Hill Companies, Inc., 1221 Avenue of the Americas, New York, NY, 10020. Copyright © 2006, 2002, 1997, 1994, 1989, 1984, 1979, 1970, 1964, 1957 by The McGraw-Hill Companies, Inc. All rights reserved. No part of this publication may be reproduced or distributed in any form or by any means, or stored in a database or retrieval system, without the prior written consent of The McGraw-Hill Companies, Inc., including, but not limited to, in any network or other electronic storage or transmission, or broadcast for distance learning.

Some ancillaries, including electronic and print components, may not be available to customers outside the United States.

This book is printed on acid-free paper.

Printed in the United States
 7 8 9 0 WDQ/WDQ 12 11 10
ISBN-13: 978-0-07-296340-3
ISBN-10: 0-07-296340-9

Editorial director: *John E. Biernat*
Publisher: *Linda Schreiber*
Sponsoring editor: *Doug Hughes*
Developmental editor: *Tammy Higham*
Developmental editor: *Megan Gates*
Marketing manager: *Keari Bedford*
Lead producer, Media technology: *Victoria Bryant*
Lead project manager: *Pat Frederickson*
Freelance project manager: *Rich Wright*
Senior production supervisor: *Michael R. McCormick*
Lead designer: *Matthew Baldwin*
Photo research coordinator: *Lori Kramer*
Senior supplement producer: *Susan Lombardi*
Senior digital content specialist: *Brian Nacik*
Cover design: *Subtle Intensity*
Interior design: *Matthew Baldwin*
Typeface: *11/12 Times Roman*
Compositor: *Seven Worldwide Publishing Solutions*
Printer: *Worldcolor*

www.mhhe.com

CONTENTS

Preface v
Introduction to the Student vii
About Your Book ix
Reference Manual R-1–R-22

**PART ONE:
The Alphabet, Number, and Symbol Keys**

UNIT 1 KEYBOARDING: THE ALPHABET 2
1 Home Keys: Space Bar Enter A S D F J K L ; 3
2 New Keys: H E O R 5
3 New Keys: M T P C 7
4 New Keys: Right Shift V . W 9
5 Review 11

UNIT 2 KEYBOARDING: THE ALPHABET 13
6 New Keys: I Left Shift - G 14
7 New Keys: U B : X 16
8 New Keys: Y , Q / 18
9 New Keys: N Z ? Tab 20
10 Review 23

UNIT 3 KEYBOARDING: THE NUMBERS 25
11 Number Keys: 5 7 3 9 26
12 Review 28
13 Number Keys: 8 2 0 30
14 Number Keys: 4 6 1 32
15 Review 34

UNIT 4 KEYBOARDING: THE SYMBOLS 36
16 Symbol Keys: $ ( ) ! 37
17 Review 39
18 Symbol Keys: * # ' 41
19 Symbol Keys: & % " @ 43
20 Review 46

SKILLBUILDING

Diagnostic Practice: Symbols and Punctuation SB-2–SB-4
Diagnostic Practice: Numbers SB-5–SB-6
Progressive Practice: Alphabet SB-7–SB-10
Progressive Practice: Numbers SB-11–SB-13
Paced Practice SB-14–SB-27
Supplementary Timed Writings SB-28–SB-36

APPENDIX

Ten-Key Numeric Keypad A-1–A-3

INDEX I-1–I-6

McGraw-Hill/Irwin and the GDP author team would like to acknowledge the participants of the 2004 Focus Group for their efforts in making the 10th edition the best it can be:

Special thanks goes to Ken Baker for his work as the tech editor on GDP.

Kim Aylett
Branford Hall Career Institute
Southington, CT

Ken Baker
Sinclair Community College
Dayton, OH

Lenette Baker
Valencia Community College
Orlando, FL

Joyce Crawford
Central Piedmont Community College
Charlotte, NC

Martha Gwatney
Northern Virginia Community College
Annandale, VA

Marijean Harmonis
Community College of Philadelphia
Philadelphia, PA

Mary Hedberg
Johnson County Community College
Overland Park, KS

Kay Ono
Leeward Community College
Pearl City, HI

Marcia Polanis
Forsyth Tech Community College
Winston-Salem, NC

Photo Credits
Ryan McVay/Getty Images iii, R-23, 42; Royalty Free/Getty Images R-2

PREFACE

Gregg College Keyboarding & Document Processing Lessons 1–120, 10th Edition, is a multi-component instructional program designed to give the student and the instructor a high degree of flexibility and a high degree of success in meeting their respective goals. For student and instructor convenience, the core components of this instructional system are available in either a kit format or a book format. *Gregg College Keyboarding Lessons 1–20, 10th Edition,* is also available for the development of touch-typing skills for use in shorter computer keyboarding classes.

The Kit Format

Gregg College Keyboarding & Document Processing Lessons 1–120, 10th Edition, provides a complete kit of materials for both courses in the keyboarding curriculum generally offered by colleges. Each kit, which is briefly described below, contains a softcover textbook and a student word processing manual.

Kit 1: Lessons 1–60. This kit provides the text and word processing manual for the first course. Since this kit is designed for the beginning student, its major objectives are to develop touch control of the keyboard and proper typing techniques, to build basic speed and accuracy, and to provide practice in applying those basic skills to the formatting of reports, letters, memos, tables, and other kinds of personal and business communications.

Kit 2: Lessons 61–120. This kit provides the text and word processing manual for the second course. This course continues developing of basic typing skills and emphasizes the formatting of various kinds of business correspondence, reports, tables, electronic forms, and desktop publishing projects from arranged, unarranged, and rough-draft sources.

The Book Format

For the convenience of those who wish to obtain the core instructional materials in separate volumes, *Gregg College Keyboarding & Document Processing Lessons 1–120, 10th Edition,* offers textbooks for the first course: *Gregg College Keyboarding & Document Processing Lessons 1–60, 10th Edition,* or *Gregg College Keyboarding Lessons 1–20, 10th Edition.* For the second course, *Gregg College Document Processing Lessons 61–120* is offered, and for the two-semester course, *Gregg College Keyboarding & Document Processing Lessons 1–120* is available. In each instance, the content of the textbooks is identical to that of the corresponding textbooks in kit format. Third semester instruction is available in *Gregg College Document Processing Lessons 121–180.*

Supporting Materials

Gregg College Keyboarding & Document Processing Lessons 1–120, 10th Edition, includes the following additional components:

Instructional Materials. Supporting materials are provided for instructor use with either the kits or the textbooks. The special Instructor Wraparound Edition (IWE) offers lesson plans and reduced-size student pages to enhance classroom instruction. Distance-learning tips, instructional methodology, adult learner strategies, and special needs features are also included in this wraparound edition. Solution keys for all of the formatting exercises in Lessons 1–180 are contained in separate booklets used with this program. Finally, test booklets are available with the objective tests and alternative document processing tests for each part.

Computer Software. PC-compatible computer software is available for the entire program. The computer software provides complete lesson-by-lesson instruction for the entire 120 lessons.

Structure

Gregg College Keyboarding & Document Processing, 10th Edition, opens with a two-page part opener that introduces students to the focus of the instruction. Objectives are presented, and opportunities within career clusters are highlighted. The unit opener familiarizes students with the lesson content to be presented in the five lessons in the unit.

Every lesson begins with a Warmup that should be typed as soon as students are settled at the keyboard. In the New Keys Section, all alphabet, number, and symbol keys are introduced in the first 20 lessons. Drill lines in this section provide the practice necessary to achieve keyboarding skills.

An easily identifiable Skillbuilding section can be found in every lesson. Each drill presents to the student a variety of different activities designed to improve speed and accuracy. Skillbuilding exercises include Technique Timings, Diagnostic Practice, Paced Practice, Progressive Practice, MAP (Misstroke Analysis and Prescription), and Timed Writings, which progress from 1 to 5 minutes in length.

Many of the Skillbuilding sections also include a Pretest/Practice/Posttest routine. This routine is designed to build speed and accuracy skills as well as confidence. The Pretest helps identify speed and accuracy needs. The Practice activities consist of a variety of intensive enrichment drills. Finally, the Posttest measures improvement.

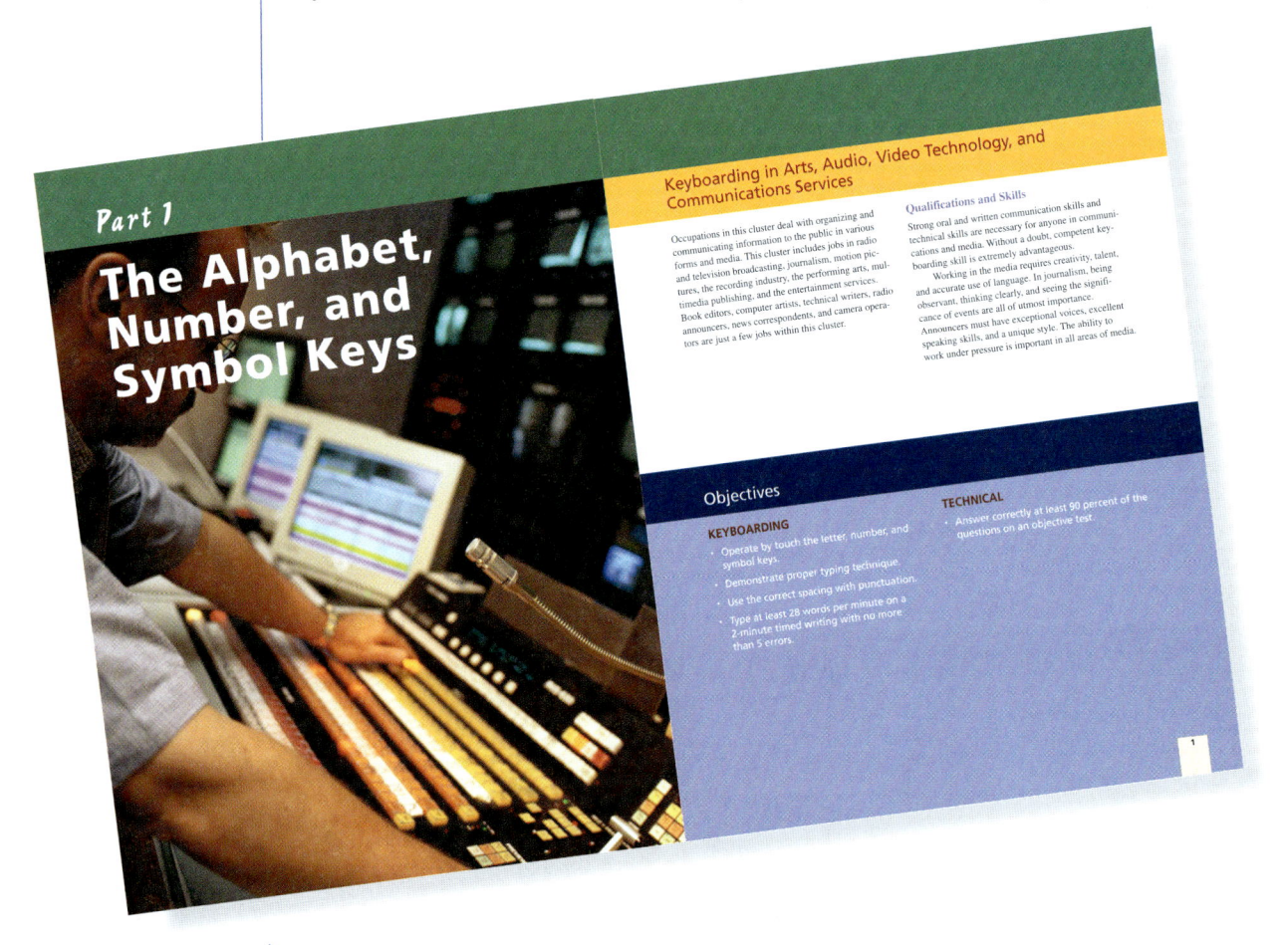

INTRODUCTION TO THE STUDENT

Goals
- Type at least 30wpm/3'/5e
- Format one-page business reports

Starting a Lesson

Each lesson begins with the goals for that lesson. Read the goals carefully so that you understand the purpose of your practice. In the example at the left (from Lesson 26), the goals for the lesson are to type 30wpm (words per minute) on a 3-minute timed writing with no more than 5 errors and to format one-page business reports.

Building Straight-Copy Skill

Warmups. Each lesson begins with a Warmup that reinforces learned alphabet, number, and/or symbol keys.

Skillbuilding. The Skillbuilding portion of each lesson includes a variety of drills to individualize your keyboarding speed and accuracy development. Instructions for completing the drills are always provided beside each activity.

Additional Skillbuilding drills are included in the back of the textbook. These drills are intended to help you meet your individual goals.

Measuring Straight-Copy Skill

Straight-copy skill is measured in wpm. All timed writings are the exact length needed to meet the speed goal for the lesson. If you finish a timed writing before time is up, you have automatically reached your speed goal for the lesson.

Counting Errors. Specific criteria are used for counting errors. Count an error when:

1. Any stroke is incorrect.
2. Any punctuation after a word is incorrect or omitted. Count the word before the punctuation as incorrect.
3. The spacing after a word or after its punctuation is incorrect. Count the word as incorrect.
4. A letter or word is omitted.
5. A letter or word is repeated.
6. A direction about spacing, indenting, and so on, is violated.
7. Words are transposed.

(**Note:** Only one error is counted for each word, no matter how many errors it may contain.)

Determining Speed. Typing speed is measured in wpm. To compute wpm, count every 5 strokes, including spaces, as 1 "word." Horizontal word scales below an activity divide lines into 5-stroke words. Vertical word scales beside an activity show the number of words in each line cumulatively totaled. For example, in the illustration below, if you complete a line, you have typed 8 words. If you complete 2 lines, you have typed 16 words. Use the bottom word scale to determine the word count of a partial line. Add that number to the cumulative total for the last complete line.

```
23  Ada lost her letter; Dee lost her card.         8
24  Dave sold some of the food to a market.        16
25  Alva asked Walt for three more matches.        24
26  Dale asked Seth to watch the last show.        32
    |  1  |  2  |  3  |  4  |  5  |  6  |  7  |  8  |
```

Correcting Errors

As you learn to type, you will probably make some errors. To correct an error, press BACKSPACE (shown as ← on some keyboards) to delete the incorrect character. Then type the correct character.

If you notice an error on a different line, use the up, down, left, or right arrows to move the insertion point immediately to the left or right of the error. Press BACKSPACE to delete a character to the left of the insertion point, or DELETE to delete a character to the right of the insertion point. Error-correction settings in the GDP software determine whether you can correct errors in timed writings and drills. Consult your instructor for error-correction guidelines.

Typing Technique

Correct position at the keyboard enables you to type with greater speed and accuracy and with less fatigue. When typing for a long period, rest your eyes occasionally by looking away from the screen. Change position, walk around, or stretch when your muscles feel tired. Making such movements and adjustments may help prevent your body from becoming too tired. In addition, long-term bodily damage, such as carpal tunnel syndrome, can be prevented.

If possible, adjust your workstation as follows:

Chair. Adjust the height so that your upper and lower legs form a 90-degree angle and your lower back is supported by the back of the chair.
Keyboard. Center your body opposite the J key, and lean forward slightly. Keep your forearms horizontal to the keyboard.
Screen. Position the monitor so that the top of the screen is just below eye level and about 18 to 26 inches away.
Text. Position your textbook or other copy on either side of the monitor as close to it as vertically and horizontally possible to minimize head and eye movement and to avoid neck strain.

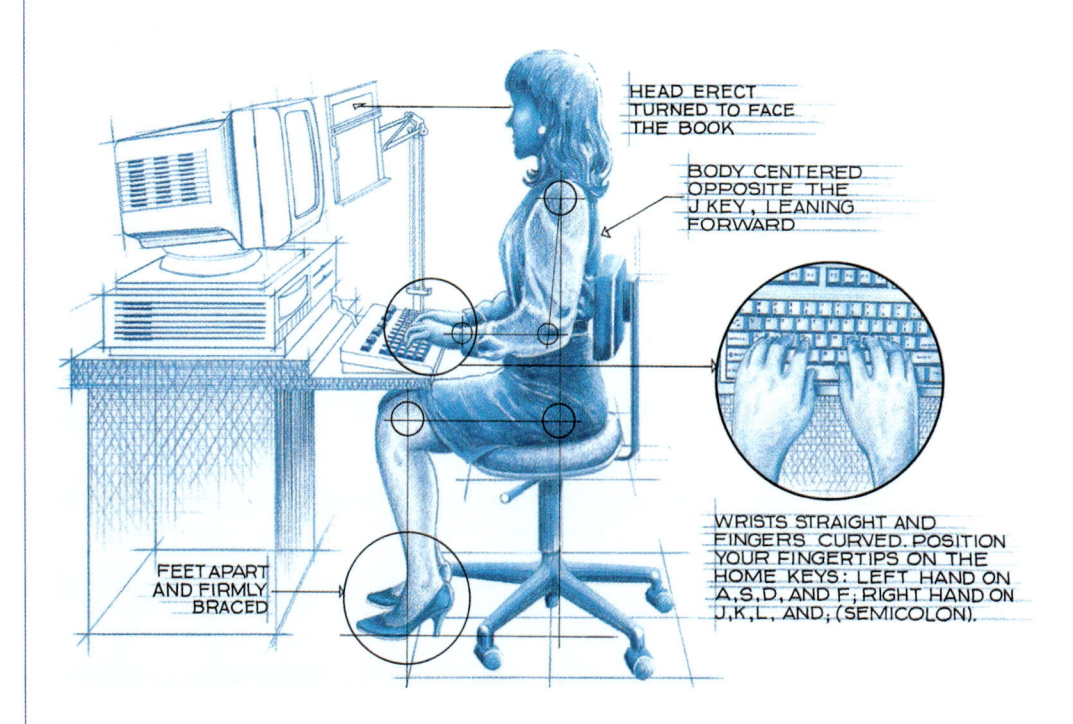

ABOUT YOUR BOOK

Unit 1

Keyboarding: The Alphabet

LESSON 1
A S D F J K L ;
ENTER   SPACE BAR

LESSON 2
H E O R

LESSON 3
M T P C

LESSON 4
RIGHT SHIFT V . W

LESSON 5
Review

> The **Unit Opener** helps you organize your study of unit concepts. The listing of the lessons clearly previews what will be taught in the unit.

New Keys

Lesson 4

Goals
- Touch-type the RIGHT SHIFT, V, period, and W keys
- Count errors
- Type at least 13wpm/1'/3e

A. Type 2 times.

A. WARMUP

1 the farmer asked her to feed the mares;
2 the late callers came to mop the floor;

NEW KEYS

B. Type each line 2 times.

Use the Sem finger.
SHIFT

B. THE RIGHT SHIFT KEY

To capitalize letters on the left half of the keyboard:
1. With the J finger at home, press and hold down the RIGHT SHIFT key with the Sem finger.
2. Press the letter key.
3. Release the RIGHT SHIFT key and return fingers to home position.

3 ;;; ;A; ;A; ;;; ;S; ;S; ;;; ;D; ;D; ;;;
4 Art Alf Ada Sal Sam Dee Dot Flo Ted Tom
   Carl Chet Elsa Fred Sara Todd Elda
   Amos took Sara Carter to the races

KEY

  fvf vfv fff fvf fvf vfv fff fvf
  Eva vet Ava vat Eve ova Vel vee
  se Vera ever vast Reva dove vest
  ted for Vassar; Val voted for me

KEY

  1.1 .1. 111 1.1 1.1 .1. 111 1.1
  ea. ea. sr. sr. Dr. Dr. Sr. Sr.
  A.D. p.m. Corp. amt. Dr. Co.
  t. Dave left. Sarah came home.

UNIT 1   Lesson 4   9

> **Color Coding** is used in the early lessons to help you differentiate which finger is used. On the keyboard chart shown at the beginning of each new-key lesson, new keys are highlighted, previously learned keys are labeled but not highlighted, and unlearned keys are blank. You will have a sense of progress as you move through the 20 new-key lessons.

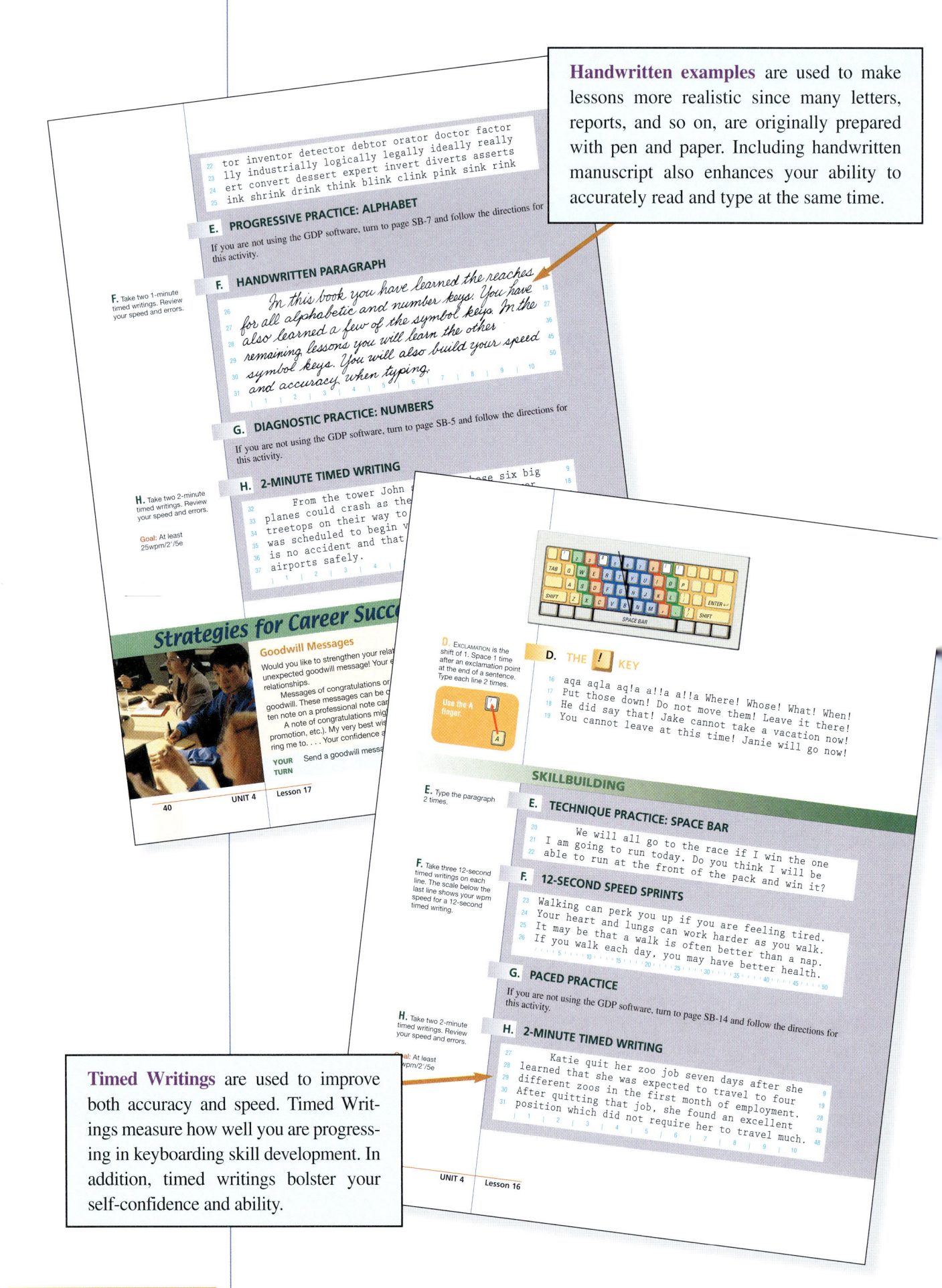

Handwritten examples are used to make lessons more realistic since many letters, reports, and so on, are originally prepared with pen and paper. Including handwritten manuscript also enhances your ability to accurately read and type at the same time.

```
22  tor inventor detector debtor orator doctor factor
23  lly industrially logically legally ideally really
24  ert convert dessert expert invert diverts asserts
25  ink shrink drink think blink clink pink sink rink
```

E. PROGRESSIVE PRACTICE: ALPHABET

If you are not using the GDP software, turn to page SB-7 and follow the directions for this activity.

F. Take two 1-minute timed writings. Review your speed and errors.

F. HANDWRITTEN PARAGRAPH

In this book you have learned the reaches for all alphabetic and number keys. You have also learned a few of the symbol keys. In the remaining lessons you will learn the other symbol keys. You will also build your speed and accuracy when typing.

G. DIAGNOSTIC PRACTICE: NUMBERS

If you are not using the GDP software, turn to page SB-5 and follow the directions for this activity.

H. 2-MINUTE TIMED WRITING

H. Take two 2-minute timed writings. Review your speed and errors.

Goal: At least 25wpm/2'/5e

```
    From the tower John ... these six big
planes could crash as the ...
treetops on their way to ...
was scheduled to begin v...
is no accident and that ...
airports safely.
```

D. EXCLAMATION is the shift of 1. Space 1 time after an exclamation point at the end of a sentence. Type each line 2 times.

Use the A finger.

D. THE ! KEY

```
16  aqa aqla aq!a a!!a a!!a Where! Whose! What! When!
17  Put those down! Do not move them! Leave it there!
18  He did say that! Jake cannot take a vacation now!
19  You cannot leave at this time! Janie will go now!
```

SKILLBUILDING

E. Type the paragraph 2 times.

E. TECHNIQUE PRACTICE: SPACE BAR

```
20      We will all go to the race if I win the one
21  I am going to run today. Do you think I will be
22  able to run at the front of the pack and win it?
```

F. Take three 12-second timed writings on each line. The scale below the last line shows your wpm speed for a 12-second timed writing.

F. 12-SECOND SPEED SPRINTS

```
23  Walking can perk you up if you are feeling tired.
24  Your heart and lungs can work harder as you walk.
25  It may be that a walk is often better than a nap.
26  If you walk each day, you may have better health.
```

G. PACED PRACTICE

If you are not using the GDP software, turn to page SB-14 and follow the directions for this activity.

H. Take two 2-minute timed writings. Review your speed and errors.

H. 2-MINUTE TIMED WRITING

Goal: At least wpm/2'/5e

```
27      Katie quit her zoo job seven days after she
28  learned that she was expected to travel to four
29  different zoos in the first month of employment.
30  After quitting that job, she found an excellent
31  position which did not require her to travel much.
```

Strategies for Career Success

Goodwill Messages

Would you like to strengthen your rela... unexpected goodwill message! Your ... relationships.

Messages of congratulations or ... goodwill. These messages can be c... ten note on a professional note car...

A note of congratulations mig... promotion, etc.). My very best wis... ring me to. . . . Your confidence a...

YOUR TURN Send a goodwill mess...

Timed Writings are used to improve both accuracy and speed. Timed Writings measure how well you are progressing in keyboarding skill development. In addition, timed writings bolster your self-confidence and ability.

Lesson 17

Review

Goal
- Type at least 25wpm/2'/5e

A. Type 2 times.

A. WARMUP
1 Yes! We object to the dumping of 25 toxic   9
2 barrels at 4098 Nix Street. A larger number (36) 19
3 were dumped on the 7th, costing us over $10,000. 28
   | 1 | 2 | 3 | 4 | 5 | 6 | 7 | 8 | 9 | 10

SKILLBUILDING

B. Type each line 2 times.

B. NUMBER PRACTICE
4 we 23 pi 08 you 697 row 492 tire 5843 power 09234
5 or 94 re 43 eye 363 top 590 quit 1785 witty 28556
6 up 70 ye 63 pit 085 per 034 root 4995 wrote 24953
7 it 85 ro 49 rip 480 two 529 tour 5974 quite 17853
8 yi 68 to 59 toy 596 rot 495 tier 5834 queue 17373
9 op 90 qo 19 wet 235 pet 035 rope 4903 quote 17953

C. Type each line 2 times.

C. WORD BEGINNINGS
10 tri trinkets tribune trifle trick trial trip trim
11 mil million mileage mildew mills milky miles mild
12 spo sponsor sponge sports spore spo
13 for forgiving forbear forwar
14 div dividend division divine
15 vic vicinity vicious victory
16 aff affliction affiliates aff
17 tab tablecloth tabulates table

D. Type each line 2 times.

D. WORD ENDINGS
18 ive repulsive explosive alive
19 est nearest invest attest wises
20 ply supply simply deeply damply
21 ver whenever forever whoever qu

Skillbuilding practice in every lesson offers an individualized plan for speed and accuracy development. A variety of skill-building exercises, including Technique Practice, Pretest/Practice/Posttest, Sustained Practice, 12-Second Speed Sprints, Diagnostic Practice, Progressive Practice, Paced Practice, and Number Practice, provide the foundation for progress in your skill development.

The Reference Manual material found in the front of the book and in the Word manual enables you to easily locate information regarding the proper way to format business letters, reports, e-mail messages, memoranda, and other forms of written communication. Elements such as line spacing and the placement of letterhead and body text are all illustrated in detail for your instructional support. In addition, 50 "must-know" rules for language arts in business contexts are included with examples in the Reference Manual to help improve writing skills.

Reference Manual

COMPUTER SYSTEM
keyboard, R-2B
parts of, R-2A

CORRESPONDENCE
application letter, R-12B
attachment notation, R-4D
blind copy notation, R-5B
block style, R-3A
body, R-3A
company name, R-5B
complimentary closing, R-3A
copy notation, R-3C, R-5B
date line, R-3A
delivery notation, R-4A, R-5B
e-mail, R-5C-D
enclosure notation, R-3B, R-5B
envelope formatting, R-6A
executive stationery, R-4A
half-page stationery, R-4B
inside address, R-3A
international address, R-3D
letter folding, R-6B
letterhead, R-3A
lists, R-3B-C, R-12C-D
memo, R-4D
modified-block style, R-3B
multipage, R-5A-B
on-arrival notation, R-5A
open punctuation, R-3B
page number, R-5B
personal-business, R-3D
postscript notation, R-5B
reference initials, R-3A, R-5B
return address, R-3D
salutation, R-3A
simplified style, R-3C
standard punctuation, R-3A, R-3D
subject line, R-3C, R-5A, R-7C
table, R-4D
window envelope, folding for, R-6B
window envelope, formatted for, R-4C
writer's identification, R-3A

EMPLOYMENT DOCUMENTS
application letter, R-12B
resume, R-12A

FORMS
R-14A

LANGUAGE ARTS
abbreviations, R-22
adjectives and adverbs, R-20
agreement, R-19
apostrophes, R-17
capitalization, R-21
colons, R-18
commas, R-15 to R-16
grammar, R-19 to R-20
hyphens, R-17
italics (or underline), R-18
mechanics, R-21 to R-22
number expression, R-21 to R-22
periods, R-18
pronouns, R-20
punctuation, R-15 to R-18
quotation marks, R-18
semicolons, R-16
sentences, R-19
underline (or italics), R-18
word usage, R-20

PROOFREADERS' MARKS
R-14C

REPORTS
academic style, R-8C-D
agenda, R-11A
APA style, R-10A-B
author/year citations, R-10A
bibliography, R-9B
business style, R-8A-B, R-9A
byline, R-8A
citations, R-9D
date, R-8A
endnotes, R-8C-D
footnotes, R-8A-B
headings, R-9D
headings, paragraph, R-8A
headings, side, R-8A
itinerary, R-11C
left-bound, R-9A
legal document, R-11D
lists, R-8A, R-8C, R-12D
margins, R-9D
memo report, R-9C
minutes of a meeting, R-11B
MLA style, R-10C-D
outline, R-7A
quotation, long, R-8B, R-8D
references page, R-10B
resume, R-12A
spacing, R-9D
subtitle, R-8A
table, R-8B
table of contents, R-7D
title, R-8A
title page, R-7B
transmittal memo, R-7C
works-cited page, R-10D

TABLES
2-line column heading, R-13B
body, R-13A
boxed, R-13A
capitalization in columns, R-13D
column headings, R-13A-D
in correspondence, R-4D, R-5A
dollar signs, R-13D
heading block, R-13D
note, R-13A
open, R-13B
percent signs, R-13D
in reports, R-8B, R-13C
ruled, R-13C
subtitle, R-13A, R-13D
table number, R-13C
table source, R-8B
title, R-13A
total line, R-13A, R13-D
vertical placement, R-13D

U.S. POSTAL SERVICE STATE ABBREVIATIONS
R-14B

Reference Manual

A. MAJOR PARTS OF A MICROCOMPUTER SYSTEM

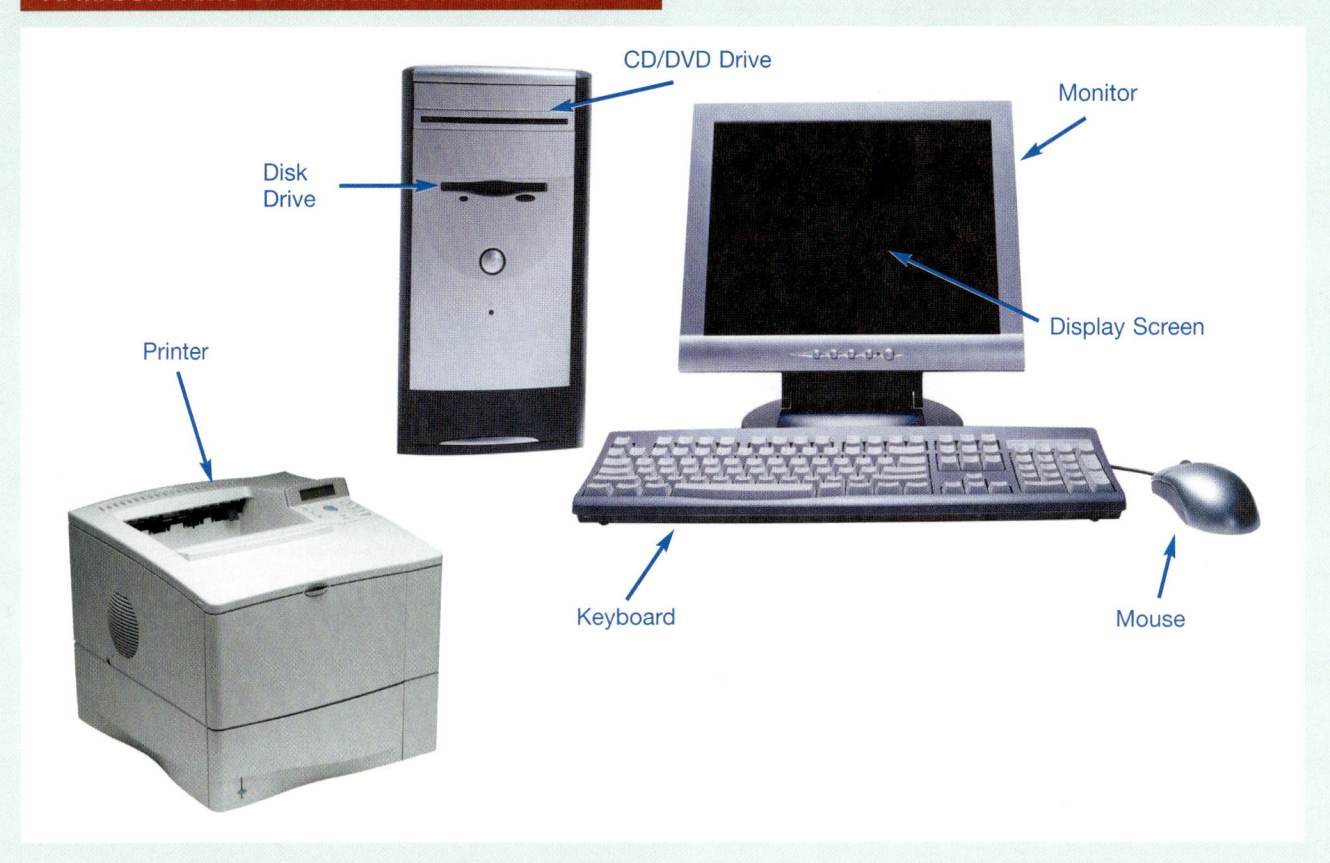

B. THE COMPUTER KEYBOARD

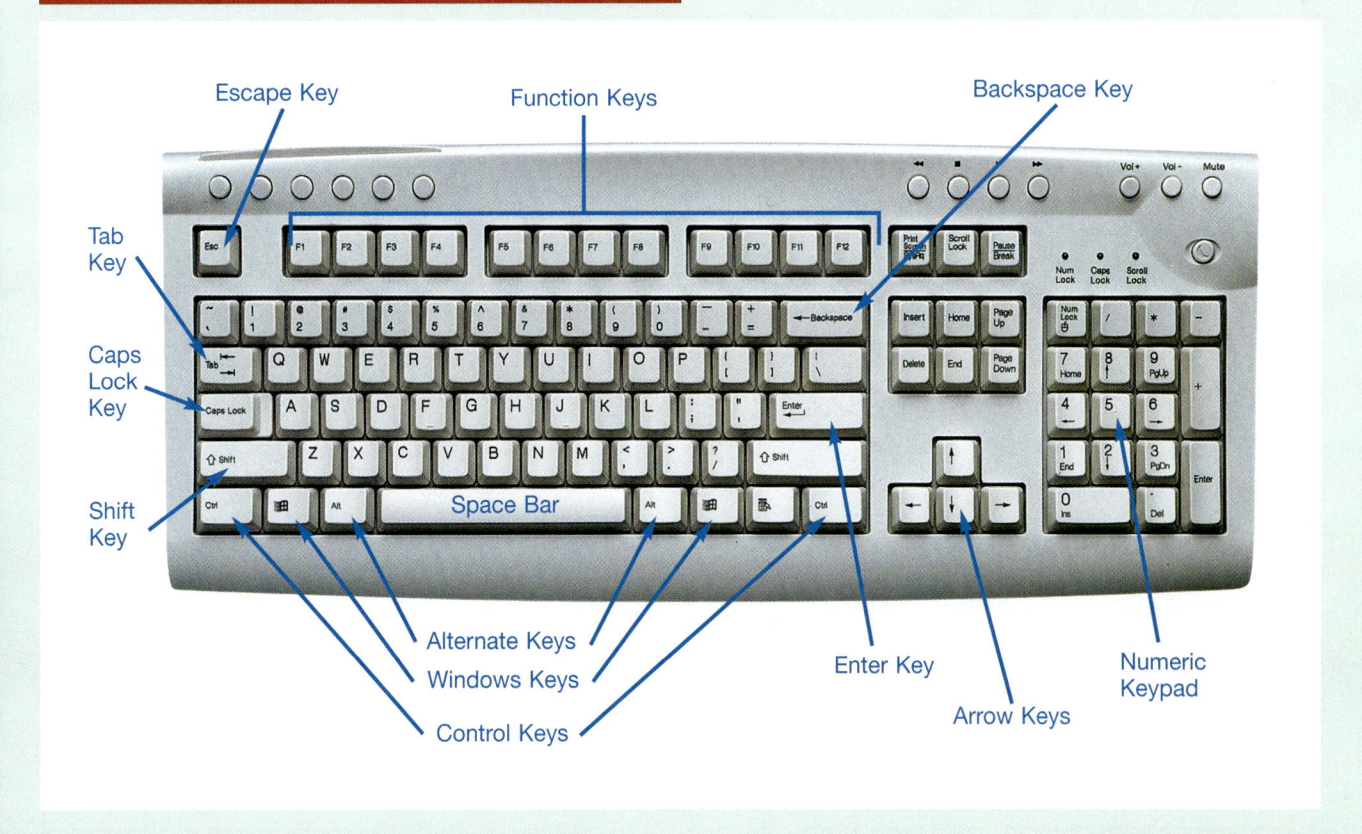

Reference Manual   R-2

Reference Manual

A. BUSINESS LETTER IN BLOCK STYLE
(with standard punctuation)

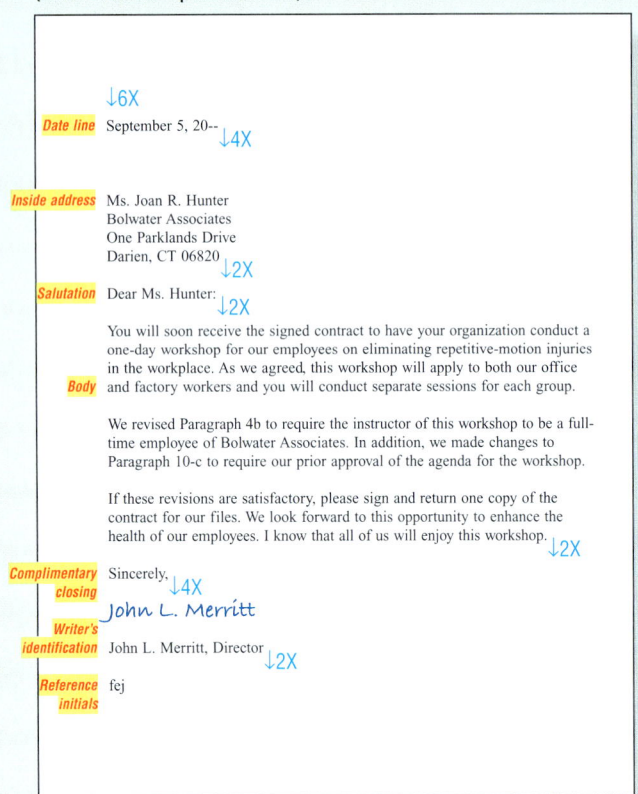

Date line — ↓6X
September 5, 20-- ↓4X

Inside address — Ms. Joan R. Hunter
Bolwater Associates
One Parklands Drive
Darien, CT 06820 ↓2X

Salutation — Dear Ms. Hunter: ↓2X

Body — You will soon receive the signed contract to have your organization conduct a one-day workshop for our employees on eliminating repetitive-motion injuries in the workplace. As we agreed, this workshop will apply to both our office and factory workers and you will conduct separate sessions for each group.

We revised Paragraph 4b to require the instructor of this workshop to be a full-time employee of Bolwater Associates. In addition, we made changes to Paragraph 10-c to require our prior approval of the agenda for the workshop.

If these revisions are satisfactory, please sign and return one copy of the contract for our files. We look forward to this opportunity to enhance the health of our employees. I know that all of us will enjoy this workshop. ↓2X

Complimentary closing — Sincerely, ↓4X

John L. Merritt

Writer's identification — John L. Merritt, Director ↓2X

Reference initials — fej

B. BUSINESS LETTER IN MODIFIED-BLOCK STYLE
(with open punctuation, multiline list, and enclosure notation)

Left tab: 3"
↓6X
→tab to centerpoint   May 15, 20-- ↓4X

Mr. Ichiro Xie
Bolwater Associates
One Parklands Drive
Darien, CT 06820 ↓2X

Dear Mr. Xie ↓2X

I am returning a signed contract to have your organization conduct a one-day workshop for our employees on eliminating repetitive-motion injuries in the workplace. We have made the following changes to the contract:

Multiline list —
1. We revised Paragraph 4b to require the instructor of this workshop to be a full-time employee of Bolwater Associates.

2. We made changes to Paragraph 10-c to require our prior approval of the agenda for the workshop.

If these revisions are satisfactory, please sign and return one copy of the contract for our files. We look forward to this opportunity to enhance the health of our employees. I know that all of us will enjoy this workshop. ↓2X

→tab to centerpoint   Sincerely ↓4X

Reinalda Guerrero

Reinalda Guerrero, Director ↓2X

pec

Enclosure notation — Enclosure

C. BUSINESS LETTER IN SIMPLIFIED STYLE
(with single-line list, enclosure notation, and copy notation)

↓6X
October 5, 20-- ↓4X

Mr. Dale P. Griffin
Bolwater Associates
One Parklands Drive
Darien, CT 06820 ↓3X

Subject line — WORKSHOP CONTRACT ↓3X

I am returning the signed contract, Ms. Hunter, to have your organization conduct a one-day workshop for our employees on eliminating repetitive-motion injuries in the workplace. We have amended the following sections of the contract:

Single-line list —
• Paragraph 4b
• Table 3
• Attachment 2

If these revisions are satisfactory, please sign and return one copy of the contract for our files. We look forward to this opportunity to enhance the health of our employees. I know that all of us will enjoy this workshop. ↓4X

Kachina Haddad

KACHINA HADDAD, DIRECTOR ↓2X

iww
Enclosure

Copy notation — c: Legal Department

D. PERSONAL-BUSINESS LETTER IN MODIFIED-BLOCK STYLE
(with international address and standard punctuation)

Left tab: 3"
↓6X
→tab to centerpoint   July 15, 20-- ↓4X

Mr. Luis Fernandez, President
Arvon Industries, Inc.
21 St. Claire Avenue East

International Address — Toronto, ON M4T IL9
CANADA ↓2X

Dear Mr. Fernandez: ↓2X

As a former employee and present stockholder of Arvon Industries, I wish to protest the planned sale of the Consumer Products Division.

According to published reports, consumer products accounted for 19 percent of last year's corporate profits, and they are expected to account for even more this year. In addition, Dun & Bradstreet predicts that consumer products nationwide will outpace the general economy for the next five years.

I am concerned about the effect that this planned sale will have on overall corporate profits, on cash dividends for investors, and on the economy of Melbourne, where the two consumer-products plants are located. Please ask your board of directors to reconsider this matter. ↓2X

→tab to centerpoint   Sincerely, ↓4X

Roger J. Michaelson

Return address — Roger J. Michaelson
901 East Benson, Apt. 3
Fort Lauderdale, FL 33301

Reference Manual

A. BUSINESS LETTER ON EXECUTIVE STATIONERY

(7.25" x 10.5"; 1" side margins; with delivery notation and standard punctuation.)

↓6X

July 18, 20-- ↓4X

Mr. Rodney Eastwood
BBL Resources
52A Northern Ridge
Fayetteville, PA 17222 ↓2X

Dear Rodney: ↓2X

I see no reason why we should continue to consider the locality around Geraldton for our new plant. Even though the desirability of this site from an economic view is undeniable, there is insufficient housing readily available for our workers.

In trying to control urban growth, the city has been turning down the building permits for new housing or placing so many restrictions on foreign investment as to make it too expensive.

Please continue to seek out other areas of exploration where we might form a joint partnership. ↓2X

Sincerely, ↓4X

Dalit Chande

Dalit Chande
Vice President for Operations ↓2X

mme
By Fax *(Delivery notation)*

B. BUSINESS LETTER ON HALF-PAGE STATIONERY

(5.5" x 8.5"; 0.75" side margins and standard punctuation)

↓4X

July 18, 20-- ↓4X

Mr. Aristeo Olivas
BBL Resources
52A Northern Ridge
Fayetteville, PA 17222 ↓2X

Dear Aristeo: ↓2X

We should continue considering Geraldton for our new plant. Even though the desirability of this site from an economic view is undeniable, there is insufficient housing readily available.

Please continue to search out other areas of new exploration where we might someday form a joint partnership. ↓2X

Sincerely, ↓4X

Mieko Nakamura

Mieko Nakamura
Vice President for Operations ↓2X

adk

C. BUSINESS LETTER FORMATTED FOR A WINDOW ENVELOPE

(with standard punctuation)

↓6X

July 18, 20-- ↓3X

Ms. Reinalda Guerrero
BBL Resources
52A Northern Ridge
Fayetteville, PA 17222 ↓3X

Dear Ms. Guerrero: ↓2X

I see no reason why we should continue to consider the locality around Geraldton for our new plant. Even though the desirability of this site from an economic view is undeniable, there is insufficient housing readily available for our workers.

In trying to control urban growth, the city has been turning down the building permits for new housing or placing so many restrictions on foreign investment as to make it too expensive.

Please continue to seek out other areas of exploration where we might form a joint partnership. ↓2X

Sincerely, ↓4X

Arlyn J. Bunch

Arlyn J. Bunch
Vice President for Operations ↓2X

woc

D. MEMO

(with table and attachment notation)

↓6X →tab

MEMO TO: Nancy Price, Executive Vice President ↓2X
FROM: Arlyn J. Bunch, Operations *ajb* ↓2X
DATE: July 18, 20-- ↓2X
SUBJECT: New Plant Site ↓2X

As you can see from the attached letter, I've informed BBL Resources that I see no reason why we should continue to consider the locality around Geraldton for our new plant. Even though the desirability of this site from an economic standpoint is undeniable, there is insufficient housing readily available. In fact, as of June 25, the number of appropriate single-family houses listed for sale within a 25-mile radius of Geraldton was as follows: ↓2X

Agent	Units
Belle Real Estate	123
Castleton Homes	11
Red Carpet	9
Geraldton Homes	5

↓1X

In addition, in trying to control urban growth, Geraldton has been either turning down building permits for new housing or placing excessive restrictions on them.

Because of this deficiency of housing for our employees, we have no choice but to look elsewhere. ↓2X

woc
Attachment *(Attachment notation)*

Reference Manual

A. MULTIPAGE BUSINESS LETTER

(page 1; with on-arrival notation, international address, subject line, table, and standard punctuation)

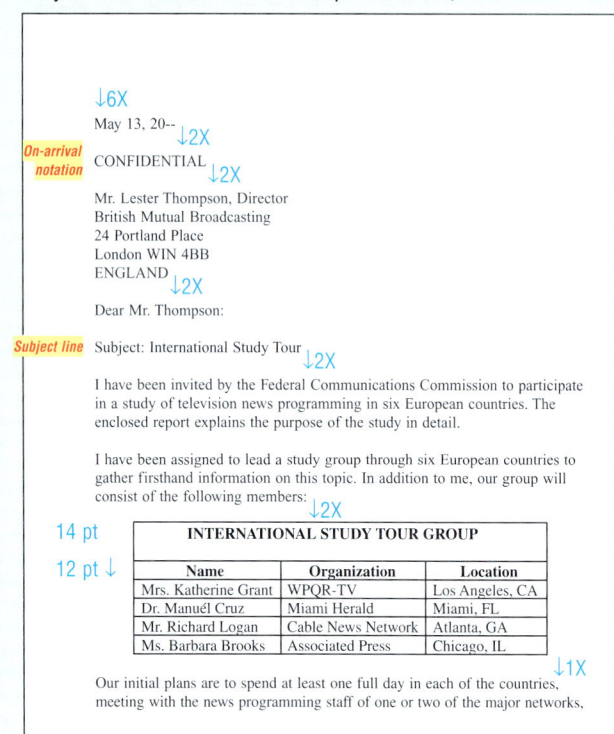

↓6X

May 13, 20-- ↓2X

On-arrival notation: CONFIDENTIAL ↓2X

Mr. Lester Thompson, Director
British Mutual Broadcasting
24 Portland Place
London WIN 4BB
ENGLAND ↓2X

Dear Mr. Thompson:

Subject line: Subject: International Study Tour ↓2X

I have been invited by the Federal Communications Commission to participate in a study of television news programming in six European countries. The enclosed report explains the purpose of the study in detail.

I have been assigned to lead a study group through six European countries to gather firsthand information on this topic. In addition to me, our group will consist of the following members: ↓2X

14 pt
12 pt ↓

INTERNATIONAL STUDY TOUR GROUP		
Name	Organization	Location
Mrs. Katherine Grant	WPQR-TV	Los Angeles, CA
Dr. Manuél Cruz	Miami Herald	Miami, FL
Mr. Richard Logan	Cable News Network	Atlanta, GA
Ms. Barbara Brooks	Associated Press	Chicago, IL

↓1X

Our initial plans are to spend at least one full day in each of the countries, meeting with the news programming staff of one or two of the major networks,

B. MULTIPAGE BUSINESS LETTER

(page 2; with company name; multiline list; enclosure, delivery, copy, postscript, blind copy notations; and standard punctuation)

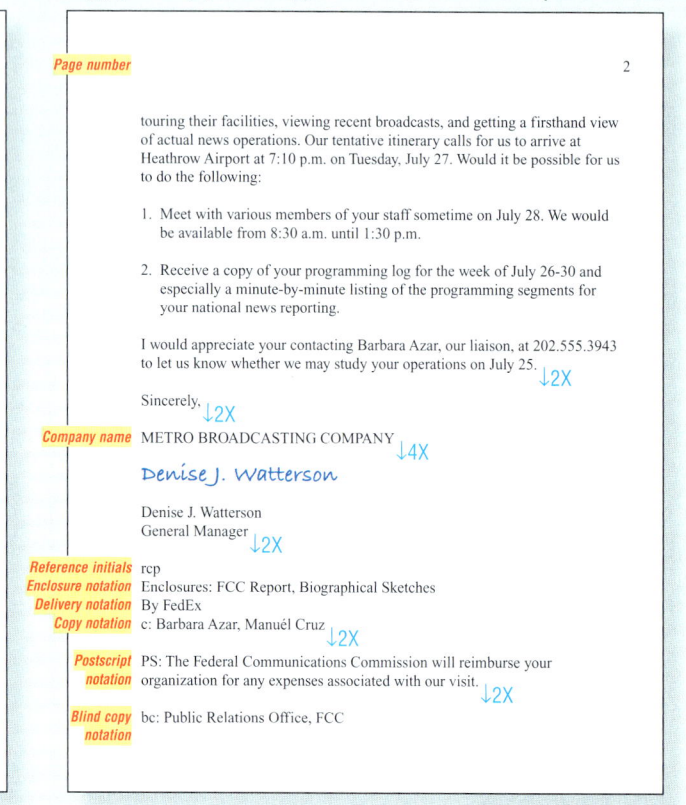

Page number   2

touring their facilities, viewing recent broadcasts, and getting a firsthand view of actual news operations. Our tentative itinerary calls for us to arrive at Heathrow Airport at 7:10 p.m. on Tuesday, July 27. Would it be possible for us to do the following:

1. Meet with various members of your staff sometime on July 28. We would be available from 8:30 a.m. until 1:30 p.m.

2. Receive a copy of your programming log for the week of July 26-30 and especially a minute-by-minute listing of the programming segments for your national news reporting.

I would appreciate your contacting Barbara Azar, our liaison, at 202.555.3943 to let us know whether we may study your operations on July 25. ↓2X

Sincerely, ↓2X

Company name: METRO BROADCASTING COMPANY ↓4X

Denise J. Watterson

Denise J. Watterson
General Manager ↓2X

Reference initials: rcp
Enclosure notation: Enclosures: FCC Report, Biographical Sketches
Delivery notation: By FedEx
Copy notation: c: Barbara Azar, Manuél Cruz ↓2X

Postscript notation: PS: The Federal Communications Commission will reimburse your organization for any expenses associated with our visit. ↓2X

Blind copy notation: bc: Public Relations Office, FCC

C. E-MAIL MESSAGE IN MICROSOFT OUTLOOK/INTERNET EXPLORER

Job Description for DTP Position - Message

To: aironey@atpi.com; clvaughan@atpi.com
Subject: Job Description for DTP Position
Attach: Job Description.doc (24 KB)

Hi, Andy and Cody:

Attached is the draft job description for the new desktop publishing position we're going to be advertising for next month. Would you please review it for accuracy, completeness, and adherence to company policy.

I'd appreciate your getting back to me with any suggested changes by Thursday so that I can get this position publicized next week.

Thanks

Sandy

Sandra R. Hill
E-mail: srhill@atpi.com
Phone: 269-555-0231

D. E-MAIL MESSAGE IN YAHOO!

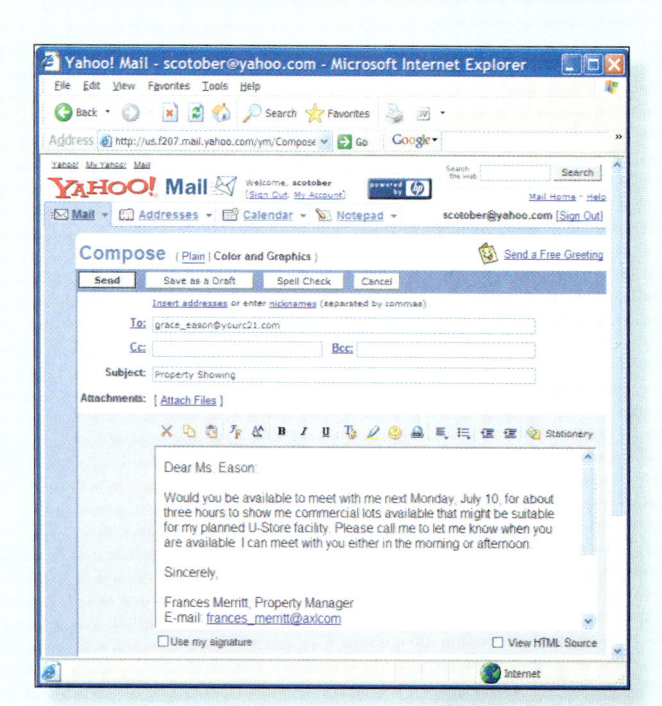

Yahoo! Mail - scotober@yahoo.com - Microsoft Internet Explorer

YAHOO! Mail — Welcome, scotober

Compose (Plain | Color and Graphics)

To: grace_eason@yourc21.com
Cc:
Bcc:
Subject: Property Showing
Attachments: [Attach Files]

Dear Ms. Eason:

Would you be available to meet with me next Monday, July 10, for about three hours to show me commercial lots available that might be suitable for my planned U-Store facility. Please call me to let me know when you are available. I can meet with you either in the morning or afternoon.

Sincerely,

Frances Merritt, Property Manager
E-mail: frances_merritt@axl.com

R-5 Reference Manual

Reference Manual

A. FORMATTING ENVELOPES

A standard large (No. 10) envelope is 9.5 by 4.125 inches. A standard small (No. 6¼) envelope is 6.5 by 3.625 inches. Although either address format shown below is acceptable, the format shown for the large envelope (all caps and no punctuation) is recommended by the U.S. Postal Service for mail that will be sorted by an electronic scanning device.

Window envelopes are often used in a word processing environment because of the difficulty of aligning envelopes correctly in some printers. A window envelope requires no formatting, since the letter is formatted and folded so that the inside address is visible through the window.

Standard Large Envelope

NATIONAL GEOGRAPHIC SOCIETY
Image Collection & Image Sales
1145 17th Street, NW
Washington, DC 20036-4688, USA

MS. JOAN R HUNTER
BOLWATER ASSOCIATES
ONE PARKLANDS DRIVE
DARIEN, CT 06820-3214

Standard Small Envelope

Roger J. Michaelson
901 East Benson, Apt. 3
Fort Lauderdale, FL 33301

MR. JOSEPH G. JENSHAK
17032 STEWART AVENUE
AUGUSTA, GA 30904

NATIONAL GEOGRAPHIC SOCIETY
Image Collection & Image Sales
1145 17th Street, NW
Washington, DC 20036-4688, USA

MS. JOAN R. HUNTER
BOLWATER ASSOCIATES
ONE PARKLANDS DRIVE
DARIEN, CT 06820-3214

Standard Window Envelope

B. FOLDING LETTERS

To fold a letter for a large envelope:

1. Place the letter *face up* and fold up the bottom third.
2. Fold the top third down to 0.5 inch from the bottom edge.
3. Insert the last crease into the envelope first, with the flap facing up.

To fold a letter for a small envelope:

1. Place the letter *face up* and fold up the bottom half to 0.5 inch from the top.
2. Fold the right third over to the left.
3. Fold the left third over to 0.5 inch from the right edge.
4. Insert the last crease into the envelope first, with the flap facing up.

To fold a letter for a window envelope:

1. Place the letter *face down* with the letterhead at the top and fold the bottom third of the letter up.
2. Fold the top third down so that the address shows.
3. Insert the letter into the envelope so that the address shows through the window.

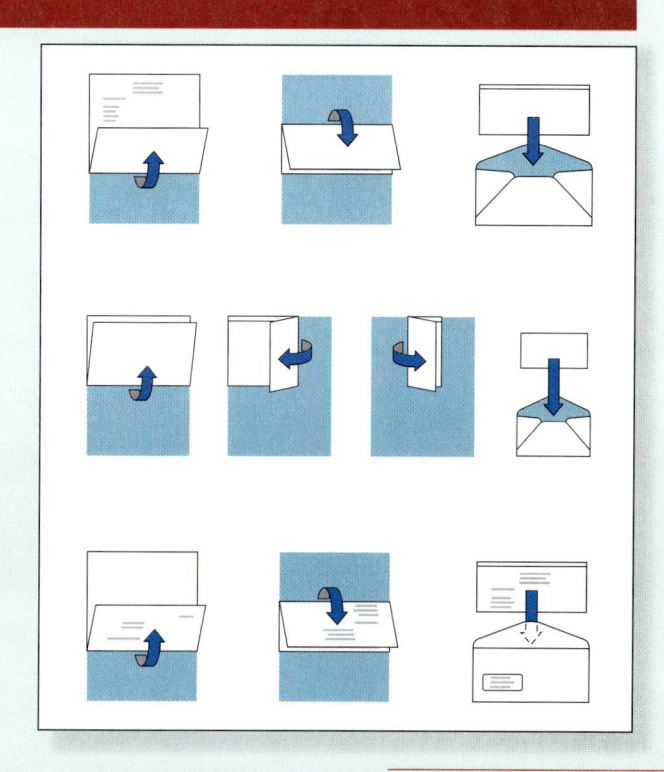

Reference Manual

A. OUTLINE

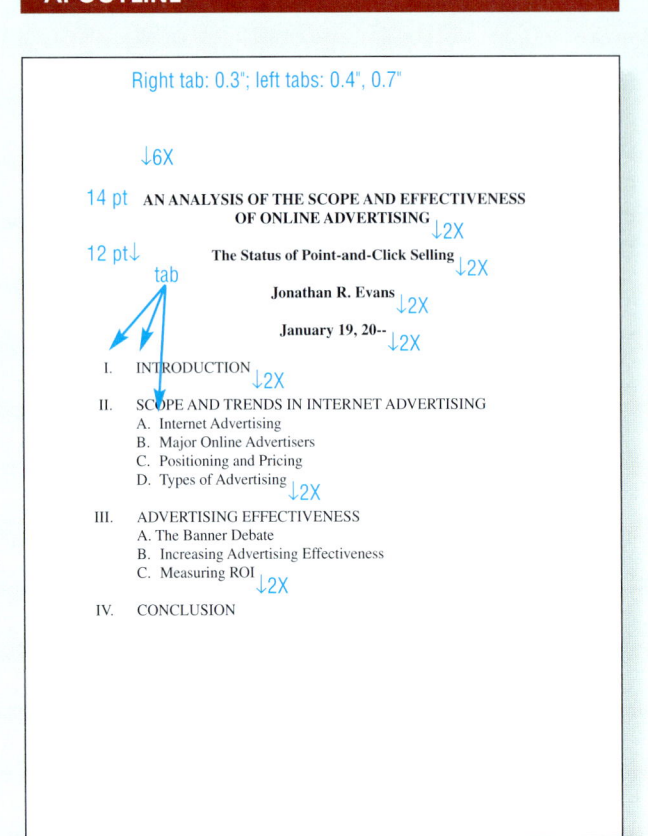

Right tab: 0.3"; left tabs: 0.4", 0.7"

↓6X

14 pt AN ANALYSIS OF THE SCOPE AND EFFECTIVENESS
OF ONLINE ADVERTISING ↓2X

12 pt↓ The Status of Point-and-Click Selling ↓2X

Jonathan R. Evans ↓2X

January 19, 20-- ↓2X

I. INTRODUCTION ↓2X

II. SCOPE AND TRENDS IN INTERNET ADVERTISING
    A. Internet Advertising
    B. Major Online Advertisers
    C. Positioning and Pricing
    D. Types of Advertising ↓2X

III. ADVERTISING EFFECTIVENESS
    A. The Banner Debate
    B. Increasing Advertising Effectiveness
    C. Measuring ROI ↓2X

IV. CONCLUSION

B. TITLE PAGE

center page↓

14 pt AN ANALYSIS OF THE SCOPE AND EFFECTIVENESS
OF ONLINE ADVERTISING ↓2X

12 pt↓ The Status of Point-and-Click Selling ↓12X

Submitted to ↓2X

Luis Torres
General Manager
ViaWorld, International ↓12X

Prepared by ↓2X

Jonathan R. Evans
Assistant Marketing Manager
ViaWorld, International ↓2X

January 19, 20--

C. TRANSMITTAL MEMO

(with 2-line subject line and attachment notation)

↓6X

→tab

MEMO TO: Luis Torres, General Manager ↓2X

FROM: Jonathan R. Evans, Assistant Marketing Manager *jre* ↓2X

DATE: January 19, 20-- ↓2X

SUBJECT: An Analysis of the Scope and Effectiveness of Online Advertising ↓2X

Here is the report analyzing the scope and effectiveness of Internet advertising that you requested on January 5, 20--.

The report predicts that the total value of the business-to-business e-commerce market will reach $1.3 trillion by 2003, up from $190 billion in 1999. New technologies aimed at increasing Internet ad interactivity and the adoption of standards for advertising response measurement and tracking will contribute to this increase. Unfortunately, as discussed in this report, the use of "rich media" and interactivity in Web advertising will create its own set of problems.

I enjoyed working on this assignment, Luis, and learned quite a bit from my analysis of the situation. Please let me know if you have any questions about the report. ↓2X

plw
Attachment

D. TABLE OF CONTENTS

Left tab: 0.5"; right dot-leader tab: 6".

↓6X

14 pt CONTENTS ↓2X

12 pt↓ INTRODUCTION .... 1 ↓2X

SCOPE AND TRENDS IN ONLINE ADVERTISING .... 3 ↓2X

→tab Internet Advertising Spending 4
    Major Online Advertisers 5
    Positioning and Pricing 7
    Types of Advertising .... 8 ↓2X

ADVERTISING EFFECTIVENESS .... 9 ↓2X

    The Banner Debate 9
    Increasing Advertising Effectiveness 11
    Measuring ROI .... 12 ↓2X

CONCLUSION .... 13 ↓2X

APPENDIX

    Sample Internet Advertising 15
    Proposed WEFA Standards .... 18 ↓2X

BIBLIOGRAPHY 19

Reference Manual

A. BUSINESS REPORT
(page 1; with footnotes and multiline list)

↓6X

Title 14 pt **AN ANALYSIS OF THE SCOPE AND EFFECTIVENESS OF ONLINE ADVERTISING** ↓2X

Subtitle 12 pt↓ The Status of Point-and-Click Selling ↓2X

Byline Jonathan R. Evans ↓2X

Date January 19, 20-- ↓2X

Over the past three years, the number of American households online has tripled, from an estimated 15 million in 1996 to 45 million in 1999. Jupiter Communications, predicts that by the year 2003, 70 million households, representing about 62 percent of all U.S. households, will be online. ↓2X

Side head **GROWTH FACTORS** ↓2X

Online business has grown in tandem with the expanding number of Internet users. Forrester Research Inc. predicts that the total value of business-to-business e-commerce will reach $109 billion in 1999 and is likely to reach $1.3 trillion by 2003.[1] ↓2X

Paragraph head **Uncertainty.** The uncertainties surrounding advertising on the Internet remain one of the major impediments to the expansion. The Internet advertising industry is today in a state of flux. ↓2X

Reasons for Not Advertising Online. A recent Association of National Advertisers survey found two main reasons cited for not advertising online:[2] ↓2X

1. The difficulty of determining return on investment, especially in terms of repeat business

2. The lack of reliable tracking and measurement data

Footnotes
[1] George Anders, "Buying Frenzy," *The Wall Street Journal*, July 12, 1999, p. R6.
[2] "eStats: Advertising Revenues and Trends," *eMarketer*, August 11, 1999, <http:www.emarketer.com/estats/ad>, accessed on January 7, 2000.

B. BUSINESS REPORT
(page 3; with long quotation and table)

3

who argue that banners have a strong potential for advertising effectiveness point out that it is not the banner format itself which presents a problem to advertising effectiveness, but rather the quality of the banner and the attention to its placement. According to Mike Windsor, president of Ogilvy Interactive: ↓2X

indent 0.5"→ **Long quotation** It's more a case of bad banner ads, just like there are bad TV ads. The space itself has huge potential. As important as using the space within the banner creatively is to aim it effectively. Unlike broadcast media, the Web offers advertisers the opportunity to reach a specific audience based on data gathered about who is surfing at a site and what their interests are[1] **←indent 0.5"**

Thus, while some analysts continue to argue that the banner advertisement is passé, there is little evidence of its abandonment. Instead, ad agencies are focusing on increasing the banner's effectiveness. ↓2X

SCOPE AND TRENDS IN ONLINE ADVERTISING ↓2X

Starting from zero in 1994, analysts agree that the volume of Internet advertising spending has risen rapidly. However, as indicated in Table 3, analysts provide a wide range of the exact amount of such advertising. ↓2X

14 pt **TABLE 3. INTERNET ADVERTISING**
12 pt↓ **1998 Estimates**

Source	Estimate
Internet Advertising Board	$1.92 billion
Forester	1.30 billion
IDC	1.20 billion
Burst! Media	560 million
Table source Source: "Advertising Age Teams with eMarketer for Research Report," *Advertising Age*, May 3, 1999, p. 24.	

↓1X

The differences in estimates of total Web advertising spending is generally attributed to the different methodologies used by the research agencies to

[1] Lisa Napoli, "Banner Ads Are Under the Gun—And On the Move," *The New York Times*, June 17, 1999, p. D1.

C. ACADEMIC REPORT
(page 1; with endnotes and multiline list)

↓3DS

14 pt **AN ANALYSIS OF THE SCOPE AND EFFECTIVENESS OF ONLINE ADVERTISING** ↓1DS

12 pt↓ The Status of Point-and-Click Selling ↓1DS

Jonathan R. Evans ↓1DS

January 19, 20-- ↓1DS

Over the past three years, the number of American households online has tripled, from an estimated 15 million in 1996 to 45 million in 1999. Jupiter Communications, predicts that by the year 2003, 70 million households, representing about 62 percent of all U.S. households, will be online. ↓1DS

GROWTH FACTORS ↓1DS

Online business has grown in tandem with the expanding number of Internet users. Forrester Research Inc. predicts that the total value of business-to-business e-commerce will reach $109 billion in 1999.[i]

Reasons for Not Advertising Online. A recent Association of National Advertisers survey found two main reasons cited for not advertising online:[ii]

1. The difficulty of determining return on investment, especially in terms of repeat business.

2. The lack of reliable tracking and measurement data.

Some analysts argue that advertising on the Internet can and should follow the same principles as advertising on television.[iii] Other visual media

D. ACADEMIC REPORT
(last page; with long quotation and endnotes)

14

advertising effectiveness, but rather the quality of the banner and the attention to its placement. According to Mike Windsor, president of Ogilvy Interactive: ↓1DS

indent 0.5"→ **Long quotation** It's more a case of bad banner ads, just like there are bad TV ads. The space itself has huge potential. As important as using the space within the banner creatively is to aim it effectively. Unlike broadcast media, the Web offers advertisers the opportunity to reach a specific audience based on data gathered about who is surfing at a site and what their interests are.[vii] **←indent 0.5"** ↓1SS

From the advertiser's perspective, the most effective Internet ads do more than just deliver information to the consumer and grab the consumer's attention—they also gather information about consumers (e.g., through "cookies" and other methodologies). From the consumer's perspective, this type of interactivity may represent an intrusion and an invasion of privacy. There appears to be a shift away from the ad-supported model and toward the transaction model, wherein users pay for the content they want and the specific transactions they perform.

Endnotes
i George Anders, "Buying Frenzy," *The Wall Street Journal*, July 12, 1999, p. R6.
ii "eStats: Advertising Revenues and Trends," *eMarketer*, August 11, 1999, <http:www.emarketer.com/estats/ad>, accessed on August 11, 1999.
iii Bradley Johnson, "Nielsen/NetRatings Index Shows 4% Rise in Web Ads," *Advertising Age*, July 19, 2003, p. 18.
iv Tom Hyland, "Web Advertising: A Year of Growth," *Internet Advertising Board*, November 13, 1999, <http:www.iab.net/advertise>, accessed on January 8, 2000.
v Adrian Mand, "Click Here: Free Ride Doles Out Freebies to Ad Surfers," *Brandweek*, March 8, 1999, p. 30.
vi Andrea Petersen, "High Price of Internet Banner Ads Slips Amid Increase in Web Sites," *The Wall Street Journal*, March 2, 1999, p. B20.
vii Lisa Napoli, "Banner Ads Are Under the Gun—And On the Move," *The New York Times*, June 17, 1999, p. D1.

Reference Manual

A. LEFT-BOUND BUSINESS REPORT
(page 1; with endnotes and single-line list)

Left margin: 1.75" Right margin: *default* (1.25")

↓6X

14 pt **AN ANALYSIS OF THE SCOPE AND EFFECTIVENESS OF ONLINE ADVERTISING** ↓2X

12 pt↓ **The Status of Point-and-Click Selling** ↓2X

Jonathan R. Evans ↓2X

January 19, 20-- ↓2X

Over the past three years, the number of American households online has tripled, from an estimated 15 million in 1996 to 45 million in 1999. Jupiter Communications predicts that by the year 2003, 70 million households will be online. ↓2X

GROWTH FACTORS ↓2X

Online business has grown in tandem with the expanding number of Internet users. Forrester Research Inc. predicts that the total value of business-to-business e-commerce will reach $109 billion in 1999 and is likely to reach $1.3 trillion by 2003.[1] ↓2X

Uncertainty. The uncertainties surrounding advertising on the Internet remain one of the major impediments to the expansion. Dating from just 1994, when the first banner ads appeared on the Hotwired home page, the Internet advertising industry is today in a state of flux. ↓2X

Some analysts argue that advertising on the Internet can and should follow the same principles as advertising on television and other visual media. Others contend that advertising on the Internet should reflect the unique characteristics of this new medium. ↓2X

Reasons for Not Advertising Online. A recent Association of National Advertisers survey found two main reasons cited for not advertising online:[ii] ↓2X

1. The difficulty of determining return on investment
2. The lack of reliable tracking and measurement data

B. BIBLIOGRAPHY
(for business or academic style using either endnotes or footnotes)

↓6X

hanging indent

12 pt↓ 14 pt **BIBLIOGRAPHY** ↓2X

Book—one author Adams, Jeffrey B., *Internet Advertising,* Brunswick Press, Boston, 2004.

Annual report AdCom Industries, *2001 Annual Report,* ACI, Inc., San Francisco, 2006.

Newspaper article Andery, George, "Buying Frenzy," *The Wall Street Journal,* July 12, 1999, p. R6.

Book—two authors Arlens, Ramon, and Seymour Stevens, *E-Tailing,* All-State, Cambridge, Mass., 2003.

Book—organization as author *Directory of Business and Financial Services,* Corporate Libraries Assoc., New York, 2003.

WWW page "eStats: Advertising Revenues and Trends," *eMarketer,* August 11, 1999, <http:www.emarketer.com/estats/ad>, accessed on January 7, 2004.

Journal article— paged continuously Ivans, Edward, "Typical ROIs in Online Advertising," *Personnel Quarterly,* Vol. 20, September 2005, pp. 804-816.

Journal article— pages each issue Johnson, Bradley, "Nielsen/NetRatings Index Shows 4% Rise in Web Ads," *Advertising Age,* July 19, 2003, p. 18.

Online database "Modern Advertising Techniques," *Advertising Encyclopedia,* N.D., <http://www.advency.com/modern_advertising_techniques.html>, accessed on January 7, 2004.

Government document National Institute of Mental Health, *Who Clicks? Four Years of Internet Advertising,* DHHS Publication No. ADM 82-1195, U.S. Government Printing Office, Washington, 2006.

E-mail Waerov, Denis V., "Reaction to Management's Offer," e-mail message, August 18, 2001.

C. MEMO REPORT
(page 1, with single-line list)

↓6X

→tab

MEMO TO: Luis Torres, General Manager ↓2X

FROM: Jonathan R. Evans, Assistant Marketing Manager *jre* ↓2X

DATE: January 19, 20-- ↓2X

SUBJECT: An Analysis of the Scope and Effectiveness of Online Advertising ↓2X

According to a July 12, 1999, Wall Street Journal article, over the past three years, the number of American households online has tripled, from an estimated 15 million in 1996 to 45 million in 1999. Jupiter Communications predicts that by the year 2003, 70 million households, representing 62 percent of all U.S. households, will be online. Online business has grown in tandem with the expanding number of Internet users. Forrester Research Inc. predicts that the total value of business-to-business e-commerce will reach $109 billion in 1999 and is likely to reach $1.3 trillion by 2003. ↓2X

UNCERTAINTY ↓2X

The uncertainties surrounding advertising on the Internet remain one of the major impediments to the expansion. Dating from just 1994, when the first banner ads appeared on the Hotwired home page, the Internet advertising industry is today in a state of flux.

Some analysts argue that advertising on the Internet can and should follow the same principles as advertising on television and other visual media. Others contend that all of the advertising on the Internet should reflect the unique characteristics of this new medium.

A recent Association of National Advertisers survey found two main reasons cited for not advertising online:

1. The difficulty of determining return on investment
2. The lack of reliable tracking and measurement data

D. REPORTS: SPECIAL FEATURES

Margins and Spacing. Use a 2-inch top margin for the first page of each section of a report (for example, the table of contents, first page of the body, and bibliography page) and a 1-inch top margin for other pages. Use default side margins (1.25 inches) and bottom margins (1 inch) for all pages. If the report is going to be bound on the left, add 0.5 inch to the left margin. Single-space business reports and double-space academic reports.

Headings. Center the report title in 14-point font (press ENTER to space down before switching to 12-point font). Single-space multiline report titles in a single-spaced report and double-space multiline titles in a double-spaced report. Insert 1 blank line before and after all parts of a heading block (consisting of the title, subtitle, author, and/or date) and format all lines in bold.

Insert 1 blank line before and after side headings and format in bold, beginning at the left margin. Format paragraph headings in bold; begin at the left margin for single-spaced reports and indent for double-spaced reports. The text follows on the same line, preceded by a period and 1 space.

Citations. For business and academic reports, format citations using your word processor's footnote (or endnote) feature. For reports formatted in APA or MLA style, use the format shown on page R-10.

Reference Manual

A. REPORT IN APA STYLE
(page 1; with author/year citations)

Top, bottom, and side margins: 1"

Online Advertising 3 [header]

An Analysis of the Scope and Effectiveness
of Online Advertising
Jonathan R. Evans

Over the past three years, the number of American households online has tripled, from an estimated 15 million in 1996 to 45 million in 1999. Jupiter Communications predicts that by the year 2003, 70 million households, which represent 62 percent of all U.S. households, will be online (Napoli, 2003).

[main head] Growth Factors

Online business has grown in tandem with the expanding number of Internet users. Forrester Research Inc. predicts that the total value of business-to-business e-commerce will reach $109 billion in 2003 (Arlens & Stevens, 2003).

[subhead] Uncertainty

The uncertainties surrounding advertising on the Internet remain one of the major impediments to the expansion. Dating from just 1994, when the first banner ads appeared on the Hotwired home page, the Internet advertising industry is today in a state of flux.

Some analysts argue that advertising on the Internet can and should follow the same principles as advertising on television and other visual media ("eStats," 2004). Others contend that advertising on the Internet should reflect

B. REFERENCES IN APA STYLE

Top, bottom, and side margins: 1"
Double-space throughout.
hanging indent

Online Advertising 14 [header]

References

[Book—one author] Adams, J. B. (2004). *Internet advertising*. Boston: Brunswick Press.

[Annual report] AdCom Industries. (2006). 2005 *annual report*. San Francisco: ACI, Inc.

[Newspaper article] Anders, G. (2003, July 12). Buying frenzy. *The Wall Street Journal*, p. R6.

[Book—two authors] Arlens, R., & Stevens, S. (2003). *E-tailing*. Cambridge, MA: All-State.

[Book—organization as author] *Directory of business and financial services*. (2003). New York: Corporate Libraries Association.

[WWW page] eStats: Advertising revenues and trends. (n.d.). New York: eMarketer. Retrieved August 11, 2004, from the World Wide Web: http://www.emarketer.com/estats/ad

[Journal article—paged continuously] Ivans, E. (2005). Typical ROIs in online advertising. *Personnel Quarterly, 20,* 804-816.

[Journal article—paged each issue] Johnson, B. (2003, July 19). Nielsen/NetRatings Index shows 4% rise in Web ads. Advertising Age, 39, 18.

[Online database] Modern advertising techniques. (1998, January). *Advertising Encyclopedia*. Retrieved January 7, 2004, from http://www.advency.com/ads.html

[Government document] National Institute of Mental Health *Who clicks? Four years of Internet advertising* (DHHS Publication No. ADM 82-1195). Washington, DC. (2006).

C. REPORT IN MLA STYLE
(page 1; with author/page citations)

Top, bottom, and side margins: 1"
Double-space throughout.

Evans 1 [header]

Jonathan R. Evans
Professor Inman
Management 302
19 January 20--

An Analysis of the Scope and Effectiveness
of Online Advertising

Over the past three years, the number of American households online has tripled, from an estimated 15 million in 1996 to 45 million in 1999. Jupiter Communications predicts that by the year 2003, 70 million households, representing about 62% of all U.S. households, will be online (Napoli D1). Online business has grown in tandem with the expanding number of Internet users. Forrester Research Inc. predicts that the total value of business-to-business e-commerce will reach $109 billion in 1999 and is likely to reach $1.3 trillion by 2003 (Arlens & Stevens 376-379).

The uncertainties surrounding advertising on the Internet remain one of the major impediments to the expansion. Dating from just 1994, when the first banner ads appeared on the Hotwired home page, the Internet advertising industry is today in a state of flux.

Some analysts argue that advertising on the Internet can and should follow the same principles as advertising on television and other visual media ("eStats"). Others contend that advertising on the Internet should reflect the

D. WORKS CITED IN MLA STYLE

Top, bottom, and side margins: 1"
Double-space throughout.
hanging indent

Evans 13 [header]

Works Cited

[Book—one author] Adams, Jeffrey B. *Internet Advertising*. Boston: Brunswick Press, 2004.

[Annual report] AdCom Industries. *2006 Annual Report*. San Francisco: ACI, Inc., 2005.

[Newspaper article] Anders, George. "Buying Frenzy," *Wall Street Journal,* July 12, 2003, p. R6.

[Book—two authors] Arlens, Ramon, and Seymour Stevens. *E-Tailing*. Cambridge, MA: All-State, 2003.

[Book—organization as author] Corporate Libraries Association. *Directory of Business and Financial Services*. New York: Corporate Libraries Association, 2003.

[WWW page] "eStats: Advertising Revenues and Trends." *eMarketer,* 11 Aug. 1999. 7 Jan. 2004. <http:www.emarketer.com/estats/ad/>.

[Journal article—paged continuously] Ivans, Edward. "Typical ROIs in Online Advertising." *Personnel Quarterly* Sep. 2005: 804-816.

[Journal article—paged each issue] Johnson, Bradley. "Nielsen/NetRatings Index Shows 4% Rise in Web Ads." *Advertising Age* 19 July 2003: 18.

[Online database] *Modern Advertising Techniques*. 2003. Advertising Encyclopedia. 7 Jan. 2004 <http://www.advency.com/modern_advertising_techniques.html>.

[Government document] National Institute of Mental Health. *Who Clicks? Four Years of Internet Advertising*. DHHS Publication No. ADM 82-1195. Washington, DC: GPO, 2006.

[E-mail] Richards, Denis V. E-mail to the author. 18 Dec. 2005.

Reference Manual

A. MEETING AGENDA

↓6X

14 pt   **MILES HARDWARE EXECUTIVE COMMITTEE** ↓2X

12 pt↓   Meeting Agenda ↓2X

June 7, 20--, 3 p.m. ↓2X

1. Call to order ↓2X
2. Approval of minutes of May 5 meeting
3. Progress report on building addition and parking lot restrictions (Norman Hodges and Anthony Pascarelli)
4. May 15 draft of Five-Year Plan
5. Review of National Hardware Association annual convention
6. Employee grievance filed by Ellen Burrows (John Landstrom)
7. New expense-report forms (Anne Richards)
8. Announcements
9. Adjournment

B. MINUTES OF A MEETING

↓6X

14 pt **RESOURCE COMMITTEE** ↓2X

12 pt↓ Minutes of the Meeting ↓2X

March 13, 20-- ↓1X

ATTENDANCE	The Resource Committee met on March 13, 20--, at the Airport Sheraton in Portland, Oregon, with all members present. Michael Davis, chairperson, called the meeting to order at 2:30 p.m. ↓1X
APPROVAL OF MINUTES	The minutes of the January 27 meeting were read and approved. ↓1X
OLD BUSINESS	The members of the committee reviewed the sales brochure on electronic copyboards and agreed to purchase one for the conference room. Cynthia Giovanni will secure quotations from at least two suppliers. ↓1X
NEW BUSINESS	The committee reviewed a request from the Purchasing Department for three new computers. After extensive discussion regarding the appropriate use of the computers and software to be purchased, the committee approved the request. ↓1X
ADJOURNMENT	The meeting was adjourned at 4:45 p.m. ↓2X Respectfully submitted, ↓4X *D. S. Madsen* D. S. Madsen, Secretary

(Note: Table shown with "Show Gridlines" active.)

C. ITINERARY

↓6X

14 pt   **ITINERARY** ↓2X

12 pt↓   For Arlene Gilsdorf ↓2X

March 12-15, 20-- ↓1X

THURSDAY, MARCH 12	↓1X
5:10 p.m.-7:06 p.m.	Flight from Detroit to Portland; Northwest 83 (Phone: 800-555-1212); e-ticket; Seat 8D; nonstop; dinner ↓2X
	Jack Weatherford (Home: 503-555-8029; Office: 503-555-7631) will meet your flight on Thursday, provide transportation during your visit, and return you to the airport on Saturday morning. ↓2X
	Airport Sheraton (503-555-4032) King-sized bed, nonsmoking room; late arrival guaranteed (Reservation No. 30ZM6-02) ↓1X
FRIDAY, MARCH 13	
9 a.m.-5:30 p.m.	Portland Sales Meeting 1931 Executive Way, Suite 10 Portland (503-555-7631)
Evening	On your own
SATURDAY, MARCH 14	
7:30 a.m.-2:47 p.m.	Flight from Portland to Detroit; Northwest 360; e-ticket; Seat 9a; nonstop; breakfast

(Note: Table shown with "Show Gridlines" active.)

D. LEGAL DOCUMENT

Left tabs: 1", 3"

↓6X

12 pt↓   POWER OF ATTORNEY ↓2X

KNOW ALL MEN BY THESE PRESENTS that I, ATTORNEY LEE FERNANDEZ, of the City of Tulia, County of Swisher, State of Texas, do hereby appoint my son, Robert Fernandez, of this City, County, and State as my attorney-in-fact to act in my name, place, and stead as my agent in the management of my business operating transactions.

     I give and grant unto my said attorney full power and authority to do and perform every act and thing requisite and necessary to be done in the said management as fully, to all intents and purposes, as I might or could do if personally present, with full power of revocation, hereby ratifying all that my said attorney shall lawfully do.

     IN WITNESS WHEREOF, I have hereunto set my hand and seal this _____ day of _____, 20--. ↓2X

5 underscores ↑   20 underscores ↑

→tab to centerpoint   _____ ↓2X

SIGNED and affirmed in the presence of: ↓4X

_____ ↓4X

_____

Reference Manual

A. RESUME

↓6X

14 pt **TERRY M. MARTINA** ↓2X
12 pt ↓ 250 Maxwell Avenue, Boulder, CO 80305
Phone: 303-555-9311; e-mail: tmartina@ecc.edu
↓1X   ↓1X

OBJECTIVE	Position in resort management anywhere in Colorado or the Southwest. ↓1X
EDUCATION	A.A. in hotel management to be awarded May 2005 Edgewood Community College, Boulder, Colorado. ↓1X
EXPERIENCE	*Assistant Manager, Burger King Restaurant* Boulder, Colorado: 2003-Present • Achieved grade point average of 3.1 (on 4.0 scale). • Received Board of Regents tuition scholarship. • Financed all college expenses. ↓2X *Student Intern, Ski Valley Haven* Aspen, Colorado: September-December 2004 • Worked as an assistant to the night manager. • Gained experience in operating First-Guest software. • Was in charge of producing daily occupancy reports. • Received Employee-of-the-Month award. ↓1X
PERSONAL	• Speak and write fluent Spanish. • Competent in Microsoft Office 2003. • Secretary of ECC Hospitality Services Association. • Special Olympics volunteer: Summer 2004. ↓1X
REFERENCES	Available upon request

(Note: Table shown with "Show Gridlines" active.)

B. APPLICATION LETTER IN BLOCK STYLE
(with standard punctuation)

↓6X

March 1, 20-- ↓4X

Mr. Lou Mansfield, Director
Human Resources Department
Rocky Resorts International
P.O. Box 1412
Denver, CO 80214 ↓2X

Dear Mr. Mansfield: ↓2X

Please consider me an applicant for the position of concierge for Suite Retreat, as advertised in last Sunday's *Denver Times*.

I will receive my A.A. degree in hotel administration from Edgewood Community College in May and will be available for full-time employment immediately. In addition to my extensive coursework in hospitality services and business, I've had experience in working for a ski lodge similar to Suite Retreats in Aspen. As a lifelong resident of Colorado and an avid skier, I would be able to provide your guests with any information they request.

After you've reviewed my enclosed resume, I would appreciate having an opportunity to discuss with you why I believe I have the right qualifications and personality to serve as your concierge. I can be reached at 303-555-9311. ↓2X

Sincerely, ↓4X

Terry M. Martina

Terry M. Martina
250 Maxwell Avenue, Apt. 8
Boulder, CO 80305 ↓2X

Enclosure

C. FORMATTING LISTS

Numbers or bullets may be used in letters, memos, and reports to call attention to items in a list. If the sequence of the items is important, use numbers rather than bullets.

❑ Begin the number or bullet at the paragraph point, that is, at the left margin for blocked paragraphs and indented 0.5 inch for indented paragraphs.
❑ Insert 1 blank line before and after the list.
❑ Within the list, use the same spacing (single or double) as is used in the rest of the document.
❑ For single-spaced documents, if all items require no more than 1 line, single-space the items in the list. If any item requires more than 1 line, single-space each item and insert 1 blank line between each item.

To format a list:

1. Type the list unformatted.
2. Select the items in the list.
3. Apply the number or bullet feature.
4. If necessary, use the Decrease Indent or Increase Indent button in Microsoft Word to adjust the position of the list.

The three bulleted and numbered lists shown at the right are all formatted correctly.

D. EXAMPLES OF DIFFERENT TYPES OF LISTS

According to PricewaterhouseCoopers and the Internet Advertising Bureau, the following are the most common types of advertising on the Internet:

• Banner ads that feature some type of animation to attract the viewer's attention.
• Sponsorship, in which an advertiser sponsors a content-based Web site.
• Interstitials, ads that flash up while a page downloads.

There is now considerable controversy about the effectiveness of banner ads. As previously noted, a central goal of banner advertisements is to increase the

* * *

According to PricewaterhouseCoopers, the following are the most common types of advertising on the Internet, shown in order of popularity:

1. Banner ads
2. Sponsorship
3. Interstitials

There is now considerable controversy about the effectiveness of banner ads. As previously noted, a central goal of banner advertisements is to increase the

* * *

According to PricewaterhouseCoopers, the following are the most common types of advertising on the Internet:

• Banner ads that feature some type of animation to attract the viewer's attention.
• Sponsorship, in which an advertiser sponsors a Web site.
• Interstitials, ads that flash up while a page downloads.

There is now considerable controversy about the effectiveness of banner advertising. As previously noted, a central goal of banner advertisements is to

Reference Manual

A. BOXED TABLE (DEFAULT STYLE)
(with subtitle, braced headings, total line, and table note.)

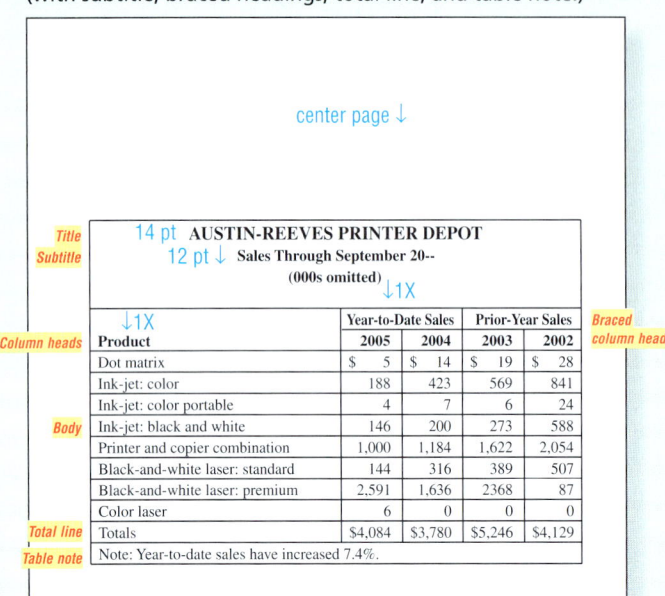

center page ↓

14 pt AUSTIN-REEVES PRINTER DEPOT
12 pt ↓ Sales Through September 20--
(000s omitted)
↓1X

Product	Year-to-Date Sales		Prior-Year Sales	
	2005	2004	2003	2002
Dot matrix	$ 5	$ 14	$ 19	$ 28
Ink-jet: color	188	423	569	841
Ink-jet: color portable	4	7	6	24
Ink-jet: black and white	146	200	273	588
Printer and copier combination	1,000	1,184	1,622	2,054
Black-and-white laser: standard	144	316	389	507
Black-and-white laser: premium	2,591	1,636	2368	87
Color laser	6	0	0	0
Totals	$4,084	$3,780	$5,246	$4,129

Note: Year-to-date sales have increased 7.4%.

Labels: Title, Subtitle, Column heads, Body, Total line, Table note, Braced column head

B. OPEN TABLE
(with subtitle, blocked column headings, and 2-line heading)

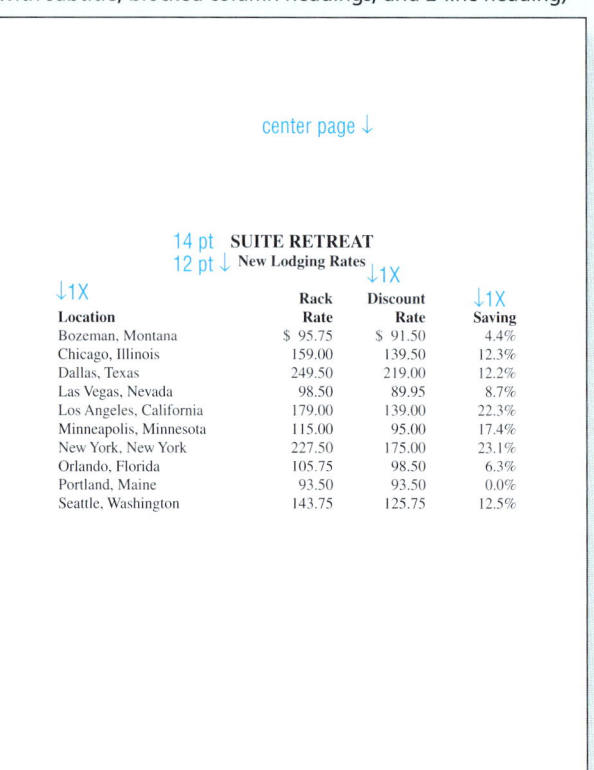

center page ↓

14 pt SUITE RETREAT
12 pt ↓ New Lodging Rates
↓1X

Location	Rack Rate	Discount Rate	Saving
Bozeman, Montana	$ 95.75	$ 91.50	4.4%
Chicago, Illinois	159.00	139.50	12.3%
Dallas, Texas	249.50	219.00	12.2%
Las Vegas, Nevada	98.50	89.95	8.7%
Los Angeles, California	179.00	139.00	22.3%
Minneapolis, Minnesota	115.00	95.00	17.4%
New York, New York	227.50	175.00	23.1%
Orlando, Florida	105.75	98.50	6.3%
Portland, Maine	93.50	93.50	0.0%
Seattle, Washington	143.75	125.75	12.5%

C. RULED TABLE
(with table number and centered column headings)

an effort to reduce errors and provide increased customer support, we have recently added numerous additional telephone support services, some of which are available 24 hours a day and others available during the workday. These are shown in Table 2. ↓2X

14 pt Table 2. COMPUTER SUPPLIES SUPPORT SERVICES
↓1X

12 pt↓

Support Service	Telephone	Hours
Product literature	800-555-3867	6 a.m. to 5 p.m.
Replacement parts	303-555-3388	24 hours a day
Technical documentation	408-555-3309	24 hours a day
Troubleshooting	800-555-8277	10 a.m. to 5 p.m.
Printer drivers	800-555-2377	6 a.m. to 5 p.m.
Software notes	800-555-3496	24 hours a day
Technical support	800-555-1205	24 hours a day
Hardware information	303-555-4289	6 a.m. to 5 p.m.

↓1X

We hope you will take advantage of these additional services to ensure that the computer hardware and software you purchase from Computer Supplies continues to provide you the quality and service you have come to expect from our company.

Sincerely,

Douglas Pullis

Douglas Pullis
General Manager

cds

D. TABLES: SPECIAL FEATURES

Vertical Placement. Vertically center a table that appears on a page by itself. Insert 1 blank line before and after a table appearing with other text.

Heading Block. Center and bold all lines of the heading, typing the title in all caps and 14-point font and the subtitle in upper- and lowercase and in 12-point font. If a table has a number, type the word *Table* in upper- and lowercase. Follow the table number with a period and 1 space.

Column Headings. If *all* columns in the table consist of text (such as words, phone numbers, or years), center all column headings and left-align all column entries. In all other situations, left-align all text column headings and text column entries and right-align all quantity column headings and quantity column entries. Regardless of the type of column, center braced headings. Use bold upper- and lowercase.

Column Capitalization. Capitalize only the first word and proper nouns in column entries.

Percentages and Dollars. Repeat the % sign for each number in a column (unless the heading identifies the data as percentages). Insert the $ sign only before the first amount and before a total amount. Align the $ sign with the longest amount in the column, inserting spaces after the $ sign as needed (leaving 2 spaces for each digit and 1 space for each comma).

Total Line. Add a border above a total line. Use the word *Total* or *Totals* as appropriate.

Reference Manual

A. FORMATTING BUSINESS FORMS

Many business forms can be created and filled in by using templates that are provided within commercial word processing software. Template forms can be used "as is" or they can be edited. Templates can also be used to create customized forms for any business.

When a template is opened, the form is displayed on screen. The user can then fill in the necessary information, including personalized company information. Data are entered into cells or fields, and you can move quickly from field to field with a single keystroke—usually by pressing TAB or ENTER.

B. U.S. POSTAL SERVICE ABBREVIATIONS

(for States, Territories, and Canadian Provinces)

States and Territories

Alabama	AL	North Carolina	NC
Alaska	AK	North Dakota	ND
Arizona	AZ	Ohio	OH
Arkansas	AR	Oklahoma	OK
California	CA	Oregon	OR
Colorado	CO	Pennsylvania	PA
Connecticut	CT	Puerto Rico	PR
Delaware	DE	Rhode Island	RI
District of Columbia	DC	South Carolina	SC
Florida	FL	South Dakota	SD
Georgia	GA	Tennessee	TN
Guam	GU	Texas	TX
Hawaii	HI	Utah	UT
Idaho	ID	Vermont	VT
Illinois	IL	Virgin Islands	VI
Indiana	IN	Virginia	VA
Iowa	IA	Washington	WA
Kansas	KS	West Virginia	WV
Kentucky	KY	Wisconsin	WI
Louisiana	LA	Wyoming	WY
Maine	ME		
Maryland	MD	**Canadian Provinces**	
Massachusetts	MA	Alberta	AB
Michigan	MI	British Columbia	BC
Minnesota	MN	Labrador	LB
Mississippi	MS	Manitoba	MB
Missouri	MO	New Brunswick	NB
Montana	MT	Newfoundland	NF
Nebraska	NE	Northwest Territories	NT
Nevada	NV	Nova Scotia	NS
New Hampshire	NH	Ontario	ON
New Jersey	NJ	Prince Edward Island	PE
New Mexico	NM	Quebec	PQ
New York	NY	Saskatchewan	SK
		Yukon Territory	YT

C. PROOFREADERS' MARKS

Proofreaders' Marks		Draft	Final Copy
⌒	Omit space	data base	database
∨ or ∧	Insert	if hes going	if he's not going,
≡	Capitalize	Maple street	Maple Street
⌿	Delete	a final draft	a draft
#	Insert space	allready to	all ready to
when	Change word	and if you	and when you
/	Use lowercase letter	our President	our president
¶	Paragraph	… to use it. We can	… to use it. We can
...	Don't delete	a true story	a true story
○	Spell out	the only 1	the only one
∽	Transpose	they all see	they see all

Proofreaders' Marks		Draft	Final Copy
ss	Single-space	ss [first line / second line]	first line second line
ds	Double-space	ds [first line / second line]	first line second line
⊐	Move right	Please send	Please send
⊏	Move left	May I	May I
∼	Bold	Column Heading	**Column Heading**
ital	Italic	ital Time magazine	*Time* magazine
u/l	Underline	u/l Time magazine	<u>Time</u> magazine readers
♂	Move as shown	readers will see	will see

Reference Manual

Language Arts for Business
(50 "must-know" rules)

PUNCTUATION

COMMAS

RULE 1
, direct address
(L. 21)

Use commas before and after a name used in direct address.
Thank you, John, for responding to my e-mail so quickly.
Ladies and gentlemen, the program has been canceled.

RULE 2
, independent clause
(L. 27)

Use a comma between independent clauses joined by a coordinate conjunction (unless both clauses are short).
Ellen left her job with IBM, and she and her sister went to Paris.
But: Ellen left her job with IBM and went to Paris with her sister.
But: John drove and I navigated.
Note: An independent clause is one that can stand alone as a complete sentence. The most common coordinate conjunctions are *and, but, or,* and *nor.*

RULE 3
, introductory expression
(L. 27)

Use a comma after an introductory expression (unless it is a short prepositional phrase).
Before we can make a decision, we must have all the facts.
But: In 2004 our nation elected a new president.
Note: An introductory expression is a group of words that come before the subject and verb of the independent clause. Common prepositions are *to, in, on, of, at, by, for,* and *with.*

RULE 4
, direct quotation
(L. 41)

Use a comma before and after a direct quotation.
James said, "I shall return," and then left.

RULE 5
, date
(L. 57)

Use a comma before and after the year in a complete date.
We will arrive on June 2, 2006, for the conference.
But: We will arrive on June 2 for the conference.

RULE 6
, place
(L. 57)

Use a comma before and after a state or country that follows a city (but not before a ZIP Code).
Joan moved to Vancouver, British Columbia, in May.
Send the package to Douglasville, GA 30135, by Express Mail.
But: Send the package to Georgia by Express Mail.

Reference Manual

RULE 7
, series
(L. 61)

Use a comma between each item in a series of three or more.

We need to order paper, toner, and font cartridges for the printer.

They saved their work, exited their program, and turned off their computers when they finished.

Note: Do not use a comma after the last item in a series.

RULE 8
, transitional expression
(L. 61)

Use a comma before and after a transitional expression or independent comment.

It is critical, therefore, that we finish the project on time.

Our present projections, you must admit, are inadequate.

But: You must admit our present projections are inadequate.

Note: Examples of transitional expressions and independent comments are *in addition to, therefore, however, on the other hand, as a matter of fact,* and *unfortunately.*

RULE 9
, nonessential expression
(L. 71)

Use a comma before and after a nonessential expression.

Andre, who was there, can verify the statement.

But: Anyone who was there can verify the statement.

Van's first book, *Crisis of Management,* was not discussed.

Van's book *Crisis of Management* was not discussed.

Note: A nonessential expression is a group of words that may be omitted without changing the basic meaning of the sentence. Always examine the noun or pronoun that comes before the expression to determine whether the noun needs the expression to complete its meaning. If it does, the expression is *essential* and does *not* take a comma.

RULE 10
, adjacent adjectives
(L. 71)

Use a comma between two adjacent adjectives that modify the same noun.

We need an intelligent, enthusiastic individual for this job.

But: Please order a new bulletin board for our main conference room.

Note: Do not use a comma after the second adjective. Also, do not use a comma if the first adjective modifies the combined idea of the second adjective and the noun (for example, *bulletin board* and *conference room* in the second example above).

SEMICOLONS

RULE 11
; no conjunction
(L. 97)

Use a semicolon to separate two closely related independent clauses that are *not* joined by a conjunction (such as *and, but, or,* or *nor*).

Management favored the vote; stockholders did not.

But: Management favored the vote, but stockholders did not.

RULE 12
; series
(L. 97)

Use a semicolon to separate three or more items in a series if any of the items already contain commas.

Staff meetings were held on Thursday, May 7; Monday, June 7; and Friday, June 12.

Note: Be sure to insert the semicolon *between* (not within) the items in a series.

Reference Manual

HYPHENS

RULE 13
- number
(L. 57)

Hyphenate compound numbers between twenty-one and ninety-nine and fractions that are expressed as words.
Twenty-nine recommendations were approved by at least three-fourths of the members.

RULE 14
- compound adjective
(L. 67)

Hyphenate compound adjectives that come before a noun (unless the first word is an adverb ending in -*ly*).
We reviewed an up-to-date report on Wednesday.
But: The report was up to date.
But: We reviewed the highly rated report.
Note: A compound adjective is two or more words that function as a unit to describe a noun.

APOSTROPHES

RULE 15
' singular noun
(L. 37)

Use *'s* to form the possessive of singular nouns.
The hurricane's force caused major damage to North Carolina's coastline.

RULE 16
' plural noun
(L. 37)

Use only an apostrophe to form the possessive of plural nouns that end in *s*.
The investors' goals were outlined in the stockholders' report.
But: The investors outlined their goals in the report to the stockholders.
But: The women's and children's clothing was on sale.

RULE 17
' pronoun
(L. 37)

Use *'s* to form the possessive of indefinite pronouns (such as *someone's* or *anybody's*); do not use an apostrophe with personal pronouns (such as *hers, his, its, ours, theirs*, and *yours*).
She could select anybody's paper for a sample.
It's time to put the file back into its cabinet.

Reference Manual

COLONS

RULE 18
: explanatory material
(L. 91)

Use a colon to introduce explanatory material that follows an independent clause.

    The computer satisfies three criteria: speed, cost, and power.

    But: The computer satisfies the three criteria of speed, cost, and power.

    Remember this: only one coupon is allowed per customer.

Note: An independent clause can stand alone as a complete sentence. Do not capitalize the word following the colon.

PERIODS

RULE 19
. polite request
(L. 91)

Use a period to end a sentence that is a polite request.

    Will you please call me if I can be of further assistance.

Note: Consider a sentence a polite request if you expect the reader to respond by doing as you ask rather than by giving a yes-or-no answer.

QUOTATION MARKS

RULE 20
" quotation
(L. 41)

Use quotation marks around a direct quotation.

    Harrison responded by saying, "Their decision does not affect us."

    But: Harrison responded by saying that their decision does not affect us.

RULE 21
" title
(L. 41)

Use quotation marks around the title of a newspaper or magazine article, chapter in a book, report, and similar terms.

    The most helpful article I found was "Multimedia for All."

ITALICS (OR UNDERLINE)

RULE 22
title
(L. 41)

Italicize (or underline) the titles of books, magazines, newspapers, and other complete published works.

    Grisham's *The Brethren* was reviewed in a recent *USA Today* article.

Reference Manual

GRAMMAR

SENTENCES

RULE 23
fragment
(L. 21)

Avoid sentence fragments.
Not: She had always wanted to be a financial manager. But had not had the needed education.
But: She had always wanted to be a financial manager but had not had the needed education.
Note: A fragment is a part of a sentence that is incorrectly punctuated as a complete sentence. In the first example above, "but had not had the needed education" is not a complete sentence because it does not contain a subject.

RULE 24
run-on
(L. 21)

Avoid run-on sentences.
Not: Mohamed is a competent worker he has even passed the MOS exam.
Not: Mohamed is a competent worker, he has even passed the MOS exam.
But: Mohamed is a competent worker; he has even passed the MOS exam.
Or: Mohamed is a competent worker. He has even passed the MOS exam.
Note: A run-on sentence is two independent clauses that run together without any punctuation between them or with only a comma between them.

AGREEMENT

RULE 25
agreement singular
agreement plural
(L. 67)

Use singular verbs and pronouns with singular subjects; use plural verbs and pronouns with plural subjects.
I was happy with my performance.
Janet and Phoenix were happy with their performance.
Among the items discussed were our raises and benefits.

RULE 26
agreement pronoun
(L. 81)

Some pronouns *(anybody, each, either, everybody, everyone, much, neither, no one, nobody,* **and** *one)* **are always singular and take a singular verb. Other pronouns** *(all, any, more, most, none,* **and** *some)* **may be singular or plural, depending on the noun to which they refer.**
Each of the employees has finished his or her task.
Much remains to be done.
Most of the pie was eaten, but most of the cookies were left.

RULE 27
agreement intervening words
(L. 81)

Disregard any intervening words that come between the subject and verb when establishing agreement.
The box containing the books and pencils has not been found.
Alex, accompanied by Tricia, is attending the conference and taking his computer.

RULE 28
agreement nearer noun
(L. 101)

If two subjects are joined by *or, either/or, neither/nor,* **or** *not only/but also,* **make the verb agree with the subject nearer to the verb.**
Neither the coach nor the players are at home.
Not only the coach but also the referee is at home.
But: Both the coach and the referee are at home.

Reference Manual

PRONOUNS

RULE 29
nominative pronoun
(L. 107)

Use nominative pronouns (such as *I, he, she, we, they,* and *who*) as subjects of a sentence or clause.
    The programmer and <u>he</u> are reviewing the code.
    Barb is a person <u>who</u> can do the job.

RULE 30
objective pronoun
(L. 107)

Use objective pronouns (such as *me, him, her, us, them,* and *whom*) as objects of a verb, preposition, or infinitive.
    The code was reviewed by the programmer and <u>him</u>.
    Barb is the type of person <u>whom</u> we can trust.

ADJECTIVES AND ADVERBS

RULE 31
adjective/adverb
(L. 101)

Use comparative adjectives and adverbs (*-er, more,* and *less*) when referring to two nouns or pronouns; use superlative adjectives and adverbs (*-est, most,* and *least*) when referring to more than two.
    The <u>shorter</u> of the <u>two</u> training sessions is the <u>more</u> helpful one.
    The <u>longest</u> of the <u>three</u> training sessions is the <u>least</u> helpful one.

WORD USAGE

RULE 32
accept/except
(L. 117)

Accept means "to agree to"; *except* means "to leave out."
    All employees <u>except</u> the maintenance staff should <u>accept</u> the agreement.

RULE 33
affect/effect
(L. 117)

Affect is most often used as a verb meaning "to influence"; *effect* is most often used as a noun meaning "result."
    The ruling will <u>affect</u> our domestic operations but will have no <u>effect</u> on our Asian operations.

RULE 34
farther/further
(L. 117)

Farther refers to distance; *further* refers to extent or degree.
    The <u>farther</u> we drove, the <u>further</u> agitated he became.

RULE 35
personal/personnel
(L. 117)

Personal means "private"; *personnel* means "employees."
    All <u>personnel</u> agreed not to use e-mail for <u>personal</u> business.

RULE 36
principal/principle
(L. 117)

Principal means "primary"; *principle* means "rule."
    The <u>principle</u> of fairness is our <u>principal</u> means of dealing with customers.

Reference Manual

MECHANICS

CAPITALIZATION

RULE 37
≡ sentence
(L. 31)

Capitalize the first word of a sentence.
　　Please prepare a summary of your activities.

RULE 38
≡ proper noun
(L. 31)

Capitalize proper nouns and adjectives derived from proper nouns.
　　Judy Hendrix drove to Albuquerque in her new Pontiac convertible.

Note: A proper noun is the official name of a particular person, place, or thing.

RULE 39
≡ time
(L. 31)

Capitalize the names of the days of the week, months, holidays, and religious days (but do not capitalize the names of the seasons).
　　On Thursday, November 25, we will celebrate Thanksgiving, the most popular holiday in the fall.

RULE 40
≡ noun #
(L. 77)

Capitalize nouns followed by a number or letter (except for the nouns *line, note, page, paragraph,* and *size*).
　　Please read Chapter 5, which begins on page 94.

RULE 41
≡ compass point
(L. 77)

Capitalize compass points (such as *north, south,* or *northeast*) only when they designate definite regions.
　　From Montana we drove south to reach the Southwest.

RULE 42
≡ organization
(L. 111)

Capitalize common organizational terms (such as *advertising department* and *finance committee*) only when they are the actual names of the units in the writer's own organization and when they are preceded by the word *the*.
　　The report from the Advertising Department is due today.
　　But: Our advertising department will submit its report today.

RULE 43
≡ course
(L. 111)

Capitalize the names of specific course titles but not the names of subjects or areas of study.
　　I have enrolled in Accounting 201 and will also take a marketing course.

NUMBER EXPRESSION

RULE 44
general
(L. 41)

In general, spell out numbers zero through ten, and use figures for numbers above ten.
　　We rented two movies for tonight.
　　The decision was reached after 27 precincts sent in their results.

Reference Manual

RULE 45
\# figure
(L. 41)

Use figures for

❑ **Dates.** (Use *st*, *d*, or *th* only if the day comes before the month.)
   The tax report is due on April 15 (*not* April 15th).
   We will drive to the camp on the 23d (or *23rd* or *23rd*) of May.

❑ **All numbers if two or more *related* numbers both above and below ten are used in the same sentence.**
   Mr. Carter sent in 7 receipts, and Ms. Cantrell sent in 22.
   But: The 13 accountants owned three computers each.

❑ **Measurements (time, money, distance, weight, and percent).**
   The $500 statue we delivered at 7 a.m. weighed 6 pounds.

❑ **Mixed numbers.**
   Our sales are up 9½ (or *9 1/2*) percent over last year.

RULE 46
\# word
(L. 57)

Spell out

❑ **A number used as the first word of a sentence.**
   Seventy-five people attended the conference in San Diego.

❑ **The shorter of two adjacent numbers.**
   We have ordered 3 two-pound cakes and one 5-pound cake for the reception.

❑ **The words *million* and *billion* in even amounts (do not use decimals with even amounts).**
   Not: A $5.00 ticket can win $28,000,000 in this month's lottery.
   But: A $5 ticket can win $28 million in this month's lottery.

❑ **Fractions.**
   Almost one-half of the audience responded to the question.
Note: When fractions and the numbers twenty-one through ninety-nine are spelled out, they should be hyphenated.

ABBREVIATIONS

RULE 47
abbreviate none
(L. 67)

In general business writing, do not abbreviate common words (such as *dept.* or *pkg.*), compass points, units of measure, or the names of months, days of the week, cities, or states (except in addresses).
   Almost one-half of the audience indicated they were at least 5 feet 8 inches tall.
Note: Do not insert a comma between the parts of a single measurement.

RULE 48
abbreviate measure
(L. 87)

In technical writing, on forms, and in tables, abbreviate units of measure when they occur frequently. Do not use periods.
   14 oz   5 ft 10 in   50 mph   2 yrs 10 mo

RULE 49
abbreviate lowercase
(L. 87)

In most lowercase abbreviations made up of single initials, use a period after each initial but no internal spaces.
   a.m.   p.m.   i.e.   e.g.   e.o.m.
   Exceptions: mph   mpg   wpm

RULE 50
abbreviate ≡
(L. 87)

In most all-capital abbreviations made up of single initials, do not use periods or internal spaces.
   OSHA   PBS   NBEA   WWW   VCR   MBA
   Exceptions: U.S.A.   A.A.   B.S.   Ph.D.   P.O.   B.C.   A.D.

Part 1

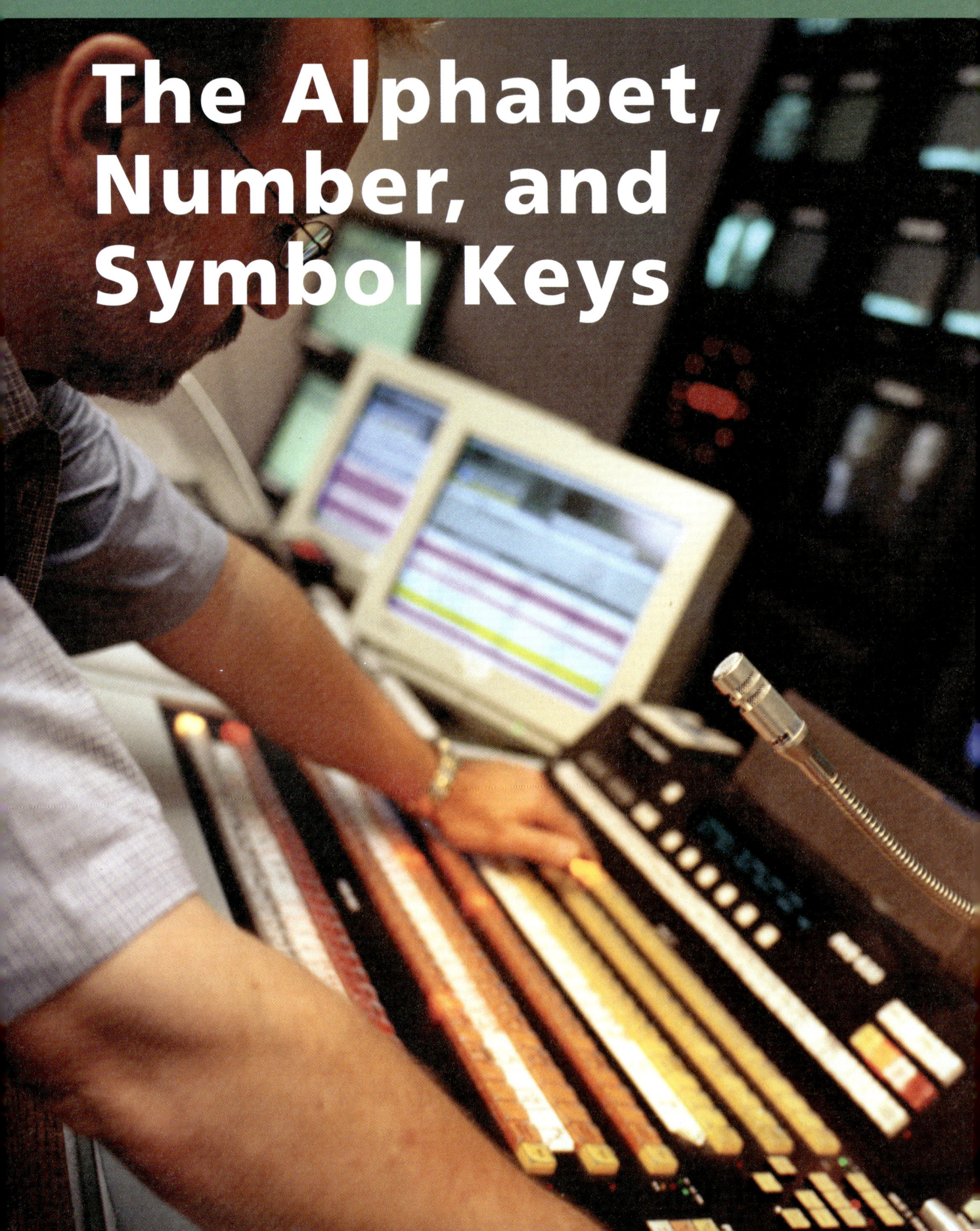

The Alphabet, Number, and Symbol Keys

Keyboarding in Arts, Audio, Video Technology, and Communications Services

Occupations in this cluster deal with organizing and communicating information to the public in various forms and media. This cluster includes jobs in radio and television broadcasting, journalism, motion pictures, the recording industry, the performing arts, multimedia publishing, and the entertainment services. Book editors, computer artists, technical writers, radio announcers, news correspondents, and camera operators are just a few jobs within this cluster.

Qualifications and Skills

Strong oral and written communication skills and technical skills are necessary for anyone in communications and media. Without a doubt, competent keyboarding skill is extremely advantageous.

Working in the media requires creativity, talent, and accurate use of language. In journalism, being observant, thinking clearly, and seeing the significance of events are all of utmost importance. Announcers must have exceptional voices, excellent speaking skills, and a unique style. The ability to work under pressure is important in all areas of media.

Objectives

KEYBOARDING

- Operate by touch the letter, number, and symbol keys.
- Demonstrate proper typing technique.
- Use the correct spacing with punctuation.
- Type at least 28 words per minute on a 2-minute timed writing with no more than 5 errors.

TECHNICAL

- Answer correctly at least 90 percent of the questions on an objective test.

Unit 1

Keyboarding: The Alphabet

LESSON 1
A S D F J K L ;
ENTER   SPACE BAR

LESSON 2
H E O R

LESSON 3
M T P C

LESSON 4
RIGHT SHIFT V . W

LESSON 5
Review

Lesson 1

Home Keys

Goals

- Touch-type the home keys (A S D F J K L ;)
- Touch-type the SPACE BAR
- Touch-type the ENTER key
- Type at least 10wpm/1'/3e

LEFT HAND			RIGHT HAND
First Finger	F	J	First Finger
Second Finger	D	K	Second Finger
Third Finger	S	L	Third Finger
Fourth Finger	A	;	Fourth Finger
		SPACE BAR	Thumb

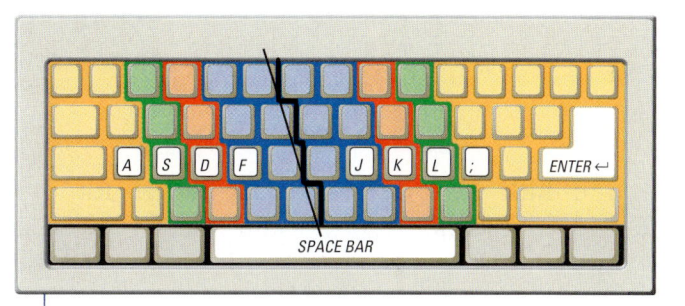

NEW KEYS

A. Follow the directions to become familiar with the home keys.

The semicolon (;) is commonly called the sem key.

A. THE HOME KEYS

The **A S D F J K L ;** keys are known as the home keys.

1. Place the fingers of your left hand on the home keys as follows: first finger on **F**; second finger on **D**; third finger on **S**; fourth finger on **A**.
2. Place the fingers of your right hand on the home keys as follows: first finger on **J**; second finger on **K**; third finger on **L**; and fourth finger on **;**.
3. Curve your fingers.
4. Using the correct fingers, type each character as you say it to yourself: `a s d f j k l ;`.
5. Remove your fingers from the keyboard and replace them on the home keys.
6. Press each home key again as you say each character: `a s d f j k l ;`.

B. THE SPACE BAR

The SPACE BAR, located beneath the letter keys, is used to space between words and after marks of punctuation.

1. With fingers held motionless on the home keys, poise your right thumb about a half inch above the SPACE BAR.
2. Type the characters and then press the SPACE BAR 1 time. Bounce your thumb off.

C. Type each line 1 time, pressing the SPACE BAR where you see a space and pressing the ENTER key at the end of a line.

C. THE ENTER KEY

The ENTER key moves the insertion point to the beginning of a new line. Reach to the ENTER key with the fourth finger of your right hand. Keep your J finger at home. Lightly press the ENTER key. Practice using the ENTER key until you can do so with confidence and without looking at your hands.

```
asdf jkl; asdf jkl; ↵
asdf jkl; asdf jkl; ↵
```

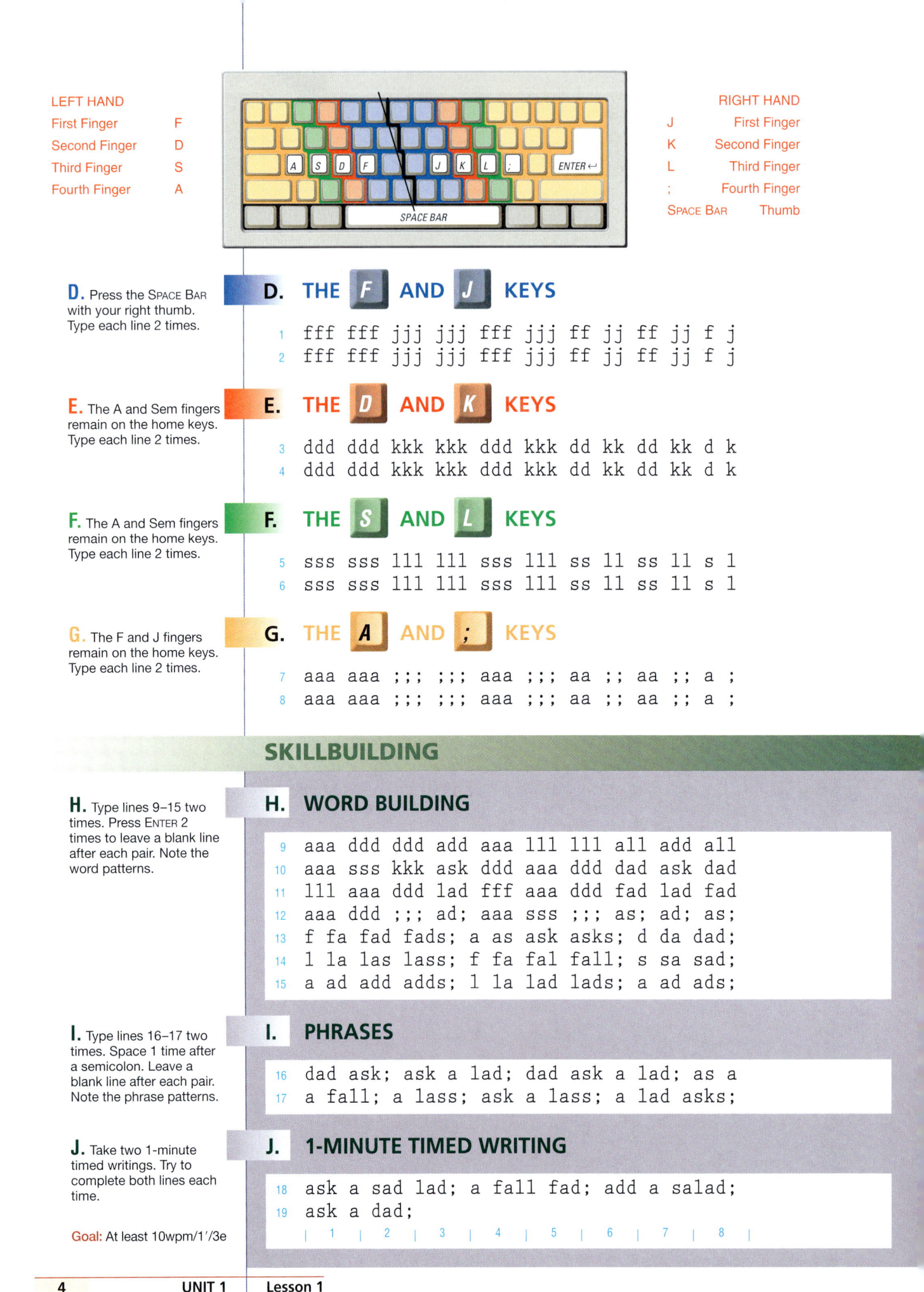

LEFT HAND			RIGHT HAND
First Finger	F	J	First Finger
Second Finger	D	K	Second Finger
Third Finger	S	L	Third Finger
Fourth Finger	A	;	Fourth Finger
		SPACE BAR	Thumb

D. Press the SPACE BAR with your right thumb. Type each line 2 times.

D. THE F AND J KEYS

```
1  fff fff jjj jjj fff jjj ff jj ff jj f j
2  fff fff jjj jjj fff jjj ff jj ff jj f j
```

E. The A and Sem fingers remain on the home keys. Type each line 2 times.

E. THE D AND K KEYS

```
3  ddd ddd kkk kkk ddd kkk dd kk dd kk d k
4  ddd ddd kkk kkk ddd kkk dd kk dd kk d k
```

F. The A and Sem fingers remain on the home keys. Type each line 2 times.

F. THE S AND L KEYS

```
5  sss sss lll lll sss lll ss ll ss ll s l
6  sss sss lll lll sss lll ss ll ss ll s l
```

G. The F and J fingers remain on the home keys. Type each line 2 times.

G. THE A AND ; KEYS

```
7  aaa aaa ;;; ;;; aaa ;;; aa ;; aa ;; a ;
8  aaa aaa ;;; ;;; aaa ;;; aa ;; aa ;; a ;
```

SKILLBUILDING

H. Type lines 9–15 two times. Press ENTER 2 times to leave a blank line after each pair. Note the word patterns.

H. WORD BUILDING

```
9   aaa ddd ddd add aaa lll lll all add all
10  aaa sss kkk ask ddd aaa ddd dad ask dad
11  lll aaa ddd lad fff aaa ddd fad lad fad
12  aaa ddd ;;; ad; aaa sss ;;; as; ad; as;
13  f fa fad fads; a as ask asks; d da dad;
14  l la las lass; f fa fal fall; s sa sad;
15  a ad add adds; l la lad lads; a ad ads;
```

I. Type lines 16–17 two times. Space 1 time after a semicolon. Leave a blank line after each pair. Note the phrase patterns.

I. PHRASES

```
16  dad ask; ask a lad; dad ask a lad; as a
17  a fall; a lass; ask a lass; a lad asks;
```

J. Take two 1-minute timed writings. Try to complete both lines each time.

Goal: At least 10wpm/1'/3e

J. 1-MINUTE TIMED WRITING

```
18  ask a sad lad; a fall fad; add a salad;
19  ask a dad;
    | 1  | 2  | 3  | 4  | 5  | 6  | 7  | 8  |
```

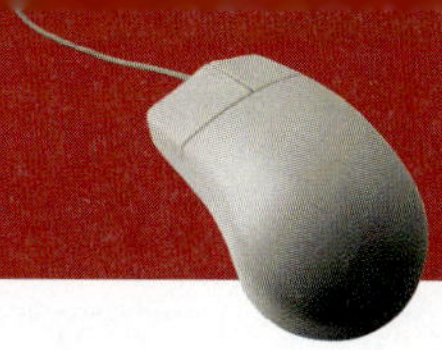

Lesson 2

New Keys

Goals

- Touch-type the H, E, O, and R keys
- Type at least 11wpm/1'/3e

Fingers are named for home keys. (Example: The middle finger of the left hand is the D finger.)

A. Type 2 times.

A. WARMUP

1 fff jjj ddd kkk sss lll aaa ;;; fff jjj
2 a salad; a lad; alas a fad; ask a lass;

NEW KEYS

B. Type each line 2 times. Space 1 time after a semicolon.

Use the J finger.

B. THE H KEY

3 jjj jhj jhj hjh jjj jhj jhj hjh jjj jhj
4 has has hah hah had had aha aha ash ash
5 hash half sash lash dash hall shad shah
6 as dad had; a lass has half; add a dash

C. Type each line 2 times. Keep your eyes on the copy as you type.

Use the D finger.

C. THE E KEY

7 ddd ded ded ede ddd ded ded ede ddd ded
8 lea led he; he see; eke fed sea lee fee
9 feed keel ease heal held seal lead fake
10 he fed a seal; she held a lease; a keel

D. Type each line 2 times. Keep fingers curved.

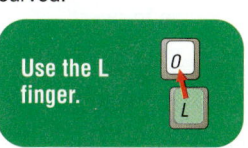

Use the L finger.

D. THE O KEY

11 lll lol lol olo lll lol lol olo lll lol
12 doe off foe hod oh; oak odd ode old sod
13 shoe look kook joke odes does solo oleo
14 he held a hook; a lass solos; old foes;

E. Type each line 2 times. Keep the A finger at home.

Use the F finger.

E. THE R KEY

```
15  fff frf frf rfr fff frf frf rfr fff frf
16  red ark ore err rah era rod oar her are
17  oars soar dear fare read role rare door
18  a dark red door; he read a rare reader;
```

SKILLBUILDING

F. Type each line 2 times. Do not type the red vertical lines.

F. WORD PATTERNS

```
19  dale kale sale hale|fold sold hold old;
20  feed deed heed seed|dash sash lash ash;
21  lake rake sake fake|dear sear rear ear;
```

G. Take two 1-minute timed writings. Try to complete both lines each time. Press ENTER only at the end of line 23.

Goal: At least 11wpm/1'/3e

G. 1-MINUTE TIMED WRITING

```
22  she asked for a rare old deed; he held
23  a red door ajar;
    |  1  |  2  |  3  |  4  |  5  |  6  |  7  |  8  |
```

Keyboarding Connection

What Is the Internet?

What is the easiest way to go to the library? Try using your fingertips! The Internet creates a "virtual library"—a library with no walls. Nothing can match the Internet as a research device. It is not just one computer but an immense connection of computers talking to one another and organizing and exchanging information.

The Internet is synonymous with cyberspace, a word describing the power and control of information. The Internet has been called "a network of networks" linked together to deliver information to users. The Internet connects more than 200 million people to over 3 million computer networks.

The Internet is considered a wide area network (WAN) because the computers on it span the entire world. Each day the Net increases at about 1000 new users every hour.

YOUR TURN List some ways the Internet, as a virtual library, enhances your research activities.

Lesson 3

New Keys

Goals
- Touch-type the M, T, P, and C keys
- Type at least 12wpm/1'/3e

A. Type 2 times.

A. WARMUP

1 aa ;; ss ll dd kk ff jj hh ee oo rr aa;
2 he held a sale for her as she had asked

NEW KEYS

B. Type each line 2 times.

Use the J finger.

B. THE M KEY

3 jjj jmj jmj mjm jjj jmj jmj mjm jjj jmj
4 mad mom me; am jam; ram dam ham mar ma;
5 arms loam lame roam make fame room same
6 she made more room for some of her ham;

C. Type each line 2 times.

Use the F finger.

C. THE T KEY

7 fff ftf ftf tft fff ftf ftf tft fff ftf
8 tar tam mat hot jot rat eat lot art sat
9 told take date late mart mate tool fate
10 he told her to set a later date to eat;

D. Type each line 2 times.

Use the Sem finger.

D. THE P KEY

11 ;;; ;p; ;p; p;p ;;; ;p; ;p; p;p ;;; ;p;
12 pat pal sap rap pet par spa lap pad mop
13 pale palm stop drop pelt plea slap trap
14 please park the red jeep past the pool;

E. THE C KEY

E. Type each line 2 times.

Use the D finger.

```
15  ddd dcd dcd cdc ddd dcd dcd cdc ddd dcd
16  cot cod sac act car coo arc ace cop cat
17  pack tack chat coat face aces deck cost
18  call her to race cool cars at the track
```

SKILLBUILDING

F. SHORT PHRASES

F. Sit in the correct position as you type these drills. Refer to the illustration in the Introduction. Type each line 2 times. Do not type the red vertical lines.

```
19  as so|she had|has met|let her|fast pace
20  to do|ask her|for the|had pop|look past
21  do as|lap top|her pad|let pat|halt them
22  as he|had for|red cap|she let|fast plot
```

G. 1-MINUTE TIMED WRITING

G. Take two 1-minute timed writings. Try to complete both lines each time. Use word wrap. Press ENTER only at the end of line 24.

```
23  the old store at home had lots of cheap
24  stools for the sale;
    | 1 | 2 | 3 | 4 | 5 | 6 | 7 | 8 |
```

Goal: At least 12wpm/1'/3e

Strategies for Career Success

Being a Good Listener

Silence is golden! Listening is essential for learning, getting along, and forming relationships.

Do you tend to forget people's names after being introduced? Do you look away from the speaker instead of making eye contact? Do you interrupt the speaker before he or she finishes talking? Do you misunderstand people? Answering yes can indicate poor listening skills.

To improve your listening skills, follow these steps. *Hear the speaker clearly.* Do not interrupt; let the speaker develop his or her ideas before you speak. *Focus on the message.* At the end of a conversation, identify major items discussed. Mentally ask questions to help you assess the points the speaker is making. *Keep an open mind.* Do not judge. Developing your listening skills benefits everyone.

YOUR TURN Assess your listening behavior. What techniques can you use to improve your listening skills? Practice them the next time you have a conversation with someone.

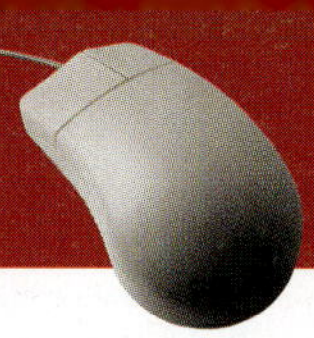

Lesson 4

New Keys

Goals
- Touch-type the RIGHT SHIFT, V, period, and W keys
- Count errors
- Type at least 13wpm/1′/3e

A. Type 2 times.

A. WARMUP

1 the farmer asked her to feed the mares;
2 the late callers came to mop the floor;

NEW KEYS

B. Type each line 2 times.

Use the Sem finger.

B. THE RIGHT SHIFT KEY

To capitalize letters on the left half of the keyboard:

1. With the J finger at home, press and hold down the RIGHT SHIFT key with the Sem finger.
2. Press the letter key.
3. Release the RIGHT SHIFT key and return fingers to home position.

3 ;;; ;A; ;A; ;;; ;S; ;S; ;;; ;D; ;D; ;;;
4 Art Alf Ada Sal Sam Dee Dot Flo Ted Tom
5 Amos Carl Chet Elsa Fred Sara Todd Elda
6 Carl Amos took Sara Carter to the races

C. Type each line 2 times.

Use the F finger.

C. THE V KEY

7   fff fvf fvf vfv fff fvf fvf vfv fff fvf
8   Val eve Eva vet Ava vat Eve ova Vel vee
9   have vase Vera ever vast Reva dove vest
10 Dave voted for Vassar; Val voted for me

D. Type each line 2 times. Space 1 time after a period following an abbreviation; do not space after a period within an abbreviation; space 1 time after a period ending a sentence.

Use the L finger.

D. THE . KEY

11 111 1.1 1.1 .1 111 1.1 1.1 .1 111 1.1
12 dr. dr. ea. ea. sr. sr. Dr. Dr. Sr. Sr.
13 a.m. acct. A.D. p.m. Corp. amt. Dr. Co.
14 Selma left. Dave left. Sarah came home.

E. THE W KEY

E. Type each line 2 times.

Use the S finger.

15 sss sws sws wsw sss sws sws wsw sss sws
16 wow sow war owe was mow woe few wee row
17 wake ward wart wave wham whom walk what
18 Wade watched Walt Shaw walk for a week.

SKILLBUILDING

F. BUILD SKILL ON SENTENCES

F. Type each line 2 times.

19 Amos Ford saw Emma Dale feed the mares.
20 Dr. Drake called Sam; he asked for Ted.
21 Vera told a tale to her old classmates.
22 Todd asked Cale to move some old rakes.

G. COUNTING ERRORS IN SENTENCES

G. Type each line 1 time. After typing all the lines, count your errors. Refer to the Introduction if you need help.

23 Ada lost her letter; Dee lost her card.
24 Dave sold some of the food to a market.
25 Alva asked Walt for three more matches.
26 Dale asked Seth to watch the last show.

H. 1-MINUTE TIMED WRITING

H. Take two 1-minute timed writings. Try to complete both lines each time.

Goal: At least 13wpm/1'/3e

27 Val asked them to tell the major to see
28 Carla at that local farm.
    | 1 | 2 | 3 | 4 | 5 | 6 | 7 | 8 |

Lesson 5

Review

Goals
- Reinforce new-key reaches
- Type at least 14wpm/1'/3e

A. Type 2 times.

A. WARMUP

1 Dave called Drew to ask for a road map.
2 Elsa took three old jars to her mother.

SKILLBUILDING

B. Type each line 2 times. Do not type the red vertical lines.

B. WORD PATTERNS

3 feed seed deed heed | fold cold mold told
4 fame tame lame same | mate late date fate
5 lace face mace race | vast last cast fast
6 park dark hark mark | rare dare fare ware

C. Type each line 2 times.

C. PHRASES

7 at the | he has | her hat | for the | come home
8 or the | he had | her top | ask the | late date
9 to the | he met | her mop | ask her | made more
10 of the | he was | her pop | ask too | fast pace

D. Type each line 2 times.

D. BUILD SKILL ON SENTENCES

11 She asked Dale to share the jar of jam.
12 Cal took the tools from store to store.
13 Darel held a sale to sell some clothes.
14 Seth watched the old cat chase the car.

E. Take a 1-minute timed writing on each line. Review your speed and errors.

E. SENTENCES

15 Carl loved to talk to the tall teacher.
16 She dashed to take the jet to her home.
17 Walt asked her to deed the farm to Ted.
   | 1 | 2 | 3 | 4 | 5 | 6 | 7 | 8 | = Number of 5-stroke words

F. Take two 1-minute timed writings on the paragraph. Press ENTER only at the end of the paragraph. Review your speed and errors.

F. PARAGRAPH

CUMULATIVE WORDS

18 Rachael asked Sal to take her to school   8
19 for two weeks. She had to meet Freda or   16
20 Walt at the school to work on the maps.   24
   | 1 | 2 | 3 | 4 | 5 | 6 | 7 | 8 |

G. Take two 1-minute timed writings. Review your speed and errors.

Goal: At least 14wpm/1'/3e

G. 1-MINUTE TIMED WRITINGS

21 Dot Crews asked Al Roper to meet her at   8
22 the tree to look for a jacket.   14
   | 1 | 2 | 3 | 4 | 5 | 6 | 7 | 8 |

Keyboarding Connection

Using Search Engines

How can you most efficiently find information on the Web? Use a search engine! A search engine guides you to the Web's resources. It analyzes the information you request, navigates the Web's many networks, and retrieves a list of relevant documents. Popular search engines include Google, Excite, Alta Vista, and Yahoo.

A search engine examines electronic databases, wire services, journals, article summaries, articles, home pages, and user group lists. It can access material found in millions of Web sites. When you request a specific keyword search, a search engine scans its large database and searches the introductory lines of text, as well as the title, headings, and subheadings of a Web page. The search engine displays the information that most closely matches your request.

YOUR TURN Try different search engines and see which ones you like best. Choose three of your favorite search engines. Then conduct a search using the keywords "touch typing." (Don't forget the quotation marks.) Compare the results for each search engine.

Unit 2

Keyboarding: The Alphabet

LESSON 6
I LEFT SHIFT - G

LESSON 7
U B : X

LESSON 8
Y , Q /

LESSON 9
N Z ? TAB

LESSON 10
Review

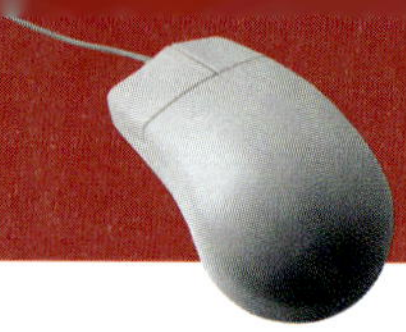

Lesson 6

New Keys

Goals
- Touch-type the I, LEFT SHIFT, hyphen, and G keys
- Type at least 15wpm/1'/3e

A. Type 2 times.

A. WARMUP

1 The major sold three wool hats at cost.
2 Dale took her cats to the vet at three.

NEW KEYS

B. Type each line 2 times.

Use the K finger.

B. THE I KEY

3 kkk kik kik iki kkk kik kik iki kkk kik
4 aid did fir him kid lid mid pit sip tip
5 chip dice itch film hide iris kite milk
6 This time he left his tie at the store.

C. Type each line 2 times.

Use the A finger.

C. THE LEFT SHIFT KEY

To capitalize letters on the right half of the keyboard:

1. With the F finger at home, press and hold down the LEFT SHIFT key with the A finger.
2. Press the letter key.
3. Release the LEFT SHIFT key and return fingers to the home position.

7 aaa Jaa Jaa aaa Kaa Kaa aaa Laa Laa aaa
8 Joe Kip Lee Hal Mat Pat Jim Kim Les Pam
9 Jake Karl Lake Hope Mark Jack Kate Hale
10 Les Lee rode with Pat Mace to the park.

D. Type each line 2 times. Do not space before or after a hyphen; keep the J finger in home position.

Use the Sem finger.

D. THE - KEY

11 ;;; ;p; ;-; ;-; -;- ;;; ;-; -;- ;;; ;-;
12 two-thirds two-fifths trade-off tip-off
13 look-alike jack-of-all-trades free-fall
14 I heard that Ms. Lee-Som is well-to-do.

E. Type each line 2 times. Keep wrists low but not resting on the keyboard.

Use the F finger.

E. THE G KEY

15 fff fgf fgf gfg fff fgf fgf gfg fff fgf
16 age cog dig fig hog jog lag peg rag sag
17 gold rage sage grow page cage gate wage
18 Gail G. Grove greeted the great golfer.

SKILLBUILDING

F. Type each line 2 times.

F. TECHNIQUE PRACTICE: SPACE BAR

19 Vic will meet. Ed is here. Ava is here.
20 See them. Do it. Make these. Hold this.
21 See Lester. See Kate. See Dad. See Mom.
22 Take this car. Make the cakes. Hide it.

G. Type each line 2 times.

G. TECHNIQUE PRACTICE: HYPHEN KEY

23 Two-thirds were well-to-do look-alikes.
24 Jo Hames-Smith is a jack-of-all-trades.
25 Phil saw the trade-offs at the tip-off.
26 Two-fifths are packed for Jo Mill-Ross.

H. Take two 1-minute timed writings. Review your speed and errors.

Goal: At least 15wpm/1'/3e

H. 1-MINUTE TIMED WRITING

                                                              WORDS
27 Al Hall left the firm two weeks ago. I   8
28 will see him at the office at three.   15
    | 1 | 2 | 3 | 4 | 5 | 6 | 7 | 8 |

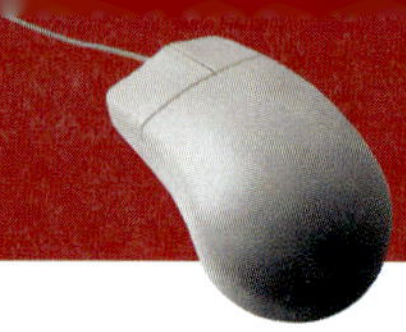

Lesson 7

New Keys

Goals

- Touch-type the U, B, colon, and X keys
- Type at least 16wpm/1′/3e

A. WARMUP

A. Type 2 times.

1. Evette jogged eight miles with Christi.
2. Philip gave Shari the award for spirit.

NEW KEYS

B. THE U KEY

B. Type each line 2 times. Keep your other fingers at home as you reach to U.

Use the J finger.

3. jjj juj juj uju jjj juj juj uju jjj juj
4. cue due hue put rut cut dug hut pup rum
5. cult duet fuel hulk just lump mule pull
6. Hugh urged us to put out the hot fires.

C. THE B KEY

C. Type each line 2 times.

Use the F finger.

7. fff fbf fbf bfb fff fbf fbf bfb fff fbf
8. bag cab bad lab bat rib bar tab beg web
9. bake back bead beef bath bail beam both
10. Bart backed Bill for a big blue bumper.

D. THE : KEY

D. The colon is the shift of the semicolon key. Type each line 2 times. Space 1 time after a period following an abbreviation and 1 time after a colon.

Use the Sem finger.

11. ;;; ;:; ;:; ;:; ;;; ;:; ;:; ;:; ;;; ;:;
12. Dr. Poole: Ms. Shu: Mr. Rose: Mrs. Tam:
13. Dear Ed: Dear Flo: Dear James: Dear Di:
14. Date: To: From: Subject: for the dates:

E. Type each line 2 times.

Use the S finger.

E. THE X KEY

15 sss sxs sxs xsx sss sxs sxs xsx sss sxs
16 box fox hex lax lux mix six tax vex wax
17 apex axle exam flax flex flux taxi text
18 Max asked six pals to fix a sixth taxi.

SKILLBUILDING

F. Type each line 2 times.

F. TECHNIQUE PRACTICE: COLON KEY

19 as follows: these people: this example:
20 Dear Sirs: Dear Madam: Dear Mrs. Smith:
21 Dear Di: Dear Bo: Dear Peter: Dear Mom:
22 for this part: as listed: the projects:

G. Type each line 2 times.

G. WORD PRACTICE

Top row
23 We were told to take our truck to Hugo.
24 There were two tired people at the hut.
25 Please write to their home to tell Tom.

Home row
26 Jake asked his dad for small red flags.
27 Sara added a dash of salt to the salad.
28 Dale said she had a fall sale at Drake.

Bottom row
29 He came to the mall at five to meet me.
30 Victoria came to vote with ample vigor.
31 Mable Baxter visited via the Marta bus.

H. Take two 1-minute timed writings. Review your speed and errors.

Goal: At least 16wpm/1'/3e

H. 1-MINUTE TIMED WRITING

WORDS
32 Dear Jack: Fred would like to take Jill   8
33 Wells to the home game at five tomorrow.   16
   | 1 | 2 | 3 | 4 | 5 | 6 | 7 | 8 |

UNIT 2   Lesson 7   17

Lesson 8

New Keys

Goals
- Touch-type the Y, comma, Q, and slash keys
- Type at least 17wpm/1′/3e

A. Type 2 times.

A. WARMUP

1 Jack asked Philip if Charlie came home.
2 Kim had a short meal with Victor Baker.

NEW KEYS

B. Type each line 2 times.

Use the J finger.

B. THE Y KEY

3 jjj jyj jyj yjy jjj jyj jyj yjy jjj jyj
4 boy cry day eye fly guy hay joy key may
5 yard year yelp yoke yolk your yule play
6 Peggy told me that she may try to stay.

C. Type each line 2 times.

Use the K finger.

C. THE , KEY

7 kkk k,k k,k ,k, kkk k,k k,k ,k, kkk k,k
8 as, at, do, if, is, it, of, oh, or, so,
9 if so, if it is, what if, what of, too,
10 Dale, Barbra, Sadie, or Edith left too.

D. Type each line 2 times.

Use the A finger.

D. THE Q KEY

11 aaa aqa aqa qaq aaa aqa aqa qaq aaa aqa
12 quip quit quack quail quake quart quash
13 quest quick quilts quotes quaver queasy
14 Four quiet squires quilted aqua quilts.

E. Type each line 2 times. Do not space before or after a slash.

Use the Sem finger.

E. THE / KEY

15 ;;; ;/; ;/; /;/ ;;; ;/; ;/; /;/ ;;; ;/;
16 his/her him/her he/she either/or ad/add
17 do/due/dew hale/hail fir/fur heard/herd
18 Ask him/her if he/she chose true/false.

SKILLBUILDING

F. Type each line 2 times.

F. PHRASES

19 if it is|she will do|will he come|he is
20 he said so|who left them|will she drive
21 after all|he voted|just wait|to ask her
22 some said it|for that firm|did she seem

G. Type each line 2 times.

G. TECHNIQUE PRACTICE: SHIFT KEY

23 Ada, Idaho; Kodiak, Alaska; Lima, Ohio;
24 Lula, Georgia; Sully, Iowa; Alta, Utah;
25 Mr. Ray Tims; Mr. Ed Chu; Mr. Cal York;
26 Ms. Vi Close; Ms. Di Ray; Ms. Sue Ames;

H. Take two 1-minute timed writings. Review your speed and errors.

Goal: At least 17wpm/1'/3e

H. 1-MINUTE TIMED WRITING

27 George predicted that Lu will have five   8
28 boxed quilts. David Quayle was to pack   16
29 a mug.   17
    | 1 | 2 | 3 | 4 | 5 | 6 | 7 | 8 |

UNIT 2   Lesson 8   19

Lesson 9

New Keys

Goals

- Touch-type the N, Z, question mark, and TAB keys
- Type at least 18wpm/1'/3e

A. Type 2 times.

A. WARMUP

1. I quit the sales job at Huber, Georgia.
2. Alice packed two boxes of silver disks.

NEW KEYS

B. Type each line 2 times.

Use the J finger.

B. THE N KEY

3. jjj jnj jnj njn jjj jnj jnj njn jjj jnj
4. and ban can den end fan nag one pan ran
5. aunt band chin dent find gain hang lawn
6. Al and Dan can enter the main entrance.

C. Type each line 2 times. Keep the F finger at home as you reach to the Z.

Use the A finger.

C. THE Z KEY

7. aaa aza aza zaz aaa aza aza zaz aaa aza
8. zap zig buzz gaze haze jazz mazes oozes
9. zip zoo zinc zing zone zoom blaze craze
10. The size of the prized pizza amazed us.

D. The question mark is the shift of the slash. Space 1 time after a question mark at the end of a sentence. Type each line 2 times.

Use the Sem finger.

D. THE ? KEY

11. ;;; ;?; ;?; ?;? ;;; ;?; ;?; ?;? ;;; ;?;
12. Can John go? If not Jane, who? Can Ken?
13. Who will see? Can this be? Is that you?
14. Why not quilt? Can they go? Did he ask?

E. THE TAB KEY

E. The word counts in this book credit you with 1 stroke for each paragraph indention in a timed writing. Press the TAB key after the timing starts.

Use the A finger.

The TAB key is used to indent paragraphs. Reach to the TAB key with the A finger. Keep your other fingers on the home keys as you quickly press the TAB key. Pressing the TAB key moves the insertion point 0.5 inch (the default setting) to the right.

F. PRACTICE THE TAB KEY

F. Type each paragraph 2 times. Press ENTER only at the end of the paragraph.

```
15  Each    day     set     your    goal
16  to      type    with    more    speed.

17  You     will    soon    reach   your
18  goal    if      you     work    hard.
```

SKILLBUILDING

G. TECHNIQUE PRACTICE: QUESTION MARK

G. Type each line 2 times.

```
19  Who? Why? How? When? What? True? False?
20  Is it Mo? Why not? What for? Which one?
21  Did Mary go? Is Clinton ready? Why not?
22  Who competed with me? Dana? James? Kay?
```

H. PHRASES

H. Type each line 2 times.

```
23  and the|for the|she is able|can they go
24  for him|ask him|they still|did they fly
25  of them|with us|can he send|ought to be
26  has been able|they need it|he will call
```

I. Type each paragraph 2 times.

I. TECHNIQUE PRACTICE: HYPHEN

Hyphens are used:

- To show that a word is divided (lines 27 and 31).
- To make a dash using two hyphens with no space before or after (lines 28 and 31).
- To join words in a compound word (lines 29, 30, and 32).

```
27      Can Larry go to the next tennis tourna-
28 ment? I am positive he--like Lane--will find
29 the event to be a first-class sports event.
30 If he can go, I will get first-rate seats.
31      Larry--like Ella--enjoys going to tourna-
32 ments that are always first-rate, first-class
33 sporting events.
```

J. Space 1 time after a semicolon, colon, and comma and 1 time after a period and question mark at the end of a sentence. Type each line 2 times.

J. PUNCTUATION PRACTICE

```
34 Kate writes; John sings. Are they good?
35 Send these items: pens, pencils, clips.
36 Hal left; she stayed. Will they attend?
37 Wes made these stops: Rome, Bern, Kiev.
```

K. Take two 1-minute timed writings. Review your speed and errors.

Goal: At least 18wpm/1'/3e

K. 1-MINUTE TIMED WRITING

```
38      Zelda judged six typing contests        7
39 that a local firm held in Piqua. Vick       14
40 Bass was a winner.                          18
   | 1 | 2 | 3 | 4 | 5 | 6 | 7 | 8 |
```

Strategies for Career Success

Preparing a Job Interview Portfolio

Don't go empty-handed to that job interview! Take a portfolio of items with you. Definitely include copies of your resume and your list of references, with at least three professional references. Your academic transcript is useful, especially if you are asked to complete a company application form. Appropriate work samples and copies of certificates and licenses are also helpful portfolio items.

The interview process provides you the opportunity to interview the organization. Include a list of questions you want to ask during the interview.

A comprehensive portfolio of materials will benefit you by giving you a measure of control during the interview process.

YOUR TURN Start today to compile items for your interview portfolio. Include copies of your resume, your reference list, and copies of certificates and licenses. Begin developing a list of interview questions. Think about appropriate work samples to include in your portfolio.

Lesson 10

Review

Goals
- Reinforce new key reaches
- Type at least 19wpm/1'/3e

A. Type 2 times.

A. WARMUP

```
1    She expects to work hard at her job.
2    Keith had a very quiet, lazy afternoon.
```

SKILLBUILDING

B. Take a 1-minute timed writing on each paragraph. Review your speed and errors.

B. SHORT PARAGRAPHS

```
3       You can utilize your office skills       7
4    to complete tasks. Some types of jobs      15
5    require more skills.                       19

6       You will be amazed at how easily         7
7    and quickly you complete your task when    15
8    you can concentrate.                       19
     | 1 | 2 | 3 | 4 | 5 | 6 | 7 | 8 |
```

C. Type each line 2 times.

C. WORD PATTERNS

```
9    banister minister adapter filter master
10   disable disband discern discord discuss
11   embargo emerge embody empty employ emit
12   enforce endure energy engage engine end
13   precept precise predict preside premier
14   subtract subject subsist sublime subdue
15   teamster tearful teaches teak team tear
16   theater theirs theory thefts therm them
17   treason crimson season prison bison son
18   tribune tribute tripod trial tribe trim
```

UNIT 2   Lesson 10   23

D. Type each line 2 times. Keep fingers curved and wrists low but not resting on the keyboard as you practice these lines.

D. ALPHABET REVIEW

19 Alda asked Alma Adams to fly to Alaska.
20 Both Barbara and Bill liked basketball.
21 Carl can accept a classic car in Cairo.
22 David dined in a dark diner in Detroit.
23 Elmo said Eddie edited the entire text.
24 Five friars focused on the four fables.
25 Guy gave a bag of green grapes to Gina.
26 Haughty Hugh hoped Hal had helped Seth.
27 Irene liked to pickle pickles in brine.
28 Jon Jones joined a junior jogging team.
29 Kenny kept a kayak for a trek to Akron.
30 Lowell played a well-planned ball game.
31 Monica made more money on many markups.
32 Ned knew ten men in a main dining room.
33 Opal Orem opened four boxes of oranges.
34 Pat paid to park the plane at the pump.
35 Quincy quickly quit his quarterly quiz.
36 Robin read rare books in their library.
37 Sam signed, sealed, and sent the lease.
38 Todd caught trout in the little stream.
39 Uncle Rubin urged Julie to go to Utica.
40 Viva Vista vetoed the five voice votes.
41 Walt waited while Wilma went to Weston.
42 Xu mixed extra extract exactly as told.
43 Yes, your young sister played a cymbal.
44 Zesty zebras zigzagged in the Ohio zoo.

E. Take two 1-minute timed writings. Review your speed and errors.

Goal: At least 19wpm/1'/3e

E. 1-MINUTE TIMED WRITING

45　　　Zoe expected a quiet morning to do　　7
46　all of her work. Jean Day was to bring　15
47　five of the tablets.　　　　　　　　　　19
　　| 1 | 2 | 3 | 4 | 5 | 6 | 7 | 8 |

Unit 3

Keyboarding: The Numbers

LESSON 11
5 7 3 9

LESSON 12
Review

LESSON 13
8 2 0

LESSON 14
4 6 1

LESSON 15
Review

Lesson 11

Number Keys

Goals
- Touch-type the 5, 7, 3, and 9 keys
- Type at least 19wpm/2′/5e

A. Type 2 times.

A. WARMUP

1   The law firm of Quayle, Buster, Given, and   9
2 Rizzo processed all the cases last June and July;   19
3 however, we will seek a new law firm next summer.   29

   | 1 | 2 | 3 | 4 | 5 | 6 | 7 | 8 | 9 | 10 |

NEW KEYS

B. Type each line 2 times.

Use the F finger.

B. THE 5 KEY

4 fr5f fr5f f55f f55f f5f5 f5f5 5 55 555 5,555 5:55
5 55 fibs 55 foes 55 fibs 55 fads 55 furs 55 favors
6 The 55 students read the 555 pages in 55 minutes.
7 He found Item 55 that weighed 55 pounds 5 ounces.

C. Type each line 2 times.

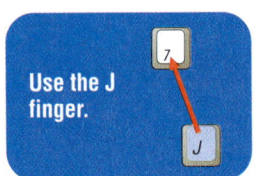

Use the J finger.

C. THE 7 KEY

8 ju7j ju7j j77j j77j j7j/ j7j7 7 77 777 7,777 7:77
9 77 jigs 77 jobs 77 jugs 77 jets 77 jars 77 jewels
10 The 77 men bought Items 77 and 777 for their job.
11 Joe had 57 books and 77 tablets for a 7:57 class.

D. Type each line 2 times.

Use the D finger.

D. THE 3 KEY

12 de3d de3d d33d d33d d3d3 d3d3 3 33 333 3,333 3:33
13 33 dots 33 dies 33 dips 33 days 33 dogs 33 drains
14 The 33 vans moved 73 cases in less than 33 hours.
15 Add 55 to 753; subtract 73 to get a total of 735.

E. Type each line 2 times.

Use the L finger.

E. THE 9 KEY

16 1o91 1o91 1991 1991 1919 1919 9 99 999 9,999 9:99
17 99 lads 99 lights 99 labs 99 legs 99 lips 99 logs
18 Their 99 cans of No. 99 were sold to 99 managers.
19 He had 39 pens, 59 pads, 97 pencils, and 9 clips.

SKILLBUILDING

F. Type each line 2 times.

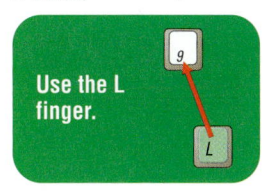

F. NUMBER PRACTICE: 5, 7, 3, AND 9

20 The 57 tickets were for the April 3 show at 9:59.
21 Mary was to read pages 33, 57, 95, and 97 to him.
22 Kate planted 53 tulips, 39 mums, and 97 petunias.
23 Only 397 of the 573 coeds could register at 5:39.

G. Type each line 2 times. Keep other fingers at home as you reach to the SHIFT keys.

G. TECHNIQUE PRACTICE: SHIFT KEY

24 Vera Rosa Tao Fay Jae Tab Pat Yuk Sue Ann Sal Joe
25 Andre Fidel Pedro Chong Alice Mike Juan Fern Dick
26 Carlos Caesar Karen Ojars Julie Marta Scott Maria
27 Marge Jerry Joan Mary Bill Ken Bob Ray Ted Mel Al

H. PROGRESSIVE PRACTICE: ALPHABET

If you are not using the GDP software, turn to page SB-7 and follow the directions for this activity.

I. Take two 2-minute timed writings. Review your speed and errors.

Goal: At least 19wpm/2'/5e

I. 2-MINUTE TIMED WRITING

28   Zach paid for six seats and quit because he   9
29 could not get the views he wanted near the middle   19
30 of the field. In August he is thinking of going   29
31 to the ticket office early to purchase tickets.   38
    | 1 | 2 | 3 | 4 | 5 | 6 | 7 | 8 | 9 | 10

Lesson 12

Review

Goal
- Type at least 20wpm/2'/5e

A. Type 2 times.

A. WARMUP

1   Rex played a very quiet game of bridge with
2   Zeke. In March they played in competition with
3   39 players; in January they played with 57 more.
  | 1 | 2 | 3 | 4 | 5 | 6 | 7 | 8 | 9 | 10

SKILLBUILDING

B. Take three 12-second timed writings on each line. The scale below the last line shows your wpm speed for a 12-second timed writing.

B. 12-SECOND SPEED SPRINTS

4   A good neighbor paid for these ancient ornaments.
5   Today I sit by the big lake and count huge rocks.
6   The four chapels sit by the end of the old field.
7   The signal means help is on its way to the child.

C. Take a 1-minute timed writing on the first paragraph to establish your base speed. Then take four 1 minute timed writings on the remaining paragraphs. As soon as you equal or exceed your base speed on one paragraph, advance to the next, more difficult paragraph.

C. SUSTAINED PRACTICE: SYLLABIC INTENSITY

8   People continue to rent autos for personal   9
9   use and for their work, and car rental businesses   19
10 just keep growing. You may want to try one soon.   29

11   It is likely that a great deal of insurance   9
12 protection is part of the standard rental cost to   19
13 you. You may, however, make many other choices.   28

14   Perhaps this is not necessary, as you might   9
15 already have the kind of protection you want in a   19
16 policy that you currently have on the automobile.   29

17   Paying separate mileage charges could evolve   9
18 into a very large bill. This will undoubtedly be   19
19 true if your trip involves distant destinations.   29

D. Type each line 2 times.

D. ALPHABET PRACTICE

20 Packing jam for the dozen boxes was quite lively.
21 Fay quickly jumped over the two dozen huge boxes.
22 We vexed Jack by quietly helping a dozen farmers.
23 The quick lynx from the zoo just waved a big paw.
24 Lazy brown dogs do not jump over the quick foxes.

E. Type each line 2 times.

E. NUMBER PRACTICE

25 Mary was to read pages 37, 59, 75, and 93 to Zoe.
26 He invited 53 boys and 59 girls to the 7:35 show.
27 The 9:37 bus did not come to our stop until 9:55.
28 Purchase Order 53 listed Items 35, 77, 93, and 9.
29 Flight 375 will be departing Gate 37 at 9:59 p.m.

F. Type each sentence on a separate line. Type 2 times.

F. TECHNIQUE PRACTICE: ENTER KEY

30 Can he go? If so, what? We are lost. Jose is ill.
31 Did she type the memos? Tina is going. Jane lost.
32 Max will drive. Xenia is in Ohio. She is tallest.
33 Nate is fine. Ty is not. Who won? Where is Nancy?
34 No, she cannot go. Was he here? Where is Roberta?

G. Type each line 2 times. Space without pausing.

G. TECHNIQUE PRACTICE: SPACE BAR

35 a b c d e f g h i j k l m n o p q r s t u v w x y
36 an as be by go in is it me no of or to we but for
37 Do you go to Ada or Ida for work every day or so?
38 I am sure he can go with you if he has some time.
39 He is to be at the car by the time you get there.

H. Take two 2-minute timed writings. Review your speed and errors.

Goal: At least 20wpm/2'/5e

H. 2-MINUTE TIMED WRITING

40   Jack and Alex ordered six pizzas at a price   9
41 that was quite a bit lower than was the one they 19
42 ordered yesterday. They will order from the same 29
43 place tomorrow for the parties they are planning 38
44 to have.   40

| 1 | 2 | 3 | 4 | 5 | 6 | 7 | 8 | 9 | 10

Lesson 13

Number Keys

Goals
- Touch-type the 8, 2, and 0 keys
- Type at least 21wpm/2'/5e

A. Type 2 times.

A. WARMUP

1 Mary, Jenny, and Quinn packed 79 prizes in   9
2 53 large boxes for the party. They will take all   19
3 of the boxes to 3579 North Capitol Avenue today.   29

| 1 | 2 | 3 | 4 | 5 | 6 | 7 | 8 | 9 | 10

NEW KEYS

B. Type each line 2 times.

Use the K finger.

B. THE 8 KEY

4 ki8k ki8k k88k k88k k8k8 k8k8 8 88 888 8,888 8:88
5 88 inks 88 inns 88 keys 88 kits 88 kids 88 knives
6 Bus 38 left at 3:38 and arrived here at 8:37 p.m.
7 Kenny called Joe at 8:38 at 883-7878 or 585-3878.

C. Type each line 2 times.

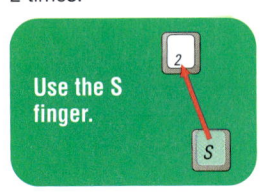

Use the S finger.

C. THE 2 KEY

8   sw2s sw2s s22s s22s s2s2 s2s2 2 22 222 2,222 2:22
9   22 seas 22 sets 22 sons 22 subs 22 suns 22 sports
10 The 22 seats sold at 2:22 to 22 coeds in Room 22.
11 He added Items 22, 23, 25, 27, and 28 on Order 2.

D. Type each line 2 times.

Use the Sem finger.

D. THE 0 KEY

12 ;p0; ;p0; ;00; ;00; ;0;0 ;0;0 0 00 000 0,000 0:00
13 20 pads 30 pegs 50 pens 70 pins 80 pits 900 parks
14 You will get 230 when you add 30, 50, 70, and 80.
15 The 80 men met at 3:05 with 20 agents in Room 90.

30   UNIT 3   Lesson 13

SKILLBUILDING

E. Type each line 2 times.

E. NUMBER PRACTICE

```
16  Jill bought 55 tickets for the 5:50 or 7:50 show.
17  Maxine called from 777-7370 or 777-7570 for Mary.
18  Sally had 23 cats, 23 dogs, and 22 birds at home.
19  Items 35, 37, 38, and 39 were sent on October 30.
20  Did Flight 2992 leave from Gate 39 at 9:39 today?
21  Sue went from 852 28th Street to 858 28th Street.
22  He sold 20 tires, 30 air filters, and 200 wipers.
```

F. Type each sentence on a separate line. For each sentence, press TAB, type the sentence, and then press ENTER. After you have typed all 11 sentences, insert a blank line and type them all a second time.

F. TECHNIQUE PRACTICE: TAB KEY

```
23       Casey left to go home. Where is John? Did
24  Susan go home with them?

25       Isaiah drove my car to work. Sandy parked
26  the car in the lot. They rode together.

27       Pat sold new cars for a new dealer. Dana
28  sold vans for the same dealer.

29       Nick bought the nails to finish the job.
30  Chris has the bolts. Dave has the wood.
```

G. PACED PRACTICE

If you are not using the GDP software, turn to page SB-14 and follow the directions for this activity.

H. PROGRESSIVE PRACTICE: ALPHABET

If you are not using the GDP software, turn to page SB-7 and follow the directions for this activity.

I. Take two 2-minute timed writings. Review your speed and errors.

Goal: At least 21wpm/2'/5e

I. 2-MINUTE TIMED WRITING

```
31       Jim told Bev that they must keep the liquid      9
32  oxygen frozen so that it could be used by the new    19
33  plant managers tomorrow. The oxygen will then be     29
34  moved quickly to its new location by transport or    39
35  rail on Tuesday.                                     42
      | 1 | 2 | 3 | 4 | 5 | 6 | 7 | 8 | 9 | 10
```

UNIT 3   Lesson 13

Lesson 14

Number Keys

Goals
- Touch-type the 4, 6, and 1 keys
- Type at least 22wpm/2′/5e

A. Type 2 times.

A. WARMUP

1 We quickly made 30 jars of jam and won a big
2 prize for our efforts on March 29. Six of the jam
3 jars were taken to 578 Culver Drive on April 28.

NEW KEYS

B. Type each line 2 times.

Use the F finger.

B. THE 4 KEY

4 fr4f fr4f f44f f44f f4f4 f4f4 4 44 444 4,444 4:44
5 44 fans 44 feet 44 figs 44 fins 44 fish 44 flakes
6 The 44 boys had 44 tickets for the games at 4:44.
7 Matthew read 4 books, 54 articles, and 434 lines.

C. Type each line 2 times.

Use the J finger.

C. THE 6 KEY

8 jy6j jy6j j66j j66j j6j6 j6j6 6 66 666 6,666 6:66
9 66 jabs 66 jams 66 jobs 66 jars 66 jots 66 jewels
10 Tom Lux left at 6:26 on Train 66 to go 600 miles.
11 There were 56,640 people in Bath; 26,269 in Hale.

D. Type each line 2 times.

Use the A finger.

D. THE 1 KEY

12 aq1a aq1a a11a a11a a1a1 a1a1 1 11 111 1,111 1:11
13 11 aces 11 arms 11 aims 11 arts 11 axes 11 arenas
14 Sam left here at 1:11, Sue at 6:11, Don at 11:11.
15 Eric moved from 1661 Main Street to 1116 in 1995.

SKILLBUILDING

E. Type each line 2 times. Focus on accuracy rather than speed as you practice the number drills.

E. NUMBER PRACTICE

16 Adding 10 and 20 and 30 and 40 and 70 totals 170.
17 Al selected Nos. 15, 16, 17, 18, and 19 to study.
18 The test took Sam 10 hours, 8 minutes, 3 seconds.
19 Did the 39 men drive 567 miles on Route 23 or 27?
20 The 18 shows were sold out by 8:37 on October 18.
21 On April 29-30 we will be open from 7:45 to 9:30.

F. PROGRESSIVE PRACTICE: NUMBERS

If you are not using the GDP software, turn to page SB-11 and follow the directions for this activity.

G. Take two 1-minute timed writings. Review your speed and errors.

G. HANDWRITTEN PARAGRAPH

22 Good writing skills are critical for success   9
23 in business. Numerous studies have shown   18
24 that these skills are essential for job advancement.   27

| 1 | 2 | 3 | 4 | 5 | 6 | 7 | 8 | 9 | 10 |

H. PACED PRACTICE

If you are not using the GDP software, turn to page SB-14 and follow the directions for this activity.

I. Take two 2-minute timed writings. Review your speed and errors.

Goal: At least 22wpm/2'/5e

I. 2-MINUTE TIMED WRITING

25   James scheduled a science quiz next week for   9
26 George, but he did not let him know what time the   19
27 exam was to be taken. George must score well on   29
28 this exam in order to be admitted to the class   38
29 at the Mount Garland Academy.   44

| 1 | 2 | 3 | 4 | 5 | 6 | 7 | 8 | 9 | 10 |

Lesson 15

Review

Goal
- Type at least 23wpm/2'/5e

A. Type 2 times.

A. WARMUP

1 Jeffrey Mendoza quickly plowed six fields so 9
2 that he could plant 19 rows of beets, 28 rows of 19
3 corn, 37 rows of grapes, and 45 rows of olives. 28

| 1 | 2 | 3 | 4 | 5 | 6 | 7 | 8 | 9 | 10 |

SKILLBUILDING

B. Take three 12-second timed writings on each line. The scale below the last line shows your wpm speed for a 12-second timed writing.

B. 12-SECOND SPEED SPRINTS

4 The lane to the lake might make the auto go away.
5 They go to the lake by bus when they work for me.
6 He just won and lost, won and lost, won and lost.
7 The man and the girl rush down the paths to town.

  5   10   15   20   25   30   35   40   45   50

C. Press TAB 1 time between columns. Type 2 times.

C. TECHNIQUE PRACTICE: TAB KEY

8	aisle	Tab→	break	Tab→	crank	Tab→	draft	Tab→	earth
9	Frank		Guinn		Henry		Ivan		Jacob
10	knack		learn		mason		night		ocean
11	print		quest		rinse		slide		title
12	Umberto		Victor		Wally		Xavier		Zenger

D. Type each line 2 times. Try not to slow down for the capital letters.

D. TECHNIQUE PRACTICE: SHIFT KEY

13 Sue, Pat, Ann, and Gail left for Rome on June 10.
14 The St. Louis Cardinals and New York Mets played.
15 Dave Herr took Flight 481 for Memphis and Toledo.
16 An address for Karen Cook is 5 Bar Street, Provo.
17 Harry Truman was born in Missouri on May 8, 1884.

E. Type each line 2 times.

E. PUNCTUATION PRACTICE: HYPHEN

18 Jan Brooks-Smith was a go-between for the author.
19 The off-the-record comment led to a free-for-all.
20 Louis was a jack-of-all-trades as a clerk-typist.
21 Ask Barbara--who is in Central Data--to find out.
22 Joanne is too old-fashioned to be that outspoken.

PPP PRETEST → PRACTICE → POSTTEST

PRETEST
Take a 1-minute timed writing. Review your speed and errors.

F. PRETEST: Vertical Reaches

23   A few of our business managers attribute the   9
24 success of the bank to a judicious and scientific 19
25 reserve program. The bank cannot drop its guard. 29
   | 1 | 2 | 3 | 4 | 5 | 6 | 7 | 8 | 9 | 10

PRACTICE
Speed Emphasis:
If you made 2 or fewer errors on the Pretest, type each *individual* line 2 times.
Accuracy Emphasis:
If you made 3 or more errors, type each *group* of lines (as though it were a paragraph) 2 times.

G. PRACTICE: Up Reaches

26 at atlas plate water later batch fatal match late
27 dr draft drift drums drawn drain drama dress drab
28 ju jumpy juror junky jumbo julep judge juice just

H. PRACTICE: Down Reaches

29 ca cable cabin cadet camel cameo candy carve cash
30 nk trunk drink prank rinks brink drank crank sink
31 ba batch badge bagel baked banjo barge basis bank

POSTTEST
Repeat the Pretest timed writing and compare performance.

I. POSTTEST: Vertical Reaches

J. PROGRESSIVE PRACTICE: ALPHABET

If you are not using the GDP software, turn to page SB-7 and follow the directions for this activity.

K. Take two 2-minute timed writings. Review your speed and errors.

Goal: At least 23wpm/2'/5e

K. 2-MINUTE TIMED WRITING

32   Jeff Malvey was quite busy fixing all of the   9
33 frozen pipes so that his water supply would not 19
34 be stopped. Last winter Jeff kept the pipes from 29
35 freezing by wrapping them with an insulated tape 38
36 that protected them from snow and ice. 46
   | 1 | 2 | 3 | 4 | 5 | 6 | 7 | 8 | 9 | 10

UNIT 3   Lesson 15

Unit 4

Keyboarding: The Symbols

LESSON 16
$ ( ) !

LESSON 17
Review

LESSON 18
* # '

LESSON 19
& % " @

LESSON 20
Review

Lesson 16

Symbol Keys

Goals
- Touch-type the $ ( ) and ! keys
- Type at least 24wpm/2'/5e

A. Type 2 times.

A. WARMUP

```
1        Gill was quite vexed by that musician who         9
2   played 5 jazz songs and 13 country songs at the       18
3   fair. He wanted 8 rock songs and 4 blues songs.       28
    |  1  |  2  |  3  |  4  |  5  |  6  |  7  |  8  |  9  | 10
```

NEW KEYS

B. DOLLAR is the shift of 4. Do not space between the dollar sign and the number. Type each line 2 times.

Use the F finger.

B. THE $ KEY

```
4   frf fr4f f4f f4$f f$$f f$$f $44 $444 $4,444 $4.44
5   I quoted $48, $64, and $94 for the set of chairs.
6   Her insurance paid $150; our insurance paid $175.
7   Season concert seats were $25, $30, $55, and $75.
```

C. PARENTHESES are the shifts of 9 and 0. Do not space between the parentheses and the text within them. Type each line 2 times.

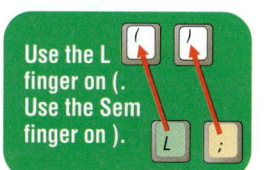

Use the L finger on (.
Use the Sem finger on).

C. THE (AND) KEYS

```
8    lo91 lo91 lo(1 lo(1 1((1 ;p0; ;p0; ;p); ;p); ;));
9    Please ask (1) Al, (2) Pat, (3) Ted, and (4) Dee.
10   Sue has some (1) skis, (2) sleds, and (3) skates.
11   Mary is (1) prompt, (2) speedy, and (3) accurate.

12   Our workers (Lewis, Jerry, and Ty) were rewarded.
13   The owner (Ms. Parks) went on Friday (August 18).
14   The Roxie (a cafe) had fish (salmon) on the menu.
15   The clerk (Ms. Fay Green) will vote yes (not no).
```

D. THE ! KEY

D. EXCLAMATION is the shift of 1. Space 1 time after an exclamation point at the end of a sentence. Type each line 2 times.

Use the A finger.

16 aqa aq1a aq!a a!!a a!!a Where! Whose! What! When!
17 Put those down! Do not move them! Leave it there!
18 He did say that! Jake cannot take a vacation now!
19 You cannot leave at this time! Janie will go now!

SKILLBUILDING

E. TECHNIQUE PRACTICE: SPACE BAR

E. Type the paragraph 2 times.

20   We will all go to the race if I win the one
21 I am going to run today. Do you think I will be
22 able to run at the front of the pack and win it?

F. 12-SECOND SPEED SPRINTS

F. Take three 12-second timed writings on each line. The scale below the last line shows your wpm speed for a 12-second timed writing.

23 Walking can perk you up if you are feeling tired.
24 Your heart and lungs can work harder as you walk.
25 It may be that a walk is often better than a nap.
26 If you walk each day, you may have better health.
        5   10   15   20   25   30   35   40   45   50

G. PACED PRACTICE

If you are not using the GDP software, turn to page SB-14 and follow the directions for this activity.

H. 2-MINUTE TIMED WRITING

H. Take two 2-minute timed writings. Review your speed and errors.

Goal: At least 24wpm/2'/5e

27   Katie quit her zoo job seven days after she   9
28 learned that she was expected to travel to four   19
29 different zoos in the first month of employment.   28
30 After quitting that job, she found an excellent   38
31 position which did not require her to travel much.   48
      1   2   3   4   5   6   7   8   9   10

Lesson 17

Review

Goal
- Type at least 25wpm/2'/5e

A. Type 2 times.

A. WARMUP

```
1        Yes! We object to the dumping of 25 toxic         9
2   barrels at 4098 Nix Street. A larger number (36)      19
3   were dumped on the 7th, costing us over $10,000.      28
    | 1  | 2  | 3  | 4  | 5  | 6  | 7  | 8  | 9  | 10
```

SKILLBUILDING

B. Type each line 2 times.

B. NUMBER PRACTICE

```
4   we 23 pi 08 you 697 row 492 tire 5843 power 09234
5   or 94 re 43 eye 363 top 590 quit 1785 witty 28556
6   up 70 ye 63 pit 085 per 034 root 4995 wrote 24953
7   it 85 ro 49 rip 480 two 529 tour 5974 quite 17853
8   yi 68 to 59 toy 596 rot 495 tier 5834 queue 17373
9   op 90 qo 19 wet 235 pet 035 rope 4903 quote 17953
```

C. Type each line 2 times.

C. WORD BEGINNINGS

```
10  tri trinkets tribune trifle trick trial trip trim
11  mil million mileage mildew mills milky miles mild
12  spo sponsor sponge sports spore spoon spool spoke
13  for forgiving forbear forward forbid forced force

14  div dividend division divine divide diving divers
15  vic vicinity vicious victory victims victor vices
16  aff affliction affiliates affirms affords affairs
17  tab tablecloth tabulates tableau tabloids tablets
```

D. Type each line 2 times.

D. WORD ENDINGS

```
18  ive repulsive explosive alive drive active strive
19  est nearest invest attest wisest nicest jest test
20  ply supply simply deeply damply apply imply reply
21  ver whenever forever whoever quiver waiver driver
```

```
22  tor inventor detector debtor orator doctor factor
23  lly industrially logically legally ideally really
24  ert convert dessert expert invert diverts asserts
25  ink shrink drink think blink clink pink sink rink
```

E. PROGRESSIVE PRACTICE: ALPHABET

If you are not using the GDP software, turn to page SB-7 and follow the directions for this activity.

F. Take two 1-minute timed writings. Review your speed and errors.

F. HANDWRITTEN PARAGRAPH

26 In this book you have learned the reaches   9
27 for all alphabetic and number keys. You have 18
28 also learned a few of the symbol keys. In the 27
29 remaining lessons you will learn the other   36
30 symbol keys. You will also build your speed   45
31 and accuracy when typing.   50

G. DIAGNOSTIC PRACTICE: NUMBERS

If you are not using the GDP software, turn to page SB-5 and follow the directions for this activity.

H. Take two 2-minute timed writings. Review your speed and errors.

Goal: At least 25wpm/2'/5e

H. 2-MINUTE TIMED WRITING

```
32       From the tower John saw that those six big      9
33  planes could crash as they zoomed quickly over      18
34  treetops on their way to the demonstration that    28
35  was scheduled to begin very soon. We hope there    37
36  is no accident and that the pilots reach their     47
37  airports safely.                                   50
```

Strategies for Career Success

Goodwill Messages

Would you like to strengthen your relationship with a customer, coworker, or boss? Send an unexpected goodwill message! Your expression of goodwill has a positive effect on business relationships.

Messages of congratulations or appreciation provide special opportunities to express goodwill. These messages can be quite brief. If your handwriting is good, send a handwritten note on a professional note card. Otherwise, send a letter or e-mail.

A note of congratulations might be "I just heard the news about your (award, promotion, etc.). My very best wishes." An appreciation note could be "Thank you for referring me to.... Your confidence and trust are sincerely appreciated."

YOUR TURN Send a goodwill message to someone to express congratulations or appreciation.

Symbol Keys

Goals
- Touch-type * # and ' keys
- Type at least 26wpm/2'/5e

A. Type 2 times.

A. WARMUP

```
1        Bill Waxmann quickly moved all 35 packs of           9
2   gear for the Amazon trip (worth $987) 26 miles           18
3   into the jungle. The move took 14 days in all.           27
    |  1  |  2  |  3  |  4  |  5  |  6  |  7  |  8  |  9  |  10
```

NEW KEYS

B. ASTERISK is the shift of 8. Type each line 2 times.

Use the K finger.

B. THE * KEY

```
4   kik ki8k k8*k k8*k k**k k**k This book* is great.
5   Use an * to show that a table source is included.
6   Asterisks keyed in a row (*******) make a border.
7   The article quoted Hanson,* Pyle,* and Peterson.*
```

C. NUMBER (if before a figure) or POUNDS (if after a figure) is the shift of 3. Type each line 2 times.

Use the D finger.

C. THE # KEY

```
 8   de3d de3#d d3#d d3#d d##d d##d #3 #33 #333 #3,333
 9   Al wants 33# of #200 and 38# of #400 by Saturday.
10   My favorite seats are #2, #34, #56, #65, and #66.
11   Please order 45# of #245 and 13# of #24 tomorrow.
```

D. Apostrophe is to the right of the semicolon. Type each line 2 times.

Use the Sem finger.

D. THE ' KEY

```
12  ;'; ';' ;'; ';' Can't we go in Sue's or Al's car?
13  It's Bob's job to cover Ted's work when he's out.
14  What's in Joann's lunch box for Sandra's dessert?
15  He's gone to Ty's banquet, which is held at Al's.
```

SKILLBUILDING

E. PACED PRACTICE

If you are not using the GDP software, turn to page SB-14 and follow the directions for this activity.

F. PROGRESSIVE PRACTICE: NUMBERS

If you are not using the GDP software, turn to page SB-11 and follow the directions for this activity.

G. Take two 1-minute timed writings. Review your speed and errors.

G. HANDWRITTEN PARAGRAPH

```
16  You have completed the first segment of      8
17  your class. You have learned to type all of   17
18  the alphabetic keys, the number keys, and some 26
19  of the symbol keys. Next you will learn the   35
20  remaining symbol keys on the top row.         42
    |  1  |  2  |  3  |  4  |  5  |  6  |  7  |  8  |  9  |  10
```

H. Take two 2-minute timed writings. Review your speed and errors.

Goal: At least 26wpm/2′/5e

H. 2-MINUTE TIMED WRITING

```
21       Max had to make one quick adjustment to his     9
22  television set before the football game began.      18
23  The picture during the last game was fuzzy and      28
24  hard to see. If he cannot fix the picture, he may   38
25  have to purchase a new television set; and that     47
26  may be difficult to do.                             52
    |  1  |  2  |  3  |  4  |  5  |  6  |  7  |  8  |  9  |  10
```

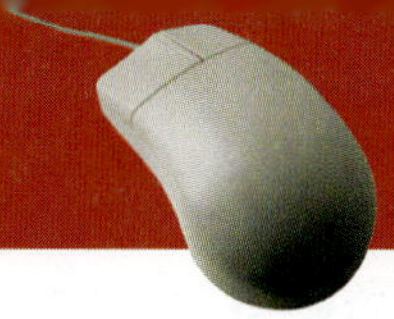

Lesson 19

Symbol Keys

Goals
- Touch-type & % " and @ keys
- Type at least 27wpm/2'/5e

A. Type 2 times.

A. WARMUP

```
1        The teacher (James Quayle) gave us some work         9
2   to do for homework for 11-28-05. Chapters 3 and 4        19
3   from our text* are to be read for a hard quiz.           28
    |  1  |  2  |  3  |  4  |  5  |  6  |  7  |  8  |  9  | 10
```

NEW KEYS

B. AMPERSAND (sign for *and*) is the shift of 7. Space before and after the ampersand. Type each line 2 times.

Use the J finger.

B. THE & KEY

```
4   juj ju7j j7j j7&j j&&j j&&j Max & Dee & Sue & Ken
5   Brown & Sons shipped goods to Crum & Lee Company.
6   Johnson & Loo brought a case against May & Green.
7   Ball & Trump vs. Vens & See is being decided now.
```

C. PERCENT is the shift of 5. Do not space between the number and the percent sign. Type each line 2 times.

Use the F finger.

C. THE % KEY

```
8   ft5f ft5%f f5%f f5%f f%%f f%%f 5% 55% 555% 5,555%
9   Robert quoted rates of 8%, 9%, 10%, 11%, and 12%.
10  Pat scored 82%, Jan 89%, and Ken 90% on the test.
11  Only 55% of the students passed 75% of the exams.
```

D. Quotation is the shift of the apostrophe. Do not space between quotation marks and the text they enclose. Type each line 2 times.

Use the Sem finger.

D. THE " KEY

12 ;'; ";" ;"; ";" "That's a super job," said Mabel.
13 The theme of the meeting is "Improving Your Job."
14 John said, "Those were good." Sharon said, "Yes."
15 Allison said, "I'll take Janice and Ed to Flint."

E. At is the shift of 2. Space before and after @ except when used in an e-mail address. Type each line 2 times.

Use the S finger.

E. THE @ KEY

16 sws sw2s s2@s s2@s s@@s s@@s Buy 15 @ $5 in June.
17 He can e-mail us at this address: projec@edu.com.
18 Order 12 items @ $14 and another 185 items @ $16.
19 Lee said, "I'll buy 8 shares @ $6 and 5 @ $7.55."

FORMATTING

F. Read these rules about the placement of quotation marks. Then type lines 20-23 two times.

F. PLACEMENT OF QUOTATION MARKS

1. The closing quotation mark is always typed *after* a period or comma but *before* a colon or semicolon.
2. The closing quotation mark is typed *after* a question mark or exclamation point if the quoted material itself is a question or an exclamation; otherwise, the quotation mark is typed *before* the question mark or exclamation point.

20 "Hello," I said. "My name is Hal; I am new here."
21 Zack read the article "Can She Succeed Tomorrow?"
22 James said, "I'll mail the check"; but he didn't.
23 Did Amy say, "We lost"? She said, "I don't know."

SKILLBUILDING

G. Type each line 2 times.

G. ALPHABET AND SYMBOL PRACTICE

24 Gaze at views of my jonquil or red phlox in back.
25 Jan quickly moved the six dozen big pink flowers.
26 Joe quietly picked six razors from the woven bag.
27 Packing jam for the dozen boxes was quite lively.

28 Mail these "Rush": #38, #45, and #67 (software).
29 No! Joe's note did not carry a rate of under 9%.
30 Lee read "The Computer Today." It's here Monday.
31 The book* cost us $48.10, 12% higher than yours.

H. Take a 1-minute timed writing on the first paragraph to establish your base speed. Then take four 1-minute timed writings on the remaining paragraphs. As soon as you equal or exceed your base speed on one paragraph, advance to the next, more difficult paragraph.

H. SUSTAINED PRACTICE: NUMBERS AND SYMBOLS

32   We purchased several pieces of new computer   9
33 equipment for our new store in Boston. We were   19
34 amazed at all the extra work we could get done.   28

35   For our department, we received 5 printers,   9
36 12 computers, and 3 fax machines. We heard that   19
37 the equipment cost us several thousand dollars.   28

38   Next week 6 computers (Model ZS86), 4 old   9
39 copiers (drums are broken), and 9 shredders will   18
40 need to be replaced. Total cost will be high.   28

41   Last year $150,890 was spent on equipment   9
42 for Iowa's offices. Breaman & Sims predicted a   18
43 17% to 20% increase (*over '99); that's amazing.   28

| 1 | 2 | 3 | 4 | 5 | 6 | 7 | 8 | 9 | 10 |

I. Take two 2-minute timed writings. Review your speed and errors.

Goal: At least 27wpm/2'/5e

I. 2-MINUTE TIMED WRITING

44   Topaz and onyx rings were for sale at a very   9
45 reasonable price last week. When Jeanette saw the   19
46 rings with these stones, she quickly bought them   29
47 both for her sons. These jewels were difficult to   39
48 find, and Jeanette was pleased she could purchase   49
49 those rings when she did.   54

| 1 | 2 | 3 | 4 | 5 | 6 | 7 | 8 | 9 | 10 |

Lesson 20

Review

Goal
- Type at least 28wpm/2'/5e

A. Type 2 times.

A. WARMUP

```
 1      Vin went to see Exhibits #794 and #860. He        9
 2   had quickly judged these zany projects that cost    19
 3   $321 (parts & labor)--a 5% markup from last year.   29
     |  1  |  2  |  3  |  4  |  5  |  6  |  7  |  8  |  9  | 10
```

SKILLBUILDING

B. Type each line 2 times.

B. PUNCTUATION PRACTICE

period — 4   Go to Reno. Drive to Yuma. Call Mary. Get Samuel.
comma — 5   We saw Nice, Paris, Bern, Rome, Munich, and Bonn.
semicolon — 6   Type the memo; read reports. Get pens; get paper.
colon, hyphen — 7   Read the following pages: 1-10, 12-22, and 34-58.
exclamation point — 8   No! Stop! Don't look! Watch out! Move over! Jump!

question mark — 9   Can you wait? Why not? Can he drive? Where is it?
colon, apostrophe — 10 I have these reports: Susan's, Bill's, and Lou's.
dash — 11 It's the best--and cheapest! Don't lose it--ever.
quotation marks — 12 "I can," she said, "right now." Val said, "Wait!"
parentheses — 13 Quint called Rome (GA), Rome (NY), and Rome (WI).

PPP PRETEST → PRACTICE → POSTTEST

PRETEST
Take a 1-minute timed writing. Review your speed and errors.

C. PRETEST: Alternate- and One-Hand Words

```
14      The chairman should handle the tax problem       9
15   downtown. If they are reversed, pressure tactics   19
16   might have changed the case as it was discussed.   28
     |  1  |  2  |  3  |  4  |  5  |  6  |  7  |  8  |  9  | 10
```

46   UNIT 4   Lesson 20

PRACTICE
Speed Emphasis:
If you made 2 or fewer errors on the Pretest, type each *individual* line 2 times.
Accuracy Emphasis:
If you made 3 or fewer errors, type each *group* of lines (as though it were a paragraph) 2 times.

POSTTEST
Repeat the Pretest timed writing and compare performance.

G. Take three 12-second timed writings on each line. The scale below the last line shows your wpm speed for a 12-second timed writing.

H. Take two 1-minute timed writings. Review your speed and errors.

K. Take two 2-minute timed writings. Review your speed and errors.

Goal: At least 28wpm/2'/5e

D. PRACTICE: Alternate-Hand Words

17 the with girl right blame handle antique chairman
18 for wish town their panel formal problem downtown
19 pan busy they flair signs thrown signals problems

E. PRACTICE: One-Hand Words

20 lip fact yolk poplin yummy affect reverse pumpkin
21 you cast kill uphill jumpy grease wagered opinion
22 tea cage lump limply hilly served bravest minimum

F. POSTTEST: Alternate- and One-Hand Words

G. 12-SECOND SPEED SPRINTS

23 Paul likes to work for the bank while in college.
24 They will make a nice profit if the work is done.
25 The group of friends went to a movie at the mall.
26 The man sent the forms after she called for them.
    | 5 | 10 | 15 | 20 | 25 | 30 | 35 | 40 | 45 | 50

H. HANDWRITTEN PARAGRAPH

27 *In your career, you will use the*   7
28 *skills you are learning in this course.*   15
29 *However, you will soon discover that you* 23
30 *must also possess human relations skills.* 31

I. MAP

Follow the GDP software directions for this exercise in improving keystroking accuracy.

J. DIAGNOSTIC PRACTICE: NUMBERS

If you are not using the GDP software, turn to page SB-5 and follow the directions for this activity.

K. 2-MINUTE TIMED WRITING

31   Jake or Peggy Zale must quickly fix the fax   9
32 machine so that we can have access to regional   18
33 reports that we think might be sent within the   28
34 next few days. Without the fax, we will not be   37
35 able to complete all our monthly reports by the   47
36 deadlines. Please let me know of any problems.   56
    | 1 | 2 | 3 | 4 | 5 | 6 | 7 | 8 | 9 | 10

SKILLBUILDING

Diagnostic Practice: SB-2
SYMBOLS AND PUNCTUATION

Diagnostic Practice: SB-5
NUMBERS

Progressive Practice: SB-7
ALPHABET

Progressive Practice: SB-11
NUMBERS

Paced Practice   SB-14

Supplementary Timed Writings   SB-28

SKILLBUILDING

Diagnostic Practice: Symbols and Punctuation

The Diagnostic Practice: Symbols and Punctuation program is designed to diagnose and then correct your keystroking errors. You may use this program at any time throughout the course after completing Lesson 19.

Directions

1. Type one of the three Pretest/Posttest paragraphs 1 time, pushing *moderately* for speed. Review your errors.
2. Note your results—the number of errors you made on each symbol or punctuation key. For example, if you typed *75&* for *75%*, you would count 1 error on the % key.
3. For any symbol or punctuation key on which you made 2 or more errors, type the corresponding drill lines 2 times. If you made only 1 error, type the drill line 1 time.
4. If you made no errors on the Pretest/Postest paragraph, type one set of the Practice: Symbols and Punctuation lines on page SB-4.
5. Finally, retype the same Pretest/Posttest, and compare your performance with your Pretest.

PRETEST/POSTTEST

Paragraph 1

Price & Joy stock closed @ 5 1/8 yesterday; it was up 13% from yesterday. If we had sold our "high-demand" shares* (*300 of them) before 3:30 p.m., we'd have made $15,000, wouldn't we? Oh, well! I'll be in my office (#13C) crying.

Paragraph 2

The Time/CNN poll had the slate of Myers & Bassey ahead by just 5%. Weren't you surprised? I was; after all, "they"* (*meaning the crew) had ordered 60# of food @ $9.50 a pound for a victory party at 3:30 p.m. today. What a sad mix-up!

Paragraph 3

Didn't my colleague* (*Elsa Jones-Salizar) send in $50 as a 10% deposit for reserving Room #5B on Friday and/or Monday? Attached to her deposit was a note that said, "Call Tibby, & me @ 10:30 a.m."; I was surprised. She sounded desperate!

PRACTICE: Individual Reaches

Ampersand

juj ju7j j7j j7&j j&&j j&&j juj ju7j j7j j7&j j&&j j&&j &&&
Alma & Bill & Carr & Dern & Epps & Farr & Gary & Horn & Ing
Jack & Kyle & Mann & Nash & Okum & Parr & Rand & Star & Tua
Uber & Vern & Will & Xang & Year & Zack & Sons & Bros & Inc

Apostrophe

;;; ;'; ;'; ';' ';' ''' Al's Bo's Di's it's Jo's Li's Moe's
you'd he'll she'd it'll she'll they'd aren't you're they're
we're we've we'll can't you've you'll hasn't didn't they've
she's don't isn't won't hadn't wasn't here's that's what'll

SKILLBUILDING

Asterisk	kik ki8k k8*k k8*k k**k k**k ki8k k8*k k8*k k**k k**k Note* Ames* Beck* Carr* Dern* Epps* Farr* Gary* Horn* Iago* Jack* Kyle* Mann* Nash* Okum* Parr* Rand* Star* Teri* Uber* Vern* Will* Xang* Year* Zack* Note* Star* Also* List* Text* Cite*
At Sign	sws sw2s s2@s s2@s s@s s@@s and sws sw2s s2@s s2@s s@s s@@s 138 @ 34 and 89 @ 104 and 18 @ 458 and 89 @ 10 and 18 @ 340 162 & 31 and 48 & 606 and 81 @ 923 and 69 @ 42 and 54 @ 128 277 @ 89 and 57 & 369 and 70 @ 434 and 50 @ 15 and 37 @ 512
Colon	;;; ;;; ;;; :;: ::: and :/: and :?: and :p: and :-: and ::: From: Name: City: Madam: 4:30 Bill to: Address: To: cc: PS: Date: Rank: Time: Dept.: 27:1 Subject: Time in: Hi: Re: Cf: Sirs: Ext.: Apt.: State: 1:00 Ship to: Acts 4:2 FY: ID: OS:
Comma	kkk k,k k,k and ,k, and ,i, and ,8, and I,I and K,K and ,,, Ava, ebb, lac, had, foe, elf, hug, ugh, poi, raj, ink, gal, bum, Ben, ago, cop, req, far, has, dot, tau, env, wow, sax, I am, you are, he is, we are, they are, Al, Ty, Hy, Jo, Ann
Diagonal	;;; ;/; /// and p/p and /p/ and 0/0 ;;; ;/; /// and p/p /// a/c c/o B/L ft/s ac/dc and/or he/she cad/cam due/dew 1/2005 I/O n/a B/S n/30 AM/FM ob/gyn on/off lay/lie fir/fur 2/2006 p/e m/f w/o km/h d/b/a ad/add to/too set/sit him/her 3/2007
Dollar Sign	frf fr4 f4f f$f f$f f$f $40 $44 $44 f$f f4f $ff $45 $54 $$$ $40 and $82 and $90 and $13 and $33 and $56 and $86 and $25 $214 plus $882 plus $900 plus $718 plus $910 plus $112 plus $1,937.53 plus $337.89 tax $3,985.43 minus $150.75 discount
Exclamation Mark	aqa aqla aq!a a!!a a!!a aqa aqla aq!a a!!a a!!a Go! Hi! Lo! Oh! Wow! Gas! Dig! Yes! Sit! Rats! Darn! Well! Drat! Shoot! So! Eat! Air! Out! Not! Aim! Whoa! Wait! Whee! Oops! Yahoo! No! Yea! Eek! Run! Boo! Buy! Look! Help! Duck! Alas! There!
Hyphen	;;; ;p; ;-; -;- --- and -;- and -;- and -/- and -:- and -P- add-on be-all F-stop H-bomb A-frame age-old all-day boo-boo how-to in-out jam-up log-in come-on cop-out end-all fade-in mix-up no-win say-so tie-up one-act pig-out rip-off T-shirt
Number/Pound	de3d de3#d d3#d d3#d d##d d##d #33 #33 #333 de3d de3#d d3#d 45# of #245 and 837# of #013 and 31# of #981 and 2# of #013 12# of #883 and 345# of #328 and 67# of #112 and 8# of #109 54# of #542 and 378# of #310 and 13# of #189 and 6# of #657
Parentheses	1o91 1o91 1o(1 1o(1 1((1 1((1 ;p0; ;p0; ;p); ;p); ;)); ;)); (a) (b) (c) (d) (e) (f) (g) (h) (i) (j) (k) (l) (m) (n) (o) (p) (q) (r) (s) (t) (u) (v) (w) (x) (y) (z) (1) (2) (3) (4) (5) (6) (7) (8) (9) (0) (@) (#) ($) (&) (*) (-) (;) (,) (:)

Diagnostic Practice: Symbols and Punctuation

SKILLBUILDING

Percent

```
ftf ft5f f5f f5%f f%%f f%%f ftf ft5f f5f f5%f f%%f f%%f %%%
```
40% and 82% and 90% and 13% and 33% and 56% and 86% and 25%
21% and 48% and 82% and 90% and 70% and 18% and 91% and 10%
34.5% off 89% increase 12% credit 67% finished 10% discount

Period

1.1 ... and .1. and .o. and .9. and .(. and .O. and L.L ...
Jan. Feb. Mar. Apr. Jun. Jul. Aug. Sep. Oct. Nov. Dec. a.m.
Sun. Mon. Tue. Wed. Thu. Fri. Sat. Mrs. Esq. Mex. Can. D.C.
I am. I see. We do. He is. I can. Do not. Help me. Go slow.

Question Mark

;;; ;/; ;?; ??? ?;? and p?p and ?O? and ?)? and ?-? and ???
So? Who? What? Can I? Why not? Who does? Stop here? Is she?
Me? How? When? May I? Who, me? Says who? Do it now? For me?
Oh? Why? Am I? Do we? Am I up? How much? Who knows? Will I?

Quotation Mark

;'; ;"; ;"; ";" """ and ;'; ;"; ;"; ";" """ and ;"; ";" """
"Eat" "Sit" "Rest" "Stay" "Roll" "Hello" "Look" "Pet" "Dry"
"Yes" "Lie" "Halt" "Next" "Move" "Write" "Type" "Ink" "Sew"
"Beg" "See" "Walk" "Wave" "Stop" "Speak" "File" "Run" "Cry"

Semicolon

;;; ;;; and ;'; and ;"; and ;p; and ;-; and ;/; and ;?; ;;;
tea; ebb; Mac; mid; lie; arf; hug; nth; obi; Taj; ark; Hal;
dim; man; bio; hop; seq; our; Gus; let; you; Bev; row; lax;
do not cry; that is Liz; see to it; I am sad; we do; I can;

PRACTICE: SYMBOLS AND PUNCTUATION

Doe & Fry sued May & Ito; Ho & Fox sued Doe & Lee for M&Ms.
Ann's dad said he's happy she's out of school; she'd agree.
Yesterday* (*April 9), the rock star said **** right on TV.
E-mail them at glyden@sales.com to buy 3 @ $89 or 9 @ $250.

Hi, Ross: Place odds of 3:1 on the game at 10:30 and 11:15.
Tom gave Ava, Jo, Al, and Tyson a red, white, and blue car.
On 3/1/2008, he will receive a pension and/or a big buyout.
The $80 skirt was cut to $70 and then $55 for a $25 saving.

What! No ice! I'm mortified! Run, order some more. Quickly!
Jones-Lynch built an all-season add-on to her A-frame home.
Please order 500# of #684, 100# of #133, and 200# of #1341.
The answer is (a) 1, (b) 4, (c) 7, or (d) all of the above.

The car was cut 15% and then 25% for a final saving of 40%.
Mr. R. J. Dix ordered from L. L. Bean on Dec. 23 at 11 a.m.
Who? Me? Why me? Because I can type? Is that a good reason?
"Look," he said, "see that sign?" It says, "Beware of Dog."
Stop here; get out of your car; walk a foot; begin digging.

SKILLBUILDING

Diagnostic Practice: Numbers

The Diagnostic Practice: Numbers program is designed to diagnose and then correct your keystroking errors. You may use this program at any time throughout the course after completing Lesson 14.

Directions

1. Type one of the three Pretest/Posttest paragraphs 1 time, pushing *moderately* for speed. Review your errors.
2. Note your results—the number of errors you made on each key and your total number of errors. For example, if you type *24* for *25*, you would count 1 error on the number *5*.
3. For any number on which you made 2 or more errors, select the corresponding drill lines and type the drills 2 times. If you made only 1 error, type the drill 1 time.
4. If you made no errors on the Pretest/Posttest paragraph, type 1 set of the drills that contain all numbers on page SB-6.
5. Finally, retype the same Pretest/Posttest, and compare your performance with your Pretest.

PRETEST/POSTTEST

Paragraph 1   The statement dated May 24, 2004, listed 56 clamps; 15 batteries; 169 hammers; 358 screwdrivers; 1,298 pliers; and 1,475 files. The invoice numbered 379 showed 387 hoes, 406 rakes, 92 lawn mowers, 63 tillers, and 807 more lawn items.

Paragraph 2   My inventory records dated May 31, 2004, revealed that we had 458 pints; 1,069 quarts; and 8,774 gallons of paint. We had 2,953 brushes; 568 scrapers; 12,963 wallpaper rolls; 897 knives; 5,692 mixers; 480 ladders; and 371 step stools.

Paragraph 3   Almost 179 hot meals were delivered to the 35 shut-ins in April, 169 in May, and 389 in June. Several workers had volunteered 7,564 hours in 2004; 9,348 hours in 2003; 5,468 in 2002; and 6,577 in 2001. About 80 people were involved.

PRACTICE: INDIVIDUAL REACHES

1 aq aq1 aq1qa 111 ants 101 aunts 131 apples 171 animals a1
They got 11 answers correct for the 11 questions in BE 121.
Those 11 adults loaded the 711 animals between 1 and 2 p.m.
All 111 agreed that 21 of those 31 are worthy of the honor.

2 sw sw2 sw2ws 222 sets 242 steps 226 salads 252 saddles s2
The 272 summer tourists saw the 22 soldiers and 32 sailors.
Your September 2 date was all right for 292 of 322 persons.
The 22 surgeons said 221 of those 225 operations went well.

3 de de3 de3ed 333 dots 303 drops 313 demons 393 dollars d3
Bus 333 departed at 3 p.m. with the 43 dentists and 5 boys.
She left 33 dolls and 73 decoys at 353 West Addison Street.
The 13 doctors helped some of the 33 druggists in Room 336.

SKILLBUILDING

4 fr fr4 fr4rf 444 fans 844 farms 444 fishes 644 fiddles f4
My 44 friends bought 84 farms and sold over 144 franchises.
She sold 44 fish and 440 beef dinners for $9.40 per dinner.
The 1954 Ford had only 40,434 fairly smooth miles by May 4.

5 fr fr5 fr5rf 555 furs 655 foxes 555 flares 455 fingers f5
They now own 155 restaurants, 45 food stores, and 55 farms.
They ordered 45, 55, 65, and 75 yards of that new material.
Flight 855 flew over Farmington at 5:50 p.m. on December 5.

6 jy jy6 jy6yj 666 jets 266 jeeps 666 jewels 866 jaguars j6
Purchase orders numbered 6667 and 6668 were sent yesterday.
Those 66 jazz players played for 46 juveniles in Room 6966.
The 6 judges reviewed the 66 journals on November 16 or 26.

7 ju ju7 ju7uj 777 jays 377 jokes 777 joists 577 juniors j7
The 17 jets carried 977 jocular passengers above 77 cities.
Those 277 jumping beans went to 77 junior scouts on May 17.
The 7 jockeys rode 77 jumpy horses between March 17 and 27.

8 ki ki8 ki8ik 888 keys 488 kites 888 knives 788 kittens k8
My 8 kennels housed 83 dogs, 28 kids, and 88 other animals.
The 18 kind ladies tied 88 knots in the 880 pieces of rope.
The 8 men saw 88 kelp bass, 38 kingfish, and 98 king crabs.

9 lo lo9 lo9ol 999 lads 599 larks 999 ladies 699 leaders 19
All 999 leaves fell from the 9 large oaks at 389 Largemont.
The 99 linemen put 399 large rolls of tape on for 19 games.
Those 99 lawyers put 899 legal-size sheets in the 19 limos.

0 ;p ;p0 ;p0p; 100 pens 900 pages 200 pandas 800 pencils ;0
There were 1,000 people who lived in the 300 private homes.
The 10 party stores are open from 1:00 p.m. until 9:00 p.m.
They edited 500 pages in 1 book and 1,000 pages in 2 books.

All numbers

ala s2s d3d f4f f5f j6j j7j k8k 191 ;0; Add 6 and 8 and 29.
That 349-page script called for 10 actors and 18 actresses.
The check for $50 was sent to 705 Garfield Street, not 507.
The 14 researchers asked the 469 Californians 23 questions.

All numbers

ala s2s d3d f4f f5f j6j j7j k8k 191 ;0; Add 3 and 4 and 70.
They built 1,299 houses on the 345-acre site by the canyon.
Her research showed that gold was at 397 in September 2004.
For $868 extra, they bought 15 new books and 61 used books.

All numbers

ala s2s d3d f4f f5f j6j j7j k8k 191 ;0; Add 5 and 7 and 68.
A bank auditor arrived on May 26, 2004, and left on May 27.
The 4 owners open the stores from 9:30 a.m. until 6:00 p.m.
After 1,374 miles on the bus, she must then drive 185 more.

SKILLBUILDING

Progressive Practice: Alphabet

This skillbuilding routine contains a series of 30-second timed writings that range from 16wpm to 104wpm. The first time you use these timed writings, take a 1-minute timed writing on the Entry Timed Writing paragraph. Note your speed.

Select a passage that is 2wpm higher than your current speed. Then take six 30-second timed writings on the passage. Your goal each time is to complete the passage within 30 seconds with no errors. When you have achieved your goal, move on to the next passage and repeat the procedure.

Entry Timed Writing

Bev was very lucky when she found extra quality in the home she was buying. She quietly told the builder that she was extremely satisfied with the work done on her new home. The builder said she can move into her new house next week.

| 1 | 2 | 3 | 4 | 5 | 6 | 7 | 8 | 9 | 10 | 11 | 12

11
23
35
47

16wpm — The author is the creator of a document.

18wpm — Open means to access a previously saved file.

20wpm — A byte represents one character to every computer.

22wpm — A mouse may be used when running Windows on a computer.

24wpm — Soft copy is text that is displayed on your computer screen.

26wpm — Memory is the part of the word processor that stores information.

28wpm — A menu is a list of choices to direct the operator through a function.

30wpm — A sheet feeder is a device that will insert sheets of paper into a printer.

32wpm — An icon is a small picture that illustrates a function or an object in software.

34wpm — A window is a rectangular area with borders that displays the contents of open files.

36wpm — To execute means to perform an action specified by an operator or by the computer program.

38wpm — Output is the result of a word processing operation. It can be either printed or magnetic form.

40wpm — Format refers to the physical features which affect the appearance and arrangement of your document.

SKILLBUILDING

42wpm   A font is a style of type of one size or kind which includes all letters, numbers, and punctuation marks.

44wpm   Ergonomics is the science of adapting working conditions or equipment to meet the physical needs of employees.

46wpm   Home position is the starting position of a document; it is typically the upper left corner of the display monitor.

48wpm   The mouse may be used to change the size of a window and to move a window to a different location on the display screen.

50wpm   An optical scanner is a device that can read text and enter it into a word processor without the need to type the data again.

52wpm   Hardware refers to the physical equipment used, such as the central processing unit, display screen, keyboard, printer, or drives.

54wpm   A peripheral device is any piece of equipment that will extend the capabilities of a computer system but is not required for operation.

56wpm   A split screen displays two or more different images at the same time; it can, for example, display two different pages of a legal document.

58wpm   When using Windows, it's possible to place several programs on a screen and to change the size of a window or to change its position on a screen.

60wpm   With the click of a mouse, one can use a button bar or a toolbar for fast access to features that are frequently applied when using a Windows program.

62wpm   An active window can be reduced to an icon when you use Windows, enabling you to double-click another icon to open a new window for formatting and editing.

64wpm   Turnaround time is the length of time needed for a document to be keyboarded, edited, proofread, corrected if required, printed, and returned to the originator.

66wpm   A local area network is a system that uses cable or another means to allow high-speed communication among many kinds of electronic equipment within particular areas.

68wpm   To search and replace means to direct the word processor to locate a character, word, or group of words wherever it occurs in the document and replace it with newer text.

SKILLBUILDING

70wpm — Indexing is the ability of a word processor to accumulate a list of words that appear in a document, including page numbers, and then print a revised list in alphabetic order.

72wpm — When a program needs information from you, a dialog box will appear on the desktop. Once the dialog box appears, you must identify the option you desire and then choose that option.

74wpm — A facsimile is an exact copy of a document, and it is also a process by which images, such as typed letters, graphs, and signatures, are scanned, transmitted, and then printed on paper.

76wpm — Compatibility refers to the ability of a computer to share information with another computer or to communicate with some other apparatus. It can be accomplished by using hardware or software.

78wpm — Some operators like to personalize their desktops when they use Windows by making various changes. For example, they can change their screen colors and the pointer so that they will have more fun.

80wpm — Wraparound is the ability of a word processor to move words from one line to another line and from one page to the next page as a result of inserting and deleting text or changing the size of margins.

82wpm — It is possible when using Windows to evaluate the contents of different directories on the screen at the very same time. You can then choose to copy or move a particular file from one directory to another.

84wpm — List processing is a capability of a word processor to keep lists of data that can be updated and sorted in alphabetic or numeric order. A list can also be added to any document that is stored in one's computer.

86wpm — A computer is a wondrous device, which accepts data that are input and then processes the data and produces output. The computer performs its work by using one or more stored programs, which provide the instructions.

88wpm — The configuration is the components that make up your word processing system. Most systems include the keyboard that is used for entering data, a central processing unit, at least one disk drive, a monitor, and a printer.

SKILLBUILDING   Progressive Practice: Alphabet

SKILLBUILDING

90wpm Help for Windows can be used whenever you see a Help button in a dialog box or on a menu bar. Once you finish reading about a topic that you have selected, you will see a list of some related topics from which you can choose.

92wpm When you want to look at the contents of two windows when using Windows, you will want to reduce the window size. Do this by pointing to a border or a corner of a window and dragging it until the window is the size that you want.

94wpm Scrolling means to display a large quantity of text by rolling it horizontally or vertically past the display screen. As the text disappears from the top section of the monitor, new text will appear at the bottom section of the monitor.

96wpm The Windows Print Manager is used to install and configure printers, join network printers, and monitor the printing of documents. Windows requires that a default printer be identified, but you can change the designation of it at any point.

98wpm A stop code is a command that makes a printer pause while it is printing to permit an operator to insert text, change the font style, or change the kind of paper in the printer. To resume printing, the operator must use a special key or command.

100wpm A computerized message system is a class of electronic mail that enables any operator to key a message on any computer terminal and have the message stored for later retrieval by the recipient, who can then display the message on his or her terminal.

102wpm Many different graphics software programs have been brought on the market in recent years. These programs can be very powerful in helping with a business presentation. If there is any need to share data, using one of these programs could be quite helpful.

104wpm Voice mail has become an essential service that many people in the business world use. This enables anyone who places a call to your phone to leave a message if you cannot answer it at that time. This special feature helps lots of workers to be more productive.

SKILLBUILDING

Progressive Practice: Numbers

This skillbuilding routine contains a series of 30-second timed writings that range from 16wpm to 80wpm. The first time you use these timed writings, take a 1-minute timed writing on the Entry Timed Writing paragraph. Note your speed.

Select a passage that is 4 to 6wpm *lower* than your current alphabetic speed. (The reason for selecting a lower speed goal is that sentences with numbers are more difficult to type.) Take six 30-second timed writings on the passage.

Your goal each time is to complete the passage within 30 seconds with no errors. When you have achieved your goal, move on to the next passage and repeat the procedure.

Entry Timed Writing

Their bags were filled with 10 sets of jars, 23 cookie cutters, 4 baking pans, 6 coffee mugs, 25 plates, 9 dessert plates, 7 soup bowls, 125 recipe cards, and 8 recipe boxes. They delivered these 217 items to 20487 Mountain Boulevard.

| 1 | 2 | 3 | 4 | 5 | 6 | 7 | 8 | 9 | 10 | 11 | 12

16wpm There were now 21 children in Room 2110.

18wpm Fewer than 12 of the 121 boxes arrived today.

20wpm Maybe 12 of the 21 applicants met all 15 criteria.

22wpm There were 34 letters addressed to 434 West Cranbrooke.

24wpm Jane reported that there were 434 freshmen and 43 transfers.

26wpm The principal assigned 3 of those 4 students to Room 343 at noon.

28wpm Only 1 or 2 of the 34 latest invoices were more than 1 page in length.

30wpm They met 11 of the 12 players who received awards from 3 of the 4 trainers.

32wpm Those 5 vans carried 46 passengers on the first trip and 65 on the next 3 trips.

34wpm We first saw 3 and then 4 beautiful eagles on Route 65 at 5 a.m. on Tuesday, June 12.

36wpm The 16 companies produced 51 of the 62 records that received awards for 3 of 4 categories.

38wpm The 12 trucks hauled the 87 cows and 65 horses to the farm, which was about 21 miles northeast.

SKILLBUILDING

40wpm She moved from 87 Bayview Drive to 657 Cole Street and then 3 blocks south to 412 Gulbranson Avenue.

42wpm My 7 or 8 buyers ordered 7 dozen in sizes 5 and 6 after the 14 to 32 percent discounts had been bestowed.

44wpm There were 34 men and 121 women waiting in line at the gates for the 65 to 87 tickets to the Cape Cod concert.

46wpm Steve had listed 5 or 6 items on Purchase Order 241 when he saw that Purchase Requisition 87 contained 3 or 4 more.

48wpm Your items numbered 278 will sell for about 90 percent of the value of the 16 items that have code numbers shown as 435.

50wpm The managers stated that 98 of those 750 randomly selected new valves had about 264 defects, far exceeding the usual 31 norm.

52wpm Half of the 625 volunteers received over 90 percent of the charity pledges. Approximately 83 of the 147 agencies will have funds.

54wpm Merico hired 94 part-time workers to help the 378 full-time employees during the 62-day period when sales go up by 150 percent or more.

56wpm Kaye only hit 1 for 4 in the first 29 games after an 8-game streak in which she batted 3 for 4. She then hit at a .570 average for 6 games.

58wpm The mail carrier delivered 98 letters during the week to 734 Oak Street and also took 52 letters to 610 Faulkner Road as he returned on Route 58.

60wpm Pat said that about 1 in 5 of the 379 swimmers had a chance of being among the top 20. The best 6 of those 48 divers will receive the 16 best awards.

62wpm It rained from 3 to 6 inches, and 18 of those 20 farmers were fearful that 4 to 7 inches more would flood about 95 acres along 3 miles of the new Route 78.

SKILLBUILDING

64wpm   Those 7 sacks weighed 48 pounds, more than the 30 pounds that I had thought. All 24 believe the 92-pound bag is at least 15 or 16 pounds above its true weight.

66wpm   They bought 7 of the 8 options for 54 of the 63 vehicles last month. They now own over 120 dump trucks for use in 9 of the 15 new regions in the big 20-county area.

68wpm   Andy was 8 or 9 years old when they moved to 632 Glendale Street away from the 1700 block of Horseshoe Lane, which is about 45 miles directly west of Boca Raton, FL 33434.

70wpm   Doug had read 575 pages in the 760-page book by March 30; Darlene had read only 468 pages. Darlene has read 29 of those optional books since October 19, and Doug has read 18.

72wpm   That school district has 985 elementary students, 507 middle school students, and 463 high school students; the total of 1,955 is 54, or 2.84 percent, over last year's grand total.

74wpm   Attendance at last year's meeting was 10,835. The goal for this year is to have 11,764 people. This will enable us to plan for an increase of 929 participants, a rise of 8.57 percent.

76wpm   John's firm has 158 stores, located in 109 cities in the West. The company employs 3,540 males and 2,624 females, a total of 6,164 employees. About 4,750 of those employees work part-time.

78wpm   Memberships were as follows: 98 members in the Drama Guild, 90 members in Zeta Tau, 82 members in Theta Phi, 75 in the Bowling Club, and 136 in the Ski Club. This meant that 481 joined a group.

80wpm   The association had 684 members from the South, 830 members from the North, 1,023 members from the East, and 751 from the West. The total membership was 3,288; these numbers increased by 9.8 percent.

Paced Practice

SKILLBUILDING

The Paced Practice skillbuilding routine builds speed and accuracy in short, easy steps by using individualized goals and immediate feedback. You may use this program at any time after completing Lesson 9.

This section contains a series of 2-minute timed writings for speeds ranging from 16wpm to 96wpm. The first time you use these timed writings, take the 1-minute Entry Timed Writing.

Select a passage that is 2wpm higher than your current typing speed. Then use this two-stage practice pattern to achieve each speed goal: (1) concentrate on speed, and (2) work on accuracy.

Speed Goal. To determine your speed goal, take three 2-minute timed writings in total. Your goal each time is to complete the passage in 2 minutes without regard to errors. When you have achieved your speed goal, work on accuracy.

Accuracy Goal. To type accurately, you need to slow down—just a bit. Therefore, to reach your accuracy goal, drop back 2wpm from the previous passage. Take consecutive timed writings on this passage until you can complete the passage in 2 minutes with no more than 2 errors.

For example, if you achieved a speed goal of 54wpm, you should then work on an accuracy goal of 52wpm. When you have achieved 52wpm for accuracy, move up 4wpm (for example, to the 56-wpm passage) and work for speed again.

Entry Timed Writing

If you can dream it, you can live it. Follow your heart. There are many careers, from the mundane to the exotic to the sublime. Start your career planning now. Prepare for the future by exploring your talents, skills, and interests.

| 1 | 2 | 3 | 4 | 5 | 6 | 7 | 8 | 9 | 10 | 11 | 12

16wpm

Your future is now. Seize each day. After you have explored your personal interests, study the sixteen career clusters for a broad range of job possibilities.

18wpm

While exploring various job options, think about what a job means to you. A job can mean something you do simply to earn money or something you find more rewarding and challenging.

20wpm

If you have a job you enjoy, work means more than just receiving wages. It means using your talents, being among people with like interests, making a contribution, and gaining a sense of satisfaction.

SKILLBUILDING

22wpm What is the difference between a job and a career? Think carefully. A job is work that people do for money. A career is a sequence of related jobs built on a foundation of interests, knowledge, training, and experiences.

24wpm Learn more about the world of work by looking at the sixteen career clusters. Most jobs are included in one of the clusters that have been organized by the government. During your exploration of careers, list the clusters that interest you.

26wpm Once you identify your career clusters of interest, look at the jobs within each cluster. Find out what skills and aptitudes are needed, what education and training are required, what the work environment is like, and what is the possibility for advancements.

28wpm Use your career center and school or public libraries to research career choices. Search the Internet. Consult with professionals for another perspective of a specific career. As you gather information about career options, you may discover other interesting career possibilities.

30wpm Gain insights into a career by becoming a volunteer, participating in an internship, or working a part-time or temporary job within a chosen field. You will become more familiar with a specific job while developing your skills. You'll gain valuable experience, whether you choose that career or not.

32wpm Whichever path you choose, strive for a high level of pride in yourself and your work. Your image is affected by what you believe other people think of you as well as by how you view yourself. Evaluate your level of confidence in yourself. If you have self-doubts, begin to build up your self-confidence and self-esteem.

SKILLBUILDING

34wpm

    Self-esteem is essential for a positive attitude, and a positive attitude is essential for success in the world of work. While you cannot control everything that happens at work, you can control how you react. Your attitude matters. Becoming more confident and cultivating positive thoughts can bring you power in your life and on the job.

36wpm

    Several factors lead to success on the job. People who have studied the factors say that it is the personal traits that often determine who is promoted or who is not. One of the finest traits a person can possess is the trait of being likable. Being likable means a person is honest, courteous, loyal, thoughtful, pleasant, kind, and most assuredly, positive.

38wpm

    If you are likable, probably you relate well with others. Your kindness serves you well in the workplace. Developing good interpersonal relationships with coworkers will make work more enjoyable. After all, think of all the hours you will spend together. By showing that you are willing to collaborate with your coworkers, most likely you will receive their cooperation in return.

40wpm

    Cooperation begins on the first day of your new job. When you work for a company, you become part of the team. Meeting people and learning new skills can be exciting. For some people, however, any new situation can trigger anxiety. The best advice is to remain calm, do your job to the best of your ability, learn the workplace policies, be flexible, avoid being too critical, and always be positive.

SKILLBUILDING

42wpm

When you begin a new job, even if you have recently received your college diploma, chances are you will start at the bottom of the organizational chart. Each of us has to start somewhere. But don't despair. With hard work and determination, soon you will be climbing up the corporate ladder. If you are clever, you will embrace even the most tedious tasks, take everything in stride, and use every opportunity to learn.

44wpm

If you think learning is restricted to the confines of an academic institution, think again. You have plenty to learn on the job, even if it is a job for which you have been trained. As a new worker, you won't be expected to know everything. When necessary, do not hesitate to ask your employer questions. Learn all you can about your job and the company. Use the new information to enhance your job performance and to prepare for success.

46wpm

Begin every valuable workday by prioritizing all your tasks. Decide which tasks must be done immediately and which can wait. List the most important tasks first; then determine the order in which each task must be done. After you complete a task, triumphantly cross it off your priority list. Do not procrastinate; that is, don't put off work you should do. If a task needs to be done, do it. You will be on top of your task list if you use your time wisely.

48wpm

Prevent the telephone from controlling your time by learning to manage your business phone calls. Phone calls can be extremely distracting from necessary tasks. When making an outgoing call, organize the topics you want to discuss. Gather needed materials such as pencils, papers, and files. Set a time limit, and stick to business. Give concise answers, summarize the points discussed, and end the conversation politely. Efficient telephone usage will help you manage your time.

SKILLBUILDING

50wpm

As with anything, practice makes perfect, but along the way, we all make mistakes. The difference between the successful people and those who are less successful is not that the successful people make fewer mistakes. It's that they don't give up. Instead of letting mistakes bring them down, they use their mistakes as opportunities to grow. If you make a mistake, be patient with yourself. You might be able to fix your mistake. Look for more opportunities for success to be just around the corner.

52wpm

Be patient with yourself when handling problems and accepting criticism. Handling criticism gracefully and maturely may be a challenge. Still, it is vital in the workplace. Criticism presented in a way that can help you learn and grow is constructive criticism . When you see criticism as helpful, it's easier to handle. Believe it or not, there are some employees who welcome criticism. It teaches them better ways to succeed on the job. Strive to improve how you accept constructive criticism, and embrace your growth.

54wpm

People experience continuous growth during a career. Goal setting is a helpful tool along any career path. Some people believe that goals provide the motivation needed to get to the place they want to be. Setting goals encourages greater achievements. The higher we set our goals, the greater the effort we will need to reach these goals. Each time we reach a target or come closer to a goal, we see an increase in our confidence and our performance, leading to greater accomplishments. And the cycle continues to spiral onward and upward.

SKILLBUILDING

56wpm

One goal we should all strive for is punctuality. When employees are tardy or absent from the workplace, it costs the company money. If you are frequently tardy or absent, others have to do their own work and cover for you. If you are absent often, your peers will begin to resent you, causing everyone stress in the department. Being late and missing work can damage the relationship with your manager and have a negative effect on your career. To avoid these potential problems, develop a personal plan to assure that you arrive every day on time or early.

58wpm

Holding a job is a major part of being an adult. Some people begin their work careers as adolescents. From the beginning, various work habits are developed that are as crucial to success as the actual job skills and knowledge that a person brings to the job. What traits are expected of workers? What do employers look for when they evaluate their employees? Important personal traits include being confident, cooperative, positive, and dependable. If you are organized, enthusiastic, and understanding, you have many of the qualities that employers value most in their employees.

60wpm

Being dependable is a desirable trait. When a project must be completed by a specific time, a manager will be reassured to know that reliable workers are going to meet the deadline. Workers who are dependable learn to utilize their time to achieve maximum results. Dependable workers can always be counted on, have good attendance records, are well prepared, and arrive on time ready to work. If a company wants to meet its goals, it must have a team of responsible and dependable workers. You, your coworkers, your supervisors, and your managers are all team members, working to reach common goals.

SKILLBUILDING

62wpm

    The ability to organize is an important quality for the employee who wishes to display good work habits. The worker should have the ability to plan the work that needs to be completed and then be able to execute the plan in a timely manner. An employer requires a competent worker to be well organized. If an office worker is efficient, he or she handles requests swiftly and deals with correspondence without delay. The organized worker does not allow work to accumulate on the desk. Also, the organized office worker returns all phone calls immediately and makes lists of the activities that need to be done each day.

64wpm

    Efficiency is another work habit that is desired. An efficient worker completes a task quickly and begins work on the next project eagerly. He or she thinks about ways to save steps and time. For example, an efficient worker may plan a single trip to the copier with several copying jobs rather than multiple trips to do each separate job. Being efficient also means having the required supplies to successfully complete each job. An efficient employee zips along on each project, uses time wisely, and stays focused on the present task. With careful and thorough planning, a worker who is efficient can accomplish more tasks in less time.

66wpm

    Cooperation is another ideal work habit. As previously mentioned, cooperation begins on the first day on the job. Cooperation is thinking of all team members when making a decision. A person who cooperates is willing to do what is necessary for the good of the whole group. For you to be a team player, it is essential that you take extra steps to cooperate. Cooperation may mean being a good sport if you are asked to do something you would rather not do. It may mean you have to correct a mistake made by another person in the office. If every employee has the interests of the company at heart and works well as a team player, then cooperation is at work.

SKILLBUILDING

68wpm

Enthusiasm is still another work trait that is eagerly sought after by employers. Being enthusiastic means that a person has lots of positive energy. This is reflected in actions toward your work, coworkers, and employer. It has been noted that eagerness can be catching. If workers show they are eager to attempt any project, they will not only achieve the highest praise but will also be considered for career advancement. How much enthusiasm do you show at the workplace? Do you encourage people or complain to people? There will always be plenty of good jobs for employees who are known to have a wealth of zeal and a positive approach to the projects that they are assigned.

70wpm

Understanding is also a preferred work habit for every excellent worker. In today's world, virtually all business includes both men and women of different religions, races, cultures, work ethic, abilities, aptitudes, and attitudes. You'll interact with various types of people as customers, coworkers, and owners. Treat everyone fairly, openly, and honestly. Any type of prejudice is hurtful, offensive, and unacceptable. Prejudice cannot be tolerated in the office. Each employee must try to understand and accept everyone's differences. Because so many diverse groups of people work side by side in the workplace, it is essential that all coworkers maintain a high degree of mutual understanding.

72wpm

It can be concluded that certain work habits or traits can play a major role in determining the success of an employee. Most managers would be quick to agree on the importance of these traits. It is most probable that these habits would be evaluated on performance appraisal forms. Promotions, pay increases, new responsibilities, and your future with the company may be based on these evaluations. You should request regular job performance evaluations even if your company does not conduct them. This feedback will improve your job performance and career development by helping you grow. If you continually look for ways to improve your work habits and skills, then you will enjoy success in the workplace and beyond.

SKILLBUILDING

74wpm

You can be certain that no matter where you work, you will use some form of computer technology. Almost every business is dependent upon computers. Companies use such devices as voice mail, fax machines, cellular phones, and electronic schedules. Technology helps to accomplish work quickly and efficiently. A result of this rapidly changing technology is globalization, which is the establishment of worldwide communication links between people. Our world is becoming a smaller, global village. We must expand our thinking beyond the office walls. We must become aware of what happens in other parts of the world. Those events may directly affect you and your workplace. The more you know, the more valuable you will become to the company.

76wpm

Technological advancements are affecting every aspect of our lives. For example, the advent of the Internet has changed how we receive and send information. It is the world's largest information network. The Internet is often called the information superhighway because it is a vast network of computers that connect people and resources worldwide. It is an exciting medium to help you access the latest information. You can even learn about companies by visiting their Web sites. Without any doubt, we are all globally connected, and information technology services support those necessary connections. This industry offers many different employment opportunities. Keep in mind that proficiency in keyboarding is beneficial in this field and in other fields.

SKILLBUILDING

78wpm

    It is amazing to discover the many careers in which keyboarding skill is necessary today, and the use of the computer keyboard by executive chefs is a prime example. The chefs in major restaurants must prepare parts or all of the meals served while directing the work of a staff of chefs, cooks, and other kitchen staff. The computer has become a necessary tool for a variety of tasks, including tracking inventories of food supplies. By observing which items are favorites and which items are not requested, the chef can calculate food requirements, order food, and supervise the food purchases. Additionally, the computer has proven to be a very practical tool for such tasks as planning budgets, preparing purchase orders for vendors, creating menus, and printing out reports.

80wpm

    Advanced technology has opened the doors to a wider variety of amazing new products and services to sell. It seems the more complex the products, the higher the price of the products, or the greater the sales commission, the stiffer the competition. Selling these technical products requires detailed product knowledge, good verbal skills, smooth sales rapport, and proficient keyboarding skills. Business favors people with special training. For example, a pharmacy company may prefer a person with knowledge in chemistry to sell its products. Selling is for people who thrive on challenges and changes in products and services. Sales is appealing to people who enjoy using their powers of persuasion to make the sales. The potential for good earnings is very high for the well-trained salesperson.

SKILLBUILDING

82wpm

  As you travel about in your sales job or type a report at the office or create Friday night's pasta special for your five-star restaurant, always remember to put safety first. Accidents happen, but they don't have to happen regularly or to have such serious consequences. Accidents cost businesses billions of dollars annually in medical expenses, lost wages, and insurance claims. A part of your job is to make certain you're not one of the millions of people injured on the job every year. You may believe you work in a safe place, but accidents occur in all types of businesses. A few careless people cause most accidents, so ensure your safety on the job. Safety doesn't just happen. Safety is the result of the careful awareness of many people who plan and put into action a safety program that benefits everyone.

84wpm

  In today's market, you need more than the necessary skill or the personal qualities described above to succeed in the workplace. Employers also expect their employees to have ethics. Ethics are the principles of conduct governing an individual or a group. Employees who work ethically do not lie, cheat, or steal. They are honest and fair in their dealings with others. Employees who act ethically build a good reputation for themselves and their company. They are known to be dependable and trustworthy. Unethical behavior can have a spiraling effect. A single act can do a lot of damage. Even if you haven't held a job yet, you have had experience with ethical problems. Life is full of many opportunities to behave ethically. Do the right thing when faced with a decision. The ethics you practice today will carry over to your workplace.

SKILLBUILDING

86wpm

Now that you know what is expected of you on the job, how do you make sure you will get the job? Almost everyone has experienced the interview process for a job. For some, the interview is a traumatic event, but it doesn't have to be stressful. Preparation is the key. Research the company with whom you are seeking employment. Formulate a list of questions. Your interview provides you the opportunity to interview the organization. Don't go empty-handed. Take a portfolio of items with you. Include copies of your resume with a list of three or more professional references, your academic transcript, and your certificates and licenses. Be sure to wear appropriate business attire. The outcome of the interview will be positive if you have enthusiasm for the job, match your qualifications to the company's needs, ask relevant questions, and listen clearly.

88wpm

How can you be the strongest candidate for the job? Be sure that your skills in reading, writing, mathematics, speaking, and listening are solid. These basic skills will help you listen well and communicate clearly, not only during a job interview, but also at your workplace. The exchange of information between senders and receivers is called communication. It doesn't matter which occupation you choose; you will spend most of your career using these basic skills to communicate with others. You will use the basic skills as tools to gain information, solve problems, and share ideas. You will use these skills to meet the needs of your customers. The majority of jobs available during the next decades will be in the industries that will require direct customer contacts. Your success will be based upon your ability to communicate effectively with customers and coworkers.

SKILLBUILDING

90wpm

Writing effectively can help you gain a competitive edge in your job search and throughout your career. Most of us have had occasion to write business letters whether to apply for a job, to comment on a product or service, or to place an order. Often it seems easy to sit and let our thoughts flow freely. In other cases, we seem to struggle to find the proper wording while trying to express our thoughts in exactly the right way. Writing skill can improve with practice. Implement the following principles to develop your writing skill. Try to use language that you would be comfortable using in person. Use words that are simple, direct, kind, confident, and professional. When possible, use words that emphasize the positive side. Remember to proofread your work. Well-organized thoughts and proper grammar, spelling, and punctuation show the reader that you care about the quality of your work.

92wpm

Listening is an essential skill of the communication process. It is crucial for learning, getting along, and forming relationships. Do you think you are an active or passive listener? Listening is not a passive activity. Conversely, active listening is hearing what is being said and interpreting its meaning. Active listening makes you a more effective communicator because you react to what you have heard. Study the following steps to increase your listening skills. Do not cut people off; let them develop their ideas before you speak. If a message is vague, write down your questions or comments, and wait for the entire presentation or discussion to be finished. Reduce personal and environmental distractions by focusing on the message. Keep an open mind. Be attentive and maintain eye contact whenever possible. By developing these basic communication skills, you will become more confident and more effective.

SKILLBUILDING

94wpm

Speaking is also a form of communication. In the world of work, speaking is an important way in which to share information. Regardless of whether you are speaking to an audience of one or one hundred, you will want to make sure that your listeners get your message. Be clear about your purpose, your audience, and your subject. A purpose is the overall goal or reason for speaking. An audience is anyone who receives information. The subject is the main topic or key idea. Research your subject. Using specific facts and examples will give you credibility. As you speak, be brief and direct. Progress logically from point to point. Speak slowly and pronounce clearly all your words. Do people understand what you say or ask you to repeat what you've said? Is the sound of your voice friendly and pleasant or shrill and off-putting? These factors influence how your message is received. A good idea is worthless if you can't communicate it.

96wpm

Developing a career is a process. You have looked at your interests, values, skills, aptitudes, and attitudes. Your exploration into the world of work has begun. The journey doesn't stop here, for the present is the perfect place to start thinking about the future. It's where you begin to take steps toward your goals. It's where you can really make a difference. As you set personal and career goals, remember the importance of small steps. Each step toward a personal goal or career goal is a small victory. That feeling of success encourages you to take other small steps. Each step builds onto the next. Continue exploring your personal world as well as the world you share with others. Expect the best as you go forward. Expect a happy life. Expect loving relationships. Expect success in life. Expect fulfilling and satisfying work in a job you truly love. Last but not least, expect that you have something special to offer the world, because you do.

Supplementary Timed Writings

Supplementary Timed Writing 1

All problem solving, whether personal or academic, involves decision making. You make decisions in order to solve problems. On occasion, problems occur as a result of decisions you have made. For example, you may decide to smoke, but later in life, you face the problem of nicotine addiction. You may decide not to study mathematics and science because you think that they are too difficult. Because of this choice, many career opportunities will be closed to you. There is a consequence for every action. Do you see that events in your life do not just happen, but that they are the result of your choices and decisions?

How can you prepare your mind for problem solving? A positive attitude is a great start. Indeed, your attitude affects the way in which you solve a problem or make a decision. Approach your studies, such as science and math courses, with a positive and inquisitive attitude. Try to perceive academic problems as puzzles to solve rather than homework to avoid.

Critical thinking is a method of problem solving that involves decoding, analyzing, reasoning, evaluating, and processing information. It is fundamental for successful problem solving. Critical thinking is a willingness to explore, probe, question, and search for answers. Problems may not always be solved on the first try. Don't give up. Try, try again. Finding a solution takes sustained effort. Use critical thinking skills to achieve success in today's fast-paced and highly competitive world of business.

SKILLBUILDING

Supplementary Timed Writing 2

For many, the Internet is an important resource in their private and professional lives. The Internet provides quick access to countless Web sites that contain news, products, games, entertainment, and many other types of information. The Web pages on these sites can be designed, authored, and posted by anyone, anywhere around the world. Utilize critical thinking when reviewing all Web sites.

Just because something is stated on the radio, printed in the newspaper, or shown on television doesn't mean that it's true, real, accurate, or correct. This applies to information found on the Internet as well. Don't fall into the trap of believing that if it's on the Net, it must be true. A wise user of the Internet thinks critically about data found on the Net and evaluates this material before using it.

When evaluating a new Web site, think about who, what, how, when, and where. Who refers to the author of the Web site. The author may be a business, an organization, or a person. What refers to the validity of the data. Can this data be verified by a reputable source? How refers to the viewpoint of the author. Is the data presented without prejudice? When refers to the time frame of the data. Is this recent data? Where refers to the source of the data. Is this data from an accurate source? By answering these critical questions, you will learn more about the accuracy and dependability of a Web site. As you surf the Net, be very cautious. Anyone can publish on the Internet.

| 1 | 2 | 3 | 4 | 5 | 6 | 7 | 8 | 9 | 10 | 11 | 12

Supplementary Timed Writing 3

Office employees perform a variety of tasks during their workday. These tasks vary from handling telephone calls to forwarding personal messages, from sending short e-mail messages to compiling complex office reports, and from writing simple letters to assembling detailed letters with tables, graphics, and imported data. Office workers are a fundamental part of a company's structure.

The office worker uses critical thinking in order to accomplish a wide array of daily tasks. Some of the tasks are more urgent than other tasks and should be completed first. Some tasks take only a short time, while others take a lot more time. Some tasks demand a quick response, while others may be taken up as time permits or even postponed until the future. Some of the tasks require input from coworkers or managers. Whether a job is simple or complex, big or small, the office worker must decide what is to be tackled first by determining the priority of each task.

When setting priorities, critical thinking skills are essential. The office worker evaluates each aspect of the task. It is a good idea to identify the size of the task, determine its complexity, estimate its effort, judge its importance, and set its deadline. Once the office worker assesses each task that is to be finished within a certain period of time, then the priority for completing all tasks can be set. Critical thinking skills, if applied well, can save the employer money or, if executed poorly, can cost the employer.

| 1 | 2 | 3 | 4 | 5 | 6 | 7 | 8 | 9 | 10 | 11 | 12 |

SKILLBUILDING

Supplementary Timed Writing 4

Each day business managers make choices that keep businesses running smoothly, skillfully, and profitably. Each decision regarding staff, finances, operations, and resources often needs to be quick and precise. To develop sound decisions, managers must use critical thinking. They gather all the essential facts so that they can make good, well-informed choices. After making a decision, skilled managers review their thinking process. Over time, they refine their critical thinking skills. When they encounter similar problems, they use their prior experiences to help them solve problems with ease and in less time.

What type of decisions do you think managers make that involve critical thinking? Human resources managers decide whom to employ, what to pay a new employee, and where to place a new worker. In addition, human resources managers should be unbiased negotiators, resolving conflict between other employees. Office managers purchase copy machines, computers, software, and office supplies. Finance officers prepare precise, timely financial statements. Top managers control business policies, appoint mid-level managers, and assess the success of the business. Plant supervisors set schedules, gauge work quality, and evaluate workers. Sales managers study all of the new sales trends, as well as provide sales training and promotion materials.

Most managers use critical thinking to make wise, well-thought-out decisions. They carefully check their facts, analyze these facts, and make a final judgment based upon these facts. They should also be able to clearly discern fact from fiction. Through trial and error, managers learn their own ways of solving problems and finding the most effective and creative solutions.

| 1 | 2 | 3 | 4 | 5 | 6 | 7 | 8 | 9 | 10 | 11 | 12 |

Supplementary Timed Writing 5

In most classes, teachers want students to analyze situations, draw conclusions, and solve problems. Each of these tasks requires students to use thinking skills. How do students acquire these skills? What is the process students follow to develop thinking skills?

During the early years of life, children learn words and then combine these words into sentences. From there, they learn to declare ideas, share thoughts, and express feelings. Students learn numbers and simple math concepts. They may learn to read musical notes, to keep rhythm, to sing songs, and to recognize many popular and classical pieces of music. Students learn colors, identify shapes, and begin drawing. During the early years, students learn the basic problem-solving models.

One way to solve problems and apply thinking skills is to use the scientific approach. This approach requires the student to state the problem to be solved, gather all the facts about the problem, analyze the problem, and pose viable solutions. Throughout this process, teachers ask questions that force students to expand their thinking skills. Teachers may ask questions such as these: Did you clearly state the problem? Did you get all the facts? Did you get the facts from the right place? Did you assume anything? Did you pose other possible solutions? Did you keep an open mind to all solutions? Did you let your bias come into play? Did you listen to others who might have insights? Did you dig deep enough? Does the solution make sense to you?

This simple four-step process for solving problems gives students a model to use for school, for work, and for life. While the process may not be used to solve every problem, it does provide a starting point to begin using critical thinking skills.

SKILLBUILDING

Supplementary Timed Writing 6

A major goal for nearly all educators is to teach critical thinking skills to a class. Critical thinking, which is the process of reasonably or logically deciding what to do or believe, involves the ability to compare and contrast, resolve problems, make decisions, analyze and evaluate, and combine and transfer knowledge. These skills benefit the student who eventually becomes a part of the workforce. Whether someone is in a corporate setting, is in a small business, or is self-employed, the environment of today is highly competitive and skilled employees are in great demand.

One factor in achieving success in the workforce is having the ability to deal with the varied demands of the fast-paced business world. Required skills are insightful decision making, creative problem solving, and earnest communication among diverse groups. These groups could be employees, management, employers, investors, customers, or clients.

In school, we learn the details of critical thinking. This knowledge extends far beyond the boundaries of the classroom. It lasts a lifetime. We use critical thinking throughout our daily lives. We constantly analyze and evaluate music, movies, conversations, fashion, magazine or newspaper articles, and television programs. We all had experience using critical thinking skills before we even knew what they were. So keep on learning, growing, and experimenting. The classroom is the perfect setting for exploration. Take this opportunity to see how others solve problems, give each other feedback, and try out new ideas in a safe environment.

A person who has learned critical thinking skills is equipped with the essential skills for achieving success in today's workforce. There are always new goals to reach.

| 1 | 2 | 3 | 4 | 5 | 6 | 7 | 8 | 9 | 10 | 11 | 12 |

Supplementary Timed Writing 7

Use your unique creativity when applying critical thinking skills. One of the first steps in unlocking your creativity is to realize that you have control over your thinking; it doesn't control you. Creativity is using new or different methods to solve problems. Many inventions involved a breakthrough in traditional thinking, and the result was an amazing experience. For example, Einstein broke with tradition by trying lots of obscure formulas that changed scientific thought. Your attitude can form mental blocks that keep you from being creative. When you free your mind, the rest will follow.

Do your best to unleash your mind's innate creativity. Turn problems into puzzles. When you think of a task as a puzzle, a challenge, or a game instead of a difficult problem, you open your mind and encourage your creative side to operate. Creative ideas often come when you are having fun and are involved in an unrelated activity. You will find that when your defenses are down, your brain is relaxed and your subconscious is alive; then creative thoughts can flow.

Habit often restricts you from trying new approaches to problem solving. Remember, there is usually more than one solution. Empty your mind of the idea of only one way of looking at a problem and strive to see situations in a fresh, new way. How many times have you told yourself that you must follow the rules and perform tasks in a certain way? If you want to be creative, look at things in a new way, break the pattern, explore new options, and challenge the rules. If you are facing a difficult problem and can't seem to find a solution, take a quick walk or relax for a few minutes; then go back to the problem renewed. When working on homework or taking a test, always work the easiest problems first. Success builds success.

A sense of humor is key to being creative. Silly and irrelevant ideas can lead to inventive solutions. Humor generates ideas, puts you in a creative state of mind, and makes work exciting!

SKILLBUILDING

Supplementary Timed Writing 8

Keyboarding is a popular business course for many students. The major objectives of a keyboarding course are to develop touch control of the keyboard and proper typing techniques, build basic speed and accuracy, and provide practice in applying those basic skills to the formatting of letters, reports, tables, memos, and other kinds of personal and business communications. In the early part of a keyboarding course, students learn to stroke by touch using specific techniques. They learn to hit the keys in a quick and accurate way. After the keys are learned and practiced, students move into producing documents of all sizes and types for personal and vocational use.

When you first learn keyboarding, there are certain parameters, guidelines, and exercises to follow. There are rules intended to help you learn and eventually master the keyboard. Creating documents requires students to apply critical thinking. What format or layout should be used? What font and font size would be best? Are all the words spelled correctly? Does the document look neat? Are the figures accurate? Are punctuation and grammar correct?

There is a lot to learn in the world of keyboarding. Be persistent, patient, and gentle with yourself. Allow failure in class and on the job; that's how we learn. It's okay to admit mistakes. Mistakes are stepping-stones for growth and creativity. Being creative has a lot to do with risk taking and courage. It takes courage to explore new ways of thinking and to risk looking different, being silly and impractical, and even being wrong. Your path to creativity is such a vital component of your critical thinking skills. Allow your creative thoughts to flow freely when producing each of your keyboarding tasks.

Keyboarding skill and personal creativity are valuable attributes for life and on the job. The worker who can see situations and problems in a fresh way, reason logically, explore options, and come up with inventive ideas is sure to be a valuable employee.

Supplementary Timed Writing 9

One of the most important decisions we all have to face is choosing a career. The possibilities can appear overwhelming. Fear not! Your critical thinking skills will save you! Start your career planning today. Begin with self-assessment. What are your interests? Do you enjoy working indoors or outdoors? Do you prefer working with numbers or with words? Are you the independent type or would you rather work with a group? What are your favorite academic studies? Think about these questions and then create a list of your interests, skills, aptitudes, and values. What you discover about yourself will help you in finding the career that is right for you.

After you have explored your personal interests, look at the sixteen career clusters for a wide range of job prospects. Most jobs are included in one of these clusters that have been organized by the government. During your exploration, make a note of the clusters that interest you and investigate these clusters.

Gather as much information as possible by using all available resources. Scan the Help Wanted section in the major Sunday newspapers for job descriptions and salaries. Search the Net. The Internet provides electronic access to worldwide job listings. If you want to know more about a specific company, access its home page. Go to your college placement office. Sign up for interviews with companies that visit your campus. Visit your local school or county library and ask the reference librarian for occupational handbooks. Talk with people in your field of interest to ask questions and get advice. Attend chapter meetings of professional organizations to network with people working in your chosen profession. Volunteer, intern, or work a part-time or temporary job within your career choice for valuable, first-hand insight. Taking an initiative in your job search will pay off.

A career search requires the use of critical thinking skills. These skills will help you to choose the career that will match your skills and talents.

Appendix

Ten-Key Numeric Keypad

Goal

- To control the ten-key numeric keypad keys.

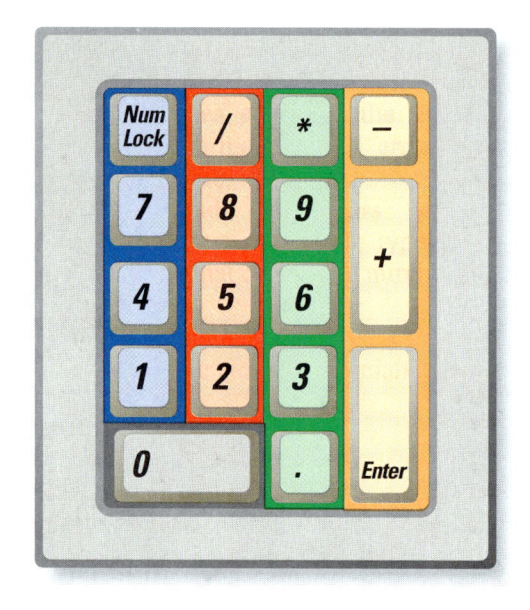

Some computer keyboards have a separate ten-key numeric keypad located to the right of the alphanumeric keyboard. The arrangement of the keypad enables you to type numbers more rapidly than you can when using the top row of the alphanumeric keyboard.

To input numbers using the ten-key numeric keypad, you must activate the Num Lock (Numeric Lock) key. Usually, an indicator light signals that the Num Lock is activated.

On the keypad, 4, 5, and 6 are the home keys. Place your fingers on the keypad home row as follows:

- First finger (J finger) on 4
- Second finger (K finger) on 5
- Third finger (L finger) on 6

The keypad keys are controlled as follows:

- First finger controls 1, 4, and 7
- Second finger controls 2, 5, and 8
- Third finger controls 3, 6, 9, and decimal point
- Right thumb controls 0
- Fourth finger controls ENTER

Since different computers have different arrangements of ten-key numeric keypads, study the arrangement of your keypad. The illustration shows the most common arrangement. If your keypad is arranged differently from the one shown in the illustration, check with your instructor for the correct placement of your fingers on the keypad.

NEW KEYS

A. Use the first finger to control the 4 key, the second finger to control the 5 key, and the third finger to control the 6 key.

Keep your eyes on the copy.

Before beginning, check to be sure the Num Lock key is activated.

Type the first column from top to bottom. Next, type the second column; then type the third column. Press ENTER after typing the final digit of each number.

A. THE 4, 5, AND 6 KEYS

444	456	454
555	654	464
666	445	546
455	446	564
466	554	654
544	556	645
566	664	666
644	665	555
655	456	444
456	654	456

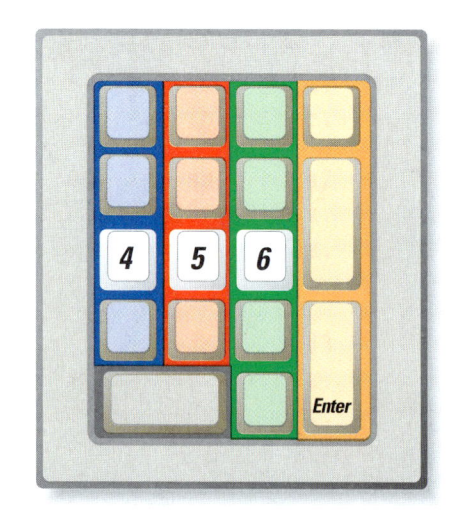

A-1　APPENDIX　Ten-Key Numeric Keypad

B. Use the 4 finger to control the 7 key, the 5 finger to control the 8 key, and the 6 finger to control the 9 key.

Keep your eyes on the copy.

Press ENTER after typing the final digit of each number.

B. THE 7, 8, AND 9 KEYS

474	585	696
747	858	969
774	885	996
447	558	669
744	855	966
477	588	699
444	555	666
747	858	969
774	885	996
747	858	969

C. Use the 4 finger to control the 1 key, the 5 finger to control the 2 key, and the 6 finger to control the 3 key.

Keep your eyes on the copy.

Press ENTER after typing the final digit of each number.

C. THE 1, 2, AND 3 KEYS

444	555	666
111	222	333
144	225	336
441	552	663
144	255	366
411	522	633
444	555	666
414	525	636
141	252	363
411	525	636

APPENDIX Ten-Key Numeric Keypad A-2

D. Use the right thumb to control the 0 key.

Keep your eyes on the copy.

Press ENTER after typing the final digit of each number.

D. THE *0* KEY

404	470	502
505	580	603
606	690	140
707	410	250
808	520	360
909	630	701
101	407	802
202	508	903
303	609	405
505	401	506

E. Use the 6 finger to control the decimal key.

Keep your eyes on the copy.

Press ENTER after typing the final digit of each number.

E. THE . KEY

4.5	7.8	1.2
6.5	9.8	3.2
4.4	7.7	1.1
4.4	7.7	1.1
5.5	8.8	2.2
5.5	8.8	2.2
6.6	9.9	3.3
6.5	9.9	3.3
4.5	7.8	1.2
6.5	8.9	1.3

INDEX

NOTE: Page numbers preceded by A- indicate material in Appendix; page numbers preceded by R- indicate material in Reference Manual; page numbers preceded by SB- indicate material in Skillbuilding supplement.

INDIVIDUAL KEYS (alphabet)

A, 3, 4
B, 16
C, 8
D, 3, 4
E, 5
F, 3, 4
G, 15
H, 5
I, 14
J, 3, 4
K, 3, 4
L, 3, 4
M, 7
N, 20
O, 5
P, 7
Q, 18
R, 6
S, 3, 4
T, 7
U, 16
V, 9
W, 10
X, 17
Y, 18
Z, 20

INDIVIDUAL KEYS (numeric)

0, 30
1, 32
2, 30
3, 26
4, 32
5, 26
6, 32
7, 26
8, 30
9, 27
decimal (.), A-3
on numeric keypad, A-1–A-3

INDIVIDUAL KEYS (punctuation, functions, and symbols)

& (ampersand), 43
' (apostrophe), 42
* (asterisk), 41
@ (at key), 44
Caps Lock Key, R-2
: (colon), 16
, (comma), 18
$ (dollar sign), 37
ENTER, 3
escape key (ESC), R-2
! (exclamation point), 38
/ (forward slash), 19
- (hyphen), 14
left SHIFT, 14
(number key), 41
Num Lock key, A-1
() (parentheses), 37
% (percent key), 43
. (period), 9
? (question mark), 20
" (quotation), 44
right SHIFT, 9
; (semicolon), 3, 4
SPACE BAR, 3
TAB key, 21

A

Abbreviations
    rules for, R-22
    U.S. Postal Service, R-14
Academic report, R-8
Accept/except, R-20
Adjectives
    adjacent, R-16
    compound, R-17
    rules for use of, R-20
Adverbs, R-20
Affect/effect, R-20
Agenda for meeting, R-11
Agreement, rules for, R-19
All-capital abbreviations, R-22
Alphabet
    home keys, 3–4
    keyboarding, 2–24
    progressive practice, SB-7–SB-10
    skillbuilding, 24, 29, 35, 45
Alternate keys, R-2
American Psychological Association (APA) style, R-9

A

Ampersand (&), 43, SB-2
Annual report citation, R-9, R-10
Apostrophe ('), R-17, 42, SB-2
Application letter in block style, R-12
Arrow keys, R-2
Asterisk (*), 41, SB-3
At key (@), 44, SB-3
Attachment notation, R-4, R-7

B

Backspace key, R-2
Bibliography, R-9
Blind copy notation, R-5
Body of letter, R-3
Body of table, R-13
Book citation, R-9, R-10
Boxed tables, R-5, R-8, R-13
Braced headings, R-13
Bulleted lists, R-12
Business forms, formatting, R-14
Business letters
   in block style, R-3
   on executive stationery, R-4
   formatted for window envelope, R-4
   on half-page stationery, R-4
   in modified-block style, R-3
   multipage, R-5
   in simplified style, R-3
Business reports, R-8, R-9
Byline, R-8

C

Capitalization
   all-capital abbreviations, R-22
   column capitalization in tables, R-13
   rules for, R-21
Caps lock key, R-2
Careers in media, 1
CD/DVD drive, R-2
Citations, in MLA style, R-9
Colon (:), R-18, 16, 17, SB-3
Column capitalization, R-13
Column headings, R-13
Comma (,), R-15–R-16, 18, SB-3
Common words, abbreviation of, R-22
Company names, R-5
Compass points, R-21
Complimentary closing, R-3
Compound adjectives, R-17
Compound numbers, R-17

Computer keyboard, R-2
Computer system, parts of, R-2
Control keys, R-2
Coordinate conjunctions, R-15
Copy notation, R-3, R-5
Course titles, R-21

D

Date, R-8, R-15
Date line, R-3
Decimal key (.), A-3
Delivery notation, R-4, R-5
Diagonals (/), 19, SB-3
Direct address, R-15
Direct quotation
   use of comma with, R-15
   use of quotation marks in, R-18
Disk drive, R-2
Display screen, R-2
Dollar sign ($), R-13, 37, SB-3
Dollars in tables, R-13

E

E-mail messages
   citation of, R-9, R-10
   in Microsoft Outlook/Internet Explorer, R-5
   in Yahoo!, R-5
Enclosure notation, R-3, R-5
Endnotes, R-8, R-9
ENTER key, R-2, 29
Envelopes
   formatting, R-6
   letters formatted for, R-4
Escape key, R-2
Exclamation point (!), 38, SB-3
Executive stationery, R-4
Explanatory material, R-18

F

Farther/further, R-20
Footnotes, R-8
Formatting
   business forms, R-14
   business letters, R-4
   envelopes, R-6
   lists, R-12
   placing quotation marks, 44

Forward slash (/), 19, SB-3
Function keys, R-2

G

Goodwill messages, 40
Government document citation, R-9, R-10
Grammar, R-19–R-20
   adjectives/adverbs, R-16, R-17, R-20
   agreement, R-19
   pronouns, R-17, R-19, R-20
   sentences, R-18, R-19, R-21
   word usage, R-20

H

Half-page stationery, R-4
Heading blocks in tables, R-13
Headings, R-8, R-9, R-13
Home keys, 3
Hyphen (-), R-17, 14, 15, 22, SB-3

I

Indefinite pronouns, possessive of, R-17
Independent clauses
   use of comma with, R-15
   use of semicolon with, R-16
Independent comments, R-16
Individual reaches, practice, SB-2–SB-6
Inside address, R-3
International address, R-3, R-5
Internet, 6
Internet Explorer, R-5
Intervening words, agreement and, R-19
Introductory expressions, R-15
Italics, R-18
Itinerary, R-11

J

Job interview portfolio, 22
Journal article citation, R-9, R-10

K

Keyboarding Connection (feature)
   Internet, 6
   search engines, 12

L

Language arts, R-15–R-22
   grammar (*See* Grammar)
   mechanics
     abbreviations, R-14, R-22
     capitalization, R-13, R-21, R-22
     number expression, R-17, R-21–R-22
   punctuation (*See* Punctuation)
Left SHIFT key, 14
Legal documents, R-11
Letterhead, R-3
Letters
   application letter in block style, R-12
   business letters (*See* Business letters)
   folding, R-6
   personal business letter in modified-block style, R-3
Listening skills, 8
Lists
   examples of, R-12
   formatting, R-12
   multiline, R-3, R-5
   single-line, R-3, R-9
Lowercase abbreviations, R-22

M

Margins, R-9
Meeting agenda, R-11
Memo report, R-9
Memos, R-4, R-7
Microcomputer system, parts of, R-2
Microsoft Outlook, R-5
Minutes of meeting, R-11
Modern Language Association (MLA) style, R-9
Monitor, R-2
Mouse, R-2
Multiline lists, R-3, R-5
Multipage business letter, R-5

N

Nearer noun, agreement with, R-19
Newspaper article citation, R-10
No. 6¼ envelopes, R-6
No. 10 envelopes, R-6
Nominative pronouns, R-20
Nonessential expressions, R-16
Nouns
   agreement with nearer noun, R-19
   capitalization rules, R-21
   plural possessive, R-17

Number expression
    hyphenation, R-17
    spelling out, R-21, R-22
    using figures, R-21, R-22
Number key (#), 41, SB-3
Numbers
    diagnostic practice, SB-5–SB-6
    keyboarding, 25–35
    in lists, R-12
    page numbers, R-5
    progressive practice, SB-11–SB-13
    skillbuilding, 27, 29, 31, 33, 39, 45
Numeric keypad, R-2
Num Lock key, A-1

O

Objective pronouns, R-20
On-arrival notation, R-5
Online database citation, R-9, R-10
Open tables, R-13
Organizational terms, R-21
Outline, R-7

P

Page numbers, R-5
Paper
    folding letters, R-6
    stationery, R-4
Paragraph heading, R-8
Paragraphs, skillbuilding, 12, 23, 33, 40, 42, 47
Parentheses (), 37, SB-3
Percentages in tables, R-13
Percent key (%), R-13, 43, SB-4
Period (.), R-18, 9, SB-4
Personal business letter in modified-block style, R-3
Personal/personnel, R-20
Phrases, skillbuilding, 4, 8, 11, 19, 21
Place names, R-15
Plural nouns, possessive, R-17
Possessives, R-17
Postscript notation, R-5
Pound sign (#), 41, SB-3
Principal/principle, R-20
Printer, R-2
Pronouns
    agreement, R-19
    possessives, R-17
    rules for use of, R-20

Proofreaders' marks, R-14
Proper nouns, R-21
Punctuation, R-15–R-18
    apostrophe, R-17
    colon, R-18
    comma, R-15–R-16
    hyphen, R-17
    italics, R-18
    period, R-18
    quotation marks, R-18
    semicolon, R-16
    underline, R-18
Punctuation practice, 17, 22, 35, 46

Q

Question mark (?), 20, 21, SB-4
Quotation marks ("), R-18, 44, SB-4
Quotations, R-8

R

Reference initials, R-3, R-5
References, in APA style, R-10
Reports
    academic report, R-8
    in APA style, R-10
    business reports, R-8, R-9
    memo report, R-9
    in MLA style, R-10
    special features, R-9
Resumes, R-12
Return address, R-3
Right SHIFT key, 9
Ruled tables, R-13
Run-on sentences, R-19

S

Salutation, R-3
Search engines, 12
Semicolon (;), R-16, 3, 4, SB-4
Sentences
    capitalization, R-21
    fragments, R-19
    rules for, R-19
    run-on, R-19
    skillbuilding, 10, 11, 12
    use of period in, R-18

Series, comma or semicolon in, R-16
SHIFT key, R-2
    left SHIFT, 14
    right SHIFT, 9
    technique practice, 19, 27, 34
Side heading, R-8
Single-line list, R-3, R-9
Skillbuilding
    alphabet practice, 29, 35, 45
    alphabet review, 24
    alternate-hand words, 46, 47
    diagnostic practice
        numbers, SB-5–SB-6
        symbols and punctuation, SB-2–SB-4
    error counting, 10
    handwritten paragraphs, 33, 40, 42, 47
    number practice, 27, 29, 31, 33, 39, 45
    one-hand words, 46, 47
    paced practice, SB-14–SB-27
    paragraphs, 12, 23
    phrases, 4, 8, 11, 19, 21
    pretest-practice-posttest
        alternate-hand words, 46, 47
        one-hand words, 46, 47
        vertical reaches, 35
    progressive practice
        alphabet, SB-7–SB-10
        numbers, SB-11–SB-13
    punctuation practice, 17, 22, 35, 46
    sentences, 10, 11, 12
    sustained practice
        numbers and symbols, 45
        syllabic intensity, 28
    symbol practice, 45
    technique practice
        colon key, 17
        ENTER key, 29
        hyphen, 15, 22
        question mark, 21
        SHIFT key, 19, 27, 34
        SPACE BAR, 15, 29, 38
        TAB key, 31, 34
    timed writings (*See* Timed writings)
    12-second speed sprints, 28, 34, 38, 47
    vertical reaches, 35
    words
        beginnings, 39
        endings, 39–40
        patterns, 6, 11, 23
        practice, 17
        word building, 4
Skills in communications and media, 1
SPACE BAR, 3, 15, 29, 38
Spacing, R-9
Strategies for Career Success (feature)
    goodwill messages, 40
    job interview portfolio, 22
    listening skills, 8
Subject line, R-3, R-5, R-7
Subtitle, R-8, R-13
Symbols
    keyboarding, 36–47
    practice, 45, SB-2–SB-4
    See also specific symbols

T

TAB key, R-2, 21, 31, 34
Table of contents, R-7
Tables
    boxed, R-5, R-8, R-13
    open, R-13
    ruled, R-13
    special features, R-13
Templates, R-14
Ten-key numeric keypad, A-1–A-3
Time, capitalization rules, R-21
Timed writings
    1-minute
        10wpm, 4
        11wpm, 6
        12wpm, 8
        13wpm, 10
        14wpm, 12
        15wpm, 15
        16wpm, 17
        17wpm, 19
        18wpm, 22
        19wpm, 24
    2-minute
        19wpm, 27
        20wpm, 29
        21wpm, 31
        22wpm, 33
        23wpm, 35
        24wpm, 38
        25wpm, 40
        26wpm, 42
        27wpm, 45
        28wpm, 47
    supplementary, SB-28–SB-36
Title page, R-7
Titles, R-8
    course titles, R-21
    subtitles, R-8, R-13

Titles *(continued)*
    use of *italics*/<u>underline</u> in, R-18
    use of quotation marks in, R-18
Total line in tables, R-13
Transitional expressions, R-16
Transmittal memo, R-7

U

<u>Underline,</u> R-18
Units of measure, R-22
U.S. Postal Service abbreviations, R-14

V

Verbs, agreement of, R-19
Vertical placement of tables, R-13

W

WAN (wide area network), 6
Web page citation, R-9, R-10
Wide area network (WAN), 6
Window envelopes, R-6
Windows keys, R-2
Word usage, R-20
Works cited, in MLA style, R-10
Writer's identification, R-3

Y

Yahoo!, R-5

Scot Ober
Ball State University

Jack E. Johnson
State University of West Georgia

Arlene Zimmerly
Los Angeles City College

Visit the *College Keyboarding* Web site at www.mhhe.com/gdp

McGraw-Hill Irwin

Boston   Burr Ridge, IL   Dubuque, IA   Madison, WI   New York   San Francisco   St. Louis
Bangkok   Bogotá   Caracas   Kuala Lumpur   Lisbon   London   Madrid   Mexico City
Milan   Montreal   New Delhi   Santiago   Seoul   Singapore   Sydney   Taipei   Toronto

This document has been prepared with the assistance of Dolphin, Inc., Voorhees, N.J.

McGraw-Hill Irwin

Student User's Guide for GDP10 Home Software for use with
COLLEGE KEYBOARDING & DOCUMENT PROCESSING
Scot Ober, Jack E. Johnson, Arlene Zimmerly

Published by McGraw-Hill/Irwin, an imprint of The McGraw-Hill Companies, Inc., 1221 Avenue of the Americas, New York, NY 10020. Copyright © 2006 by The McGraw-Hill Companies, Inc. All rights reserved.

No part of this publication may be reproduced or distributed in any form or by any means, or stored in a database or retrieval system, without the prior written consent of The McGraw-Hill Companies, Inc., including, but not limited to, in any network or other electronic storage or transmission, or broadcast for distance learning.

1 2 3 4 5 6 7 8 9 0 CSS/CSS 0 9 8 7 6 5

ISBN 0-07-299792-3

www.mhhe.com

The *McGraw·Hill* Companies

Contents

1	**Getting Started**	**1**
	1.1 WELCOME TO GDP	1
	1.2 SYSTEM REQUIREMENTS	1
	1.3 REQUIRED MATERIALS	2
	1.4 INSTALLING GDP	3
	1.5 ABOUT STUDENT DATA FILES	6
	1.5.1 Backing up Student Data Files	6
	1.5.2 If You are Using GDP Both on Campus and at Home	7
	1.6 ABOUT THIS USER'S GUIDE	7
2	**Using GDP**	**8**
	2.1 LOGGING ON FOR THE FIRST TIME	9
	2.2 SPECIFYING YOUR SETTINGS	11
	2.3 WORKING ON LESSON EXERCISES	14
	2.3.1 Exercise Screen Layout	15
	2.4 ACCESSING EXERCISES OUTSIDE OF LESSONS	17
	2.4.1 Linking to Word Outside of an Exercise	18
	2.5 VIEWING AND PRINTING STUDENT WORK	18
	2.5.1 Student Portfolio	18
	2.5.2 Performance Chart	22
	2.6 IMPORTING AND EXPORTING STUDENT DATA	23
	2.6.1 Using Import/Export to Transfer Data Files Between Campus and Home	23
	2.7 USING GDP'S WEB AND DISTANCE-LEARNING FEATURES	25
	2.7.1 E-mailing the Instructor	25
	2.7.2 Accessing the Web from GDP	25
	2.7.3 Sending Distance-Learning Student Data to the Instructor Management Web Site	26
	2.7.4 Using the Student Web Site	27
	2.7.5 Creating an HTML Version of a Student Report	32
	2.8 LESSON FEATURES	32
	2.9 TYPES OF EXERCISES IN GDP	34
	2.9.1 Warm-Ups	34
	2.9.2 New Key Drills	34
	2.9.3 Other Drills	35

	2.9.4	Timed Writings	35
	2.9.5	Pretest/Practice/Posttest	36
	2.9.6	Document Processing	36
	2.9.7	Language Arts	39
	2.9.8	Diagnostic Practice	39
	2.9.9	Progressive Practice	39
	2.9.10	Paced Practice	39
	2.9.11	Sustained Practice	40
	2.9.12	Technique Practice	40
	2.9.13	Proofreading and Spelling	41
	2.9.14	Numeric Keypad	41
	2.9.15	MAP (Misstroke Analysis and Prescription)	41
	2.9.16	Tennis Game	42
	2.9.17	Pace Car Game	43
	2.9.18	Tests	44

3 Reference Guide

3.1	**GDP DROP-DOWN MENUS**		**45**
	3.1.1 File Menu		45
	3.1.2 Options Menu		46
	3.1.3 Help Menu		46
3.2	**GDP TOOLBAR**		**47**
3.3	**KEYBOARD SHORTCUTS**		**47**
3.4	**SCORING AND ERROR MARKING**		**48**
	3.4.1	Error Marking	48
	3.4.2	One Space/Two Space Option	49
	3.4.3	Error Scores	49
	3.4.4	Speed (WPM) Calculation	49

4 Troubleshooting

4.1	**INSTALLATION AND START-UP**	**50**
4.2	**DOCUMENT PROCESSING AND SCORING**	**51**
4.3	**SOUND**	**53**
4.4	**E-MAIL/WEB**	**53**
4.5	**HELP AND REFERENCE MANUAL**	**54**
4.6	**DISTANCE LEARNING/INSTRUCTOR MANAGEMENT WEB SITE**	**54**
4.7	**DATA STORAGE LIMITS**	**56**

Index   58

Chapter 1 — Getting Started

1.1 Welcome to GDP

Gregg College Keyboarding & Document Processing (GDP) is a Windows-based program designed for use with the *Gregg College Keyboarding & Document Processing™ 10th Edition* textbook. The software and textbook mirror and reinforce each other. From new key presentations to advanced word processing, all exercises in the textbook are included in one all-encompassing program. For document processing exercises, GDP can link to Microsoft Word® 2000, 2002, and 2003.

GDP includes the following features to help you achieve keyboarding proficiency:

- An intuitive, Web-based interface provides a contemporary learning environment for today's high-tech office and makes it easy for you to use the software even if you have limited computer experience.
- Multimedia "hand" demonstrations for new key presentations allow you to visualize correct finger placement on home row keys while still being able to see all of the keys on the keyboard.
- Interactive language arts tutorials help you build the traditional language arts skills that are essential for effective business communications.
- The MAP (Misstroke Analysis and Prescription) program diagnoses accuracy problems and provides intensive, individualized remediation.
- The tennis game and the pace car game reinforce keyboarding skills in a fun setting.
- Bilingual English/Spanish instruction screens and powerful distance-learning features meet the needs of an increasingly diverse student population.

1.2 System Requirements

To run GDP, your system must meet the following minimum requirements:

- Pentium II CPU or higher

- Microsoft Windows 98, NT 4.0, 2000, Me, or XP. The specific releases are Windows 98, Second Edition, Service Pack 1.0; Windows NT Workstation 4.0, Service Pack 6.0; Windows 2000, Professional, Service Pack 3.0; Windows XP, Service Pack 2.0.
- 16 MB RAM required for Windows 98; 32 MB RAM required for Windows NT, 2000, and Me; 128 MB RAM required for Windows XP (64 MB may be sufficient)
- Hard disk drive
- Network compatible; the software can be installed on a network so that multiple users may access it at the same time. It will be compatible with most networks, including Novell Netware 5 and Windows NT 2000 servers.
- CD-ROM drive (8X or faster) required for installing the program and using Home version
- Graphics adapter, SVGA or higher; 800 x 600, True Color (24-bit or 32-bit), or High Color (16-bit) modes
- SVGA color monitor
- Data will be stored on the hard disk, data diskette or removable media such as a Zip disk for the Home version.
- Netscape Navigator 7.0 or Microsoft Internet Explorer 6.0

GDP student data can be stored in a student subdirectory on the hard disk, on a network or virtual network connection, or on floppy disk or other removable media.

1.3 Required Materials

To complete instructional activities in the program, you will need the following:

- *Gregg College Keyboarding & Document Processing™ 10th Edition* textbook for the appropriate lessons.
- *Microsoft® Word 2003 Manual for Gregg College Keyboarding & Document Processing 9th Edition Lessons 1–120* (or the manual that corresponds to your version of Microsoft® Word.)
- A blank disk, if you want to store your work on floppy disks; or removable media such as a Zip disk.

1.4 Installing GDP

GDP is designed to accommodate a host of different instructional needs and computing environments. The Home version, which is covered in this User's Guide, allows an individual student to work on GDP off campus. This is a single-user version of GDP, and it can be installed on either a standalone or an e-mail connected (distance-learning) computer.

Note | This User's Guide does not cover the Campus version of GDP. The Campus version has its own User's Guide, which is included in the GDP Campus version package.

To install the Home version of GDP on your computer:

1. Turn on the computer and start Windows.
2. Put the GDP Home version CD-ROM in the CD-ROM drive.
3. Open the Start menu (on the Windows task bar) and choose *Run....* In the Open blank, type **d:\setup** (please note that the CD-ROM drive could be e:\ on some computers). Click **OK**. The InstallShield Wizard loads, then the Welcome dialog box displays. Click **Next** to continue.
4. In the License Agreement dialog box (Figure 1-1), click **I accept**... to accept the terms of the license agreement. Click **Next** to continue. Note: You must accept the license agreement to continue with the installation process.

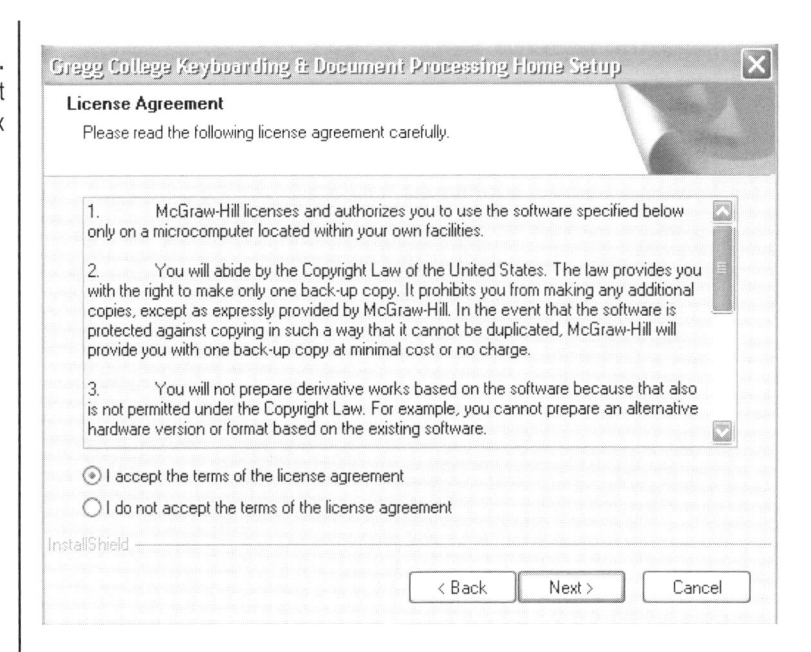

Figure 1-1.
License Agreement
Dialog Box

[Screenshot: Gregg College Keyboarding & Document Processing Home Setup - License Agreement dialog box showing McGraw-Hill license terms with "I accept the terms of the license agreement" selected, and Back/Next/Cancel buttons.]

5. In the Select Destination Location dialog box (Figure 1-2), choose the local hard-disk location where you want to install the GDP software. Click **Browse** to select a location different from the default. After you select a location, click **Next**.

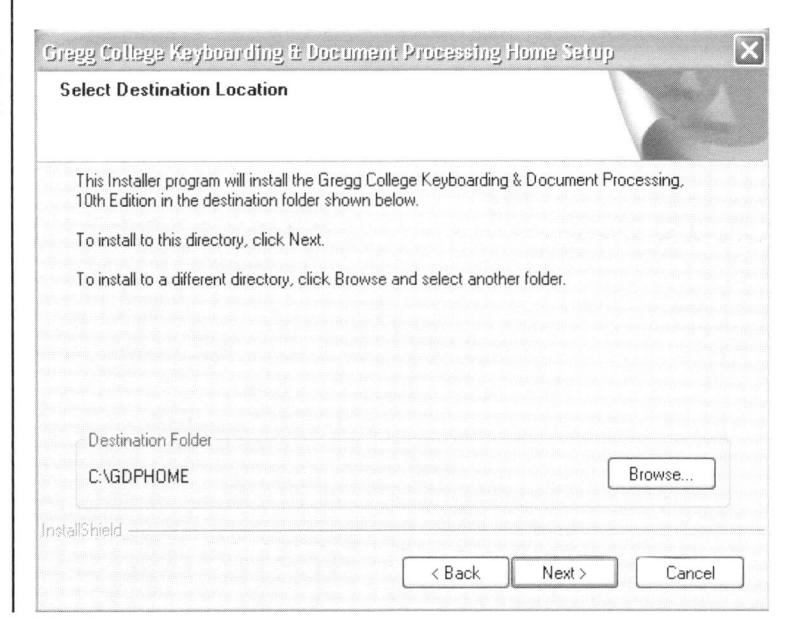

Figure 1-2.
Select Destination
Location Dialog Box

[Screenshot: Gregg College Keyboarding & Document Processing Home Setup - Select Destination Location dialog box with Destination Folder set to C:\GDPHOME, Browse button, and Back/Next/Cancel buttons.]

4 Student User's Guide for GDP/10 Home Software

6. In the Select Student Data Location dialog box (Figure 1-3), choose an option and click **Next**.

   - Select **Save student data on other media** (the default) to store student work in a data directory on the local hard disk or on other removable media such as a Zip disk. If you choose this option, the Select Student Data Path dialog box will open once you click the **Next** button.
   - Select **Save student data on floppy disk A:** if the student will store work on a floppy disk in drive A.
   - Select **Save student data on floppy disk B:** if the student will store work on a floppy disk in drive B.

Figure 1-3.
Select Student Data Location Dialog Box

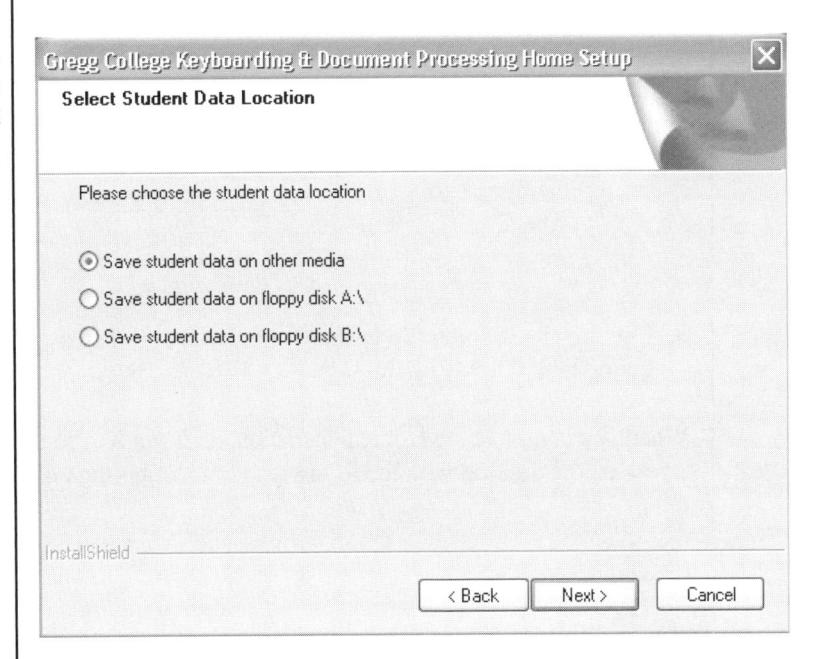

7. In the Select Student Data Path dialog box (Figure 1-4), you specify the location where student data will be stored (if you chose to save student data on other media in the previous dialog box). Click **Next** to accept the default destination folder (C:\GDPDATA), or click **Browse** to select a different location and then click **Next**.

Figure 1-4.
Select Student Data
Path Dialog Box

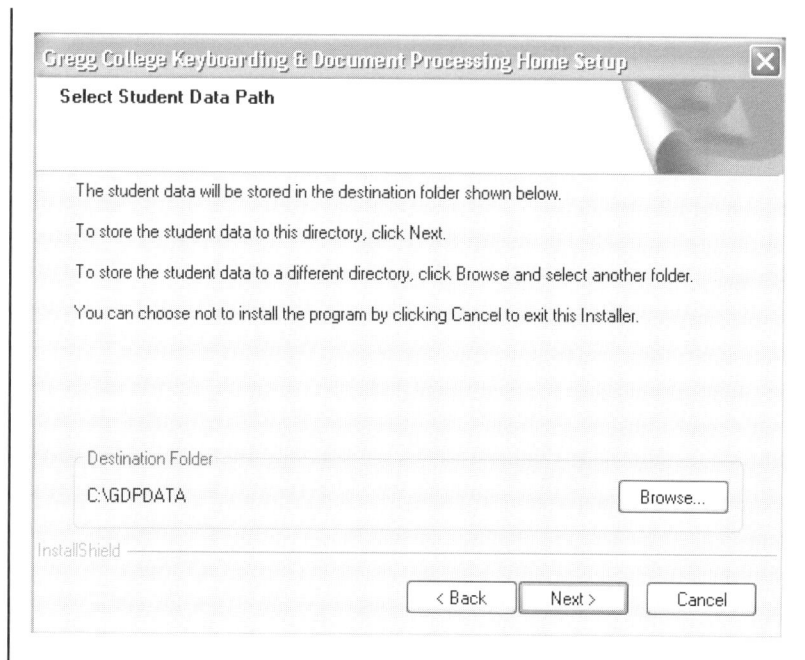

8. The installer copies file to the workstation and displays the Install Complete dialog box. Click **Finish**.

When you complete the Home installation, an Irwin Keyboarding program group opens on the desktop with the following icon for starting GDP:

1.5 About Student Data Files

The location of your data files is specified during the GDP10 installation procedure. Your work in GDP can be stored on floppy disks or other removable media, or on your local hard-disk drive. In any case, you will need approximately 5 MB of disk space.

1.5.1 Backing up Student Data Files

Remember to back up your data files regularly.

- If you use floppy disks to store your work, make back-up copies of your data disks on a regular basis.
- If you are storing your data on a hard-disk drive, it is important to make regular back-ups of the GDP data directory and the GDP program directory and all of its subdirectories. Failure to do so could result in data loss or corruption in the event of a power outage or other unforeseen system problems.

1.5.2 If You Are Using GDP Both on Campus and at Home

If you store your data files on a floppy disk and use GDP both on campus and at home, you should use the same floppy disk in both locations. If your data files are stored on the network on campus, you must use GDP's Import/Export feature to make sure that data files are up-to-date in both locations. For more information, see 2.6 Importing and Exporting Student Data on page 23.

1.6 About This User's Guide

The rest of this User's Guide provides the information you need to operate GDP.

- Chapter 2 provides an overview of how GDP works, including detailed instructions for starting the program and registering, specifying your settings, working on GDP exercises, accessing exercises outside of lessons, viewing and printing your work, and using GDP's distance-learning features. Chapter 2 also provides descriptions of all the types of exercises included in GDP.

- Chapter 3 is a reference guide, listing brief descriptions of all menu options, toolbar buttons, and shortcut keys. The reference guide also describes scoring and error marking.

- Chapter 4 is a troubleshooting guide, which lists common problems and suggested solutions.

- The Index provides a quick way to look up specific information in this User's Guide.

Chapter 2: Using GDP

Program Overview

Gregg College Keyboarding & Document Processing (GDP) is a Windows-based program with distance-learning features that is designed for use with the *Gregg College Keyboarding & Document Processing Lessons 1-120, 10th Edition* textbook. The software and textbook mirror and reinforce each other. From new key presentations to advanced document processing, all exercises in the textbook are included in one all-encompassing program. For document processing exercises, GDP links to Microsoft Word®. Distance learning features such as Upload and e-mail facilitate student data transfer and communication between students and instructors. Student work is recorded, scored, and can be reviewed in the Student Portfolio.

Program Structure

Lessons
Every lesson (with the exception of Lesson 1) begins with a Warmup that should be keyed as soon as students are settled at the keyboard. All alphabet, number, and symbol keys are introduced in the first 20 lessons. Drill lines in this section provide the practice necessary to achieve keyboarding skills.

Skillbuilding sections are found in every lesson, and can be accessed directly from the GDP button toolbar. Each drill presents a variety of different activities designed to improve speed and accuracy. Skillbuilding exercises include Technique Timings, Diagnostic Practice, Paced Practice, Progressive Practice, MAP (Misstroke Analysis and Prescription), Sustained Practice, and Timed Writings.

Many lessons also include a Pretest, Practice, and Posttest routine that identify speed and accuracy needs and measures improvement.

All of the activities contained within the lessons are also available from the navigation menu. Click the **Skillbuilding**, **Language Arts**, **Timed Writings**, **MAP**, or **Games** buttons to open the menus and directly access these activities.

Student Portfolio
All of your scores and text are stored in a portfolio that you can access at any time other than when you are working on an exercise. Your Student Portfolio is a summary report listing all the exercises and exercise scores for activities you have attempted. Detailed Reports display the scored text for exercises selected from the Student Portfolio.

Distance- Learning
You can communicate with your instructor and classmates by clicking the **E-mail** button and using GDP's e-mail feature. Use the Upload feature to send your GDP data files to the Instructor Management web site and to receive information from your instructor (for example, grades and instructor comments). Note: To receive grades and comments from your instructor in a distance-learning environment, you must download your grades using the Student Web Site. Please go to Section 2.7.4 of this document to review the Student Web Site.

Web Access
Your school web site, or any other web site your instructor chooses can be directly accessed by clicking the **Web** button on the GDP navigation toolbar. Note: In the Home version of GDP, you must specify the web link URL in your Settings (found in the Options drop-down menu).

Reference Manual
Click **Reference Manual** on the toolbar or from the *Help* menu to access a separate Help system that provides formatting instructions and examples of the types of documents taught in GDP.

2.1 Logging On for the First Time

Here is the procedure when accessing GDP for the first time:

1. Turn on the computer and start Windows.
2. If using a floppy disk to store your data, put a floppy disk in the floppy drive.
3. From the Start menu (on the Windows task bar), choose *Programs* and point to *Irwin Keyboarding*.
4. Select

5. The title screen displays for several seconds, followed by the registration screen (Figure 2-1). (To advance to the registration screen immediately, you can click anywhere on the title screen.) When accessing the GDP Home version for the first time, you will be asked to register your first and last name ("e-mail address" and "class" are optional) in the appropriate fields and then click **Save**. Subsequently when accessing the GDP Home version, you will be taken directly to the Lessons Menu (there is no log-on screen in the GDP Home version).

If you selected removable media or a floppy disk drive for data storage in the Home version of GDP (during installation) and you don't have it inserted when accessing GDP, you will be prompted with the following: "Please insert your student data disk and click **OK**. If you have not yet created your student data diskette, then click the **New Student** button." (If this is your first time accessing GDP, you will want to insert your diskette and click on the **New Student** button.)

Figure 2-1.
Registration Screen

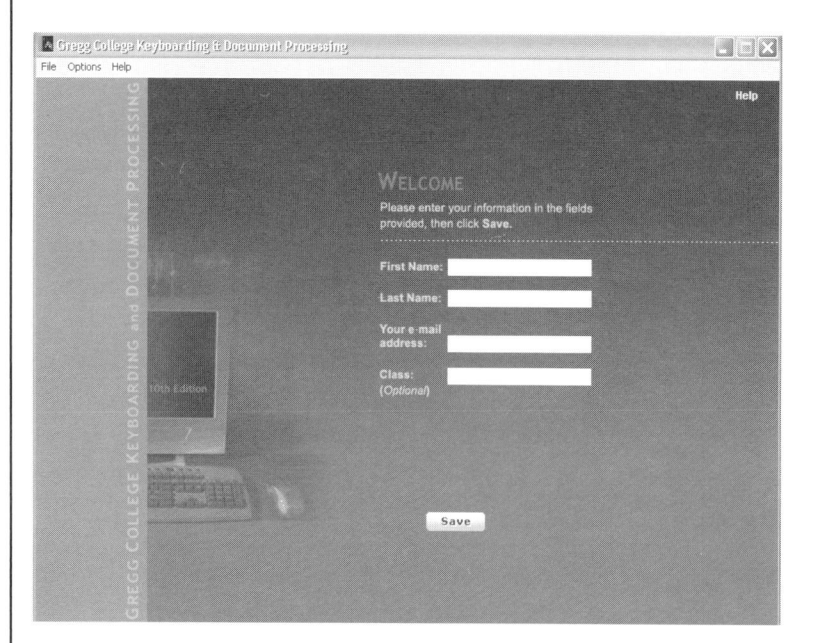

6. Complete the registration information on the log-on screen and click **Save**. Note: If you are a distance-learning student, your e-mail address must be identical to the one your instructor used to register you on the Instructor Management Web site for the Upload feature to work properly. If you enter it incorrectly, you can change it later. See 2.2 Specifying Your Settings. Your first and last name will be sent to the Instructor Management Web site, so be sure they are typed correctly. See 2.7.3 Sending Distance-Learning Student Data to the Instructor Management Web site.

7. GDP registers your information, and the Tutorial pops up in a window on the screen. The Tutorial provides first-time users an overview of how GDP works.

8. Before you start working you need to specify your settings so that GDP works properly with your system. See 2.2 Specifying Your Settings, below.

9. Now you are ready to begin working in GDP. To do so, select a lesson from the Lessons menu, which displays next. For information about working on GDP exercises, see 2.3 Working on Lesson Exercises on page 14.

Note | Subsequently when you start GDP, the program will take you directly to the Lessons menu and open the lesson upon which you last worked. If you installed GDP for use with a floppy disk and do not put the disk into the floppy disk drive before starting GDP, you will be prompted to insert the diskette. The prompt will ask you to insert your student data diskette and click **OK** or, if you haven't created your student data diskette yet, to click the **New Student** button. Insert your data diskette and click **OK**.

2.2 Specifying Your Settings

Your settings control how GDP works on your system. To specify your settings:

1. Select *Settings...* on the Options drop-down menu to open the Settings dialog box (Figure 2-2).

Figure 2-2.
Settings Dialog Box

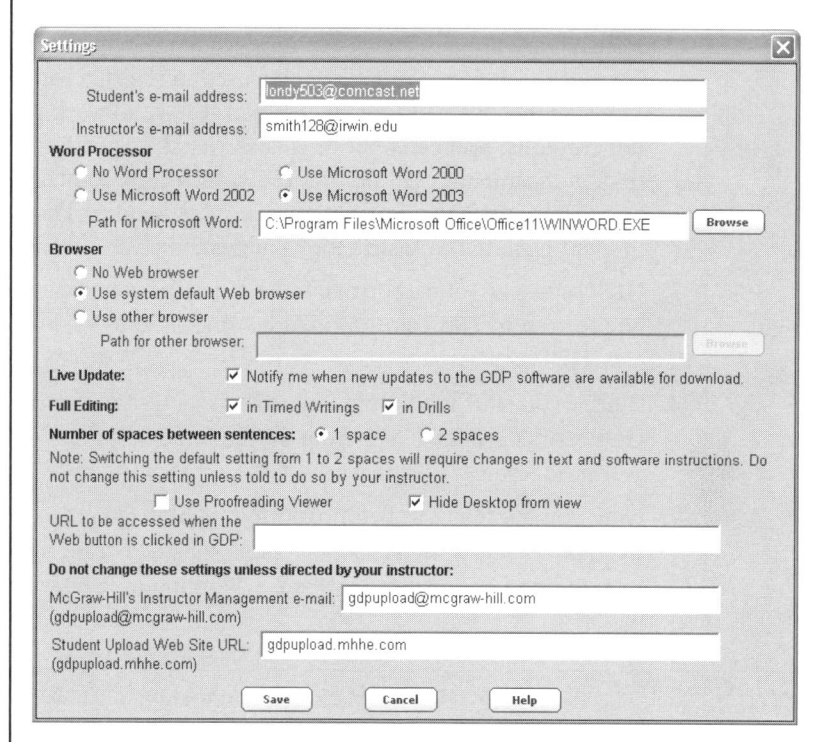

Settings

Student's e-mail address: londy503@comcast.net
Instructor's e-mail address: smith128@irwin.edu

Word Processor
- ○ No Word Processor
- ○ Use Microsoft Word 2000
- ○ Use Microsoft Word 2002
- ● Use Microsoft Word 2003

Path for Microsoft Word: C:\Program Files\Microsoft Office\Office11\WINWORD.EXE [Browse]

Browser
- ○ No Web browser
- ● Use system default Web browser
- ○ Use other browser

Path for other browser: [_____] [Browse]

Live Update: ☑ Notify me when new updates to the GDP software are available for download.
Full Editing: ☑ in Timed Writings ☑ in Drills
Number of spaces between sentences: ● 1 space ○ 2 spaces

Note: Switching the default setting from 1 to 2 spaces will require changes in text and software instructions. Do not change this setting unless told to do so by your instructor.

☐ Use Proofreading Viewer ☑ Hide Desktop from view

URL to be accessed when the Web button is clicked in GDP: [_____]

Do not change these settings unless directed by your instructor:

McGraw-Hill's Instructor Management e-mail: gdpupload@mcgraw-hill.com
(gdpupload@mcgraw-hill.com)

Student Upload Web Site URL: gdpupload.mhhe.com
(gdpupload.mhhe.com)

[Save] [Cancel] [Help]

2. Review the settings and make any necessary changes.

Student's e-mail address	This is the address you entered when you initially registered within GDP. If your address changes after initial registration, you can make the change in the Settings dialog box.
Instructor's e-mail address	This is your instructor's address, which your instructor should be able to provide to you.
Word Processor	If your computer does not have Microsoft Word 2000, 2002, or 2003 then **No Word Processor** should be selected. In this case, you will not be able to do the word processing exercises in GDP. Select the correct version of Microsoft Word and specify its full path.
Browser	If **Use system default Web browser** is selected (the default), GDP will launch the system's default Web browser when you access the campus Web site. If **No Web browser** is selected, you will not be able to access the campus Web site from GDP. If you want to access the campus Web site through GDP using a browser other than your system's default browser, **Use other browser** should be selected and the full path to it

	specified. If you do not know the full path, click **Browse** to find it.
Live Update	If this box is checked (the default), you will be notified when new GDP software updates are available for download. After you access GDP, if there is a new update available for download, the Live Update dialog box will display. If this feature is deselected, you will not receive Live Update messages.
Full Editing: in Timed Writings	If this box is checked (the default), you will be able to edit text in timed writings. If unchecked, editing will be disabled during timed writings.
Full Editing: in Drills	If this box is checked (the default), you will be able to edit text in drills. If unchecked, editing will be disabled during drills.
Number of spaces between sentences	Click on the appropriate radio button to identify whether you will use one space or two spaces following punctuation at the end of a sentence (the default is **1 Space**). **Note**: Switching the default setting from 1 to 2 spaces will require changes in text and software instructions. Do not change this setting unless told to do so by your instructor.
Use Proofreading Viewer	If this box is checked (this is **not** the default; you must select it to turn it 'on'), you will be able to view your scored text while editing a document so you can see where your errors occurred.
Hide Desktop from View	If this box is checked (the default), the **Hide Desktop from View** feature will block out the desktop behind the GDP window, while still providing access to the Start menu and task bar (In the Home version, you access the Start menu and task bar only by minimizing GDP). You must deselect this feature in order to turn it 'off'.
URL to be accessed when the Web button is clicked in GDP	If your instructor would like you to be able to access the campus Web site from GDP, he or she will provide you the correct URL to enter here.
McGraw-Hill's Instructor Management e-mail	You should not change this setting unless specifically instructed to do so by your instructor. This is the address where your uploaded data is sent when using the Distance Learning option.
Student Upload Web Site URL	Again, you should not change this setting unless specifically instructed to do so by McGraw-Hill. This is the URL used to upload your data when using the Distance-Learning option.

3. When finished working with settings, click **Save** to record changes and close the Settings dialog box.

2.3 Working on Lesson Exercises

Once you access GDP, the Lessons menu (Figure 2-3) displays the list of exercises in the current lesson. If you are using GDP for the first time, Lesson 1 exercises are listed. If you have worked with GDP previously, the exercise list is for the lesson on which you last worked. A ■ precedes exercises that have been completed. A ◳ precedes exercises that have been started but not completed.

Figure 2-3.
Lessons Menu

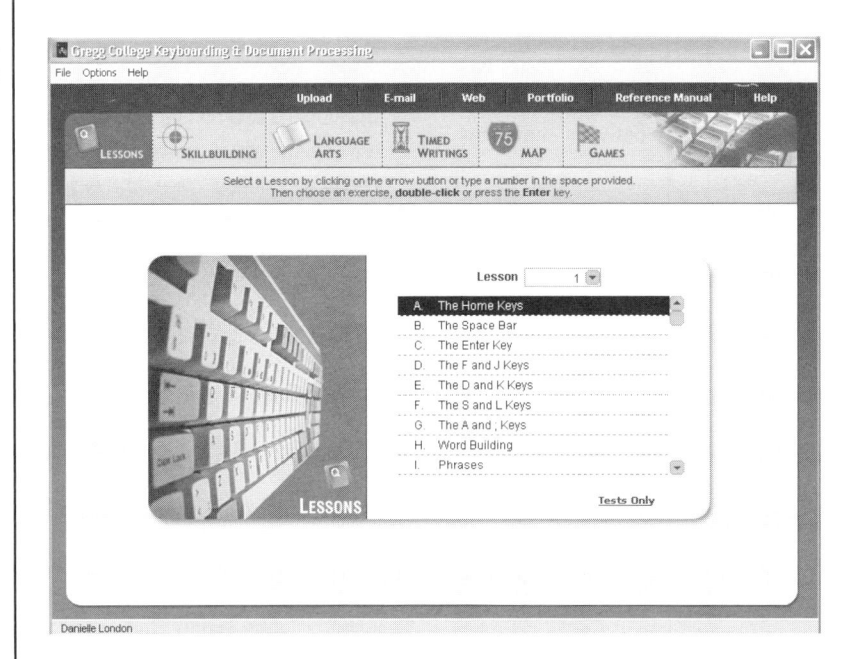

To work on an exercise:

1. Select the lesson you want to open.
    - Type the lesson number into the Lesson text box.

    or

    - Open the Lesson Text Box by clicking the ▼ button; then scroll up or down the lesson numbers.

2. Select the exercise you want to work on.
    - Highlight the name of the exercise and press **Enter** on your keyboard.

    or

- Double-click the name of the exercise.

3. Read the introductory or instruction screen(s) and turn to the appropriate page in the textbook. Type the text as instructed, and click the **Next** button at the bottom of the screen to go to the next screen in the exercise. (For more information about the exercise screen layout, see 2.3.1 Exercise Screen Layout.)

4. When you click the **Next** button at the end of an exercise, GDP goes to the next exercise in the lesson. At the end of the last exercise for a particular lesson, GDP returns to the Lessons menu.

Pressing the **Esc** key allows you to exit an exercise at any time. You can exit the program at any point by selecting *Exit GDP* on the File menu or clicking the close button (☒) at the top right.

> **Note** If you are a distance-learning student, you can send your data to the Instructor Management Web site at any time by clicking the **Upload** button on the toolbar. Your instructor must have registered you on the Instructor Management Web site before you can upload your data. When you log off GDP as a distance-learning student, GDP automatically prompts you to update your data on the Instructor Management Web site if you have done any work in GDP since your last update. For more information on uploading data to the Instructor Management Web site, see 2.7.3 Sending Distance-Learning Student Data to the Instructor Management Web Site on page 26.

2.3.1 Exercise Screen Layout

Exercise screens have the same basic layout throughout the program (see Figure 2-4).

Figure 2-4.
Exercise Screen Layout

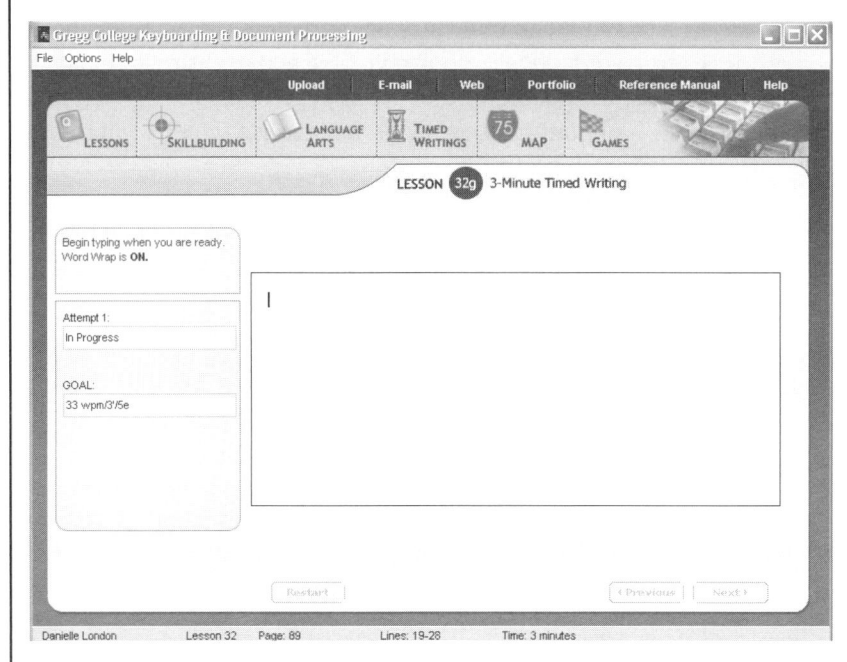

❶ **Title bar:** The title bar includes the program name and the standard window control menu (to the left) and the minimize, maximize and close buttons (to the right).

❷ **Menu bar:** The menu bar lists all of the drop-down menus. (For more information, see "Drop-Down Menus," later in this chapter.

❸ **Toolbar:** The toolbar includes buttons for frequently used features and on-screen guidance. (For more information, see 3.2 GDP Toolbar on page 47.)

❹ **Exercise header:** The exercise header specifies information about the current exercise, such as the speed and accuracy goals for a timed writing and scores on various attempts at the exercise. Goals and scores are noted as follows: number of words/number of minutes/number of errors (for example, "33wpm/3'/5e" indicates 33 words per minute for 3 minutes, with 5 errors).

❺ **Navigation menu:** The navigation menu running across the screen directly under the Toolbar includes icons for accessing GDP's activities by lesson and by activity type.

❻ **Body of the screen:** The body of the screen provides instructions or an area for typing text.

❼ **Status bar:** The status bar specifies your name, lesson number, and textbook page. Line numbers and length of a timing are indicated when applicable.

❽ Previous and Next buttons: These buttons in the bottom right corner of the screen are used to move sequentially through the screens in an exercise.

2.4 Accessing Exercises Outside of Lessons

Typically, you will follow the textbook and use the Lessons menu to work on lesson exercises sequentially. Occasionally, your instructor may want you to access exercises by type (rather than by lesson), work on special exercises to sharpen keyboarding skills, play one of the keyboarding games, or focus on particular language arts skills for a session. In such cases, use the navigation menu running across the GDP screen directly under the Toolbar.

LESSONS

SKILLBUILDING — Use this icon to go to the Skillbuilding menu, which groups exercises by type and includes all of the lesson exercises except for tests, language arts exercises, and document processing exercises. The Skillbuilding menu also includes Open Timed Writings, Custom Timed Writings, Supplementary Timed Writings, Numeric Keypad Practice, MAP, the Pace Car Game, and the Tennis Game, which are not accessible from Lessons menus.

LANGUAGE ARTS — Use this icon to go to the Language Arts menu, which displays all of the language arts exercises in the program. The Language Arts menu provides access to language arts exercises by skill area (rather than by lesson) and includes numerous interactive language arts tutorials not found in the textbook.

TIMED WRITINGS — Use this icon to go to the Timed Writings menu, which includes all of the timed writings included in lesson exercises as well as Open Timed Writings, Custom Timed Writings, and Supplementary Timed Writings.

MAP — Use this icon to go to the MAP (Misstroke Analysis and Prescription) program, which identifies keystroking problems and prescribes remedial exercises to fix those problems.

	Use this icon to go to the Games menu for quick access to the Tennis Game or Pace Car Game.
Note	The exercises accessible on the Skillbuilding, Timed Writings, and Language Arts menus work exactly the same as the corresponding exercises in the Lessons menu. The navigation menu simply provides a different way to access the exercises.

2.4.1 Linking to Word Outside of an Exercise

For documents that are included in the textbook exercises, GDP automatically links to Word 2000, 2002, or 2003, depending on the setting you selected in the Settings dialog. The *Go To Word Processor* option on the File drop-down menu is for working on other documents not included in the textbook or for printing a formatted GDP document without having to access the document through the Lessons menu. To link to the word processor outside of a textbook exercise:

1. Select *Go To Word Processor* on the File menu.
2. Word opens a new document window. You can type a new document in the blank window or open an existing document by selecting *Open* on the File menu.
3. When finished working on the document, select *Return to GDP* on the GDP menu on Word's menu bar.

Alert	The GDP program adds the GDP menu to Word's menu bar to provide you an easy, seamless route back to GDP and ensure that documents created outside of GDP exercises are saved to your data storage location. Make sure that you use this method to exit Word.

2.5 Viewing and Printing Student Work

GDP provides a chart and two types of reports to help you keep track of your progress and review completed exercises. The chart and reports can be viewed on screen and printed.

2.5.1 Student Portfolio

Your Portfolio contains two types of reports. The Portfolio itself provides a snapshot of all exercises on which you have worked, with results and completion status for each. Detailed Reports include the scored text for any exercise on which you have worked— unless you have used the *Delete Files* option from the File drop-down menu to delete some exercises.

To access your Student Portfolio:

1. Click the **Portfolio** button on the toolbar or select the *Portfolio...* option from the File drop-down menu. Your Student Portfolio lists all of the exercises attempted. To refine this list, click the **Filter Portfolio** button to specify which exercises should appear in your Student Portfolio. The Portfolio Filter dialog box (Figure 2-5) then displays.

Figure 2-5.
Portfolio Filter Dialog Box

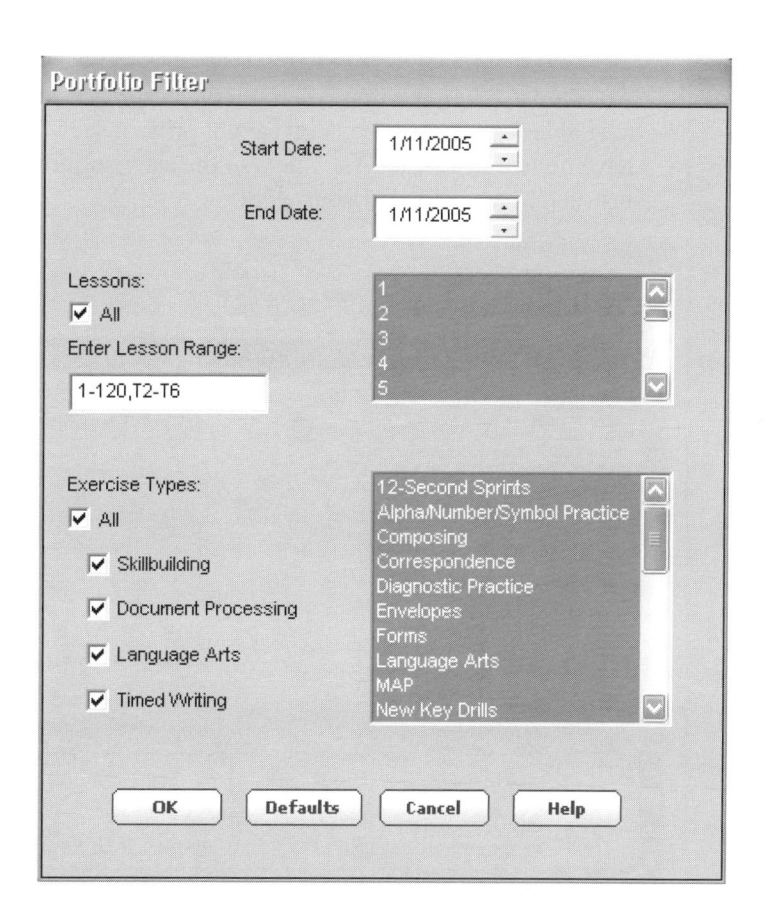

2. Specify a date range, lesson(s), and exercise type(s) to include, and then click **OK** to close the Portfolio Filter and see the filtered Student Portfolio. Click **Defaults** to select the GDP default filter (all lessons; all exercise types).

3. The Student Portfolio window (Figure 2-6) lists all of the completed exercises specified from the Portfolio Filter, one exercise per line. Each line in the Student Portfolio includes the completion date, lesson number and exercise name, score (if a scored exercise), the Total Time you spent working on the exercise, your raw grade for the exercise based on text and formatting, and your weighted average grade based on exercise type weight factors specified by your instructor. The Total Time includes time reading instruction screens, time to launch and time word processing. A question mark (**?**) indicates that a grade is not yet available. If **NA** appears in the Grade or Weighted Average columns, then your instructor has not designated that exercise as a graded activity.

An asterisk (*****) in the first column indicates that Detailed Report text is available for the exercise. You cannot print or view text for exercises that have no text available. An **A** next to the asterisk indicates that your instructor has annotated your work.

Figure 2-6.
Student Portfolio Window

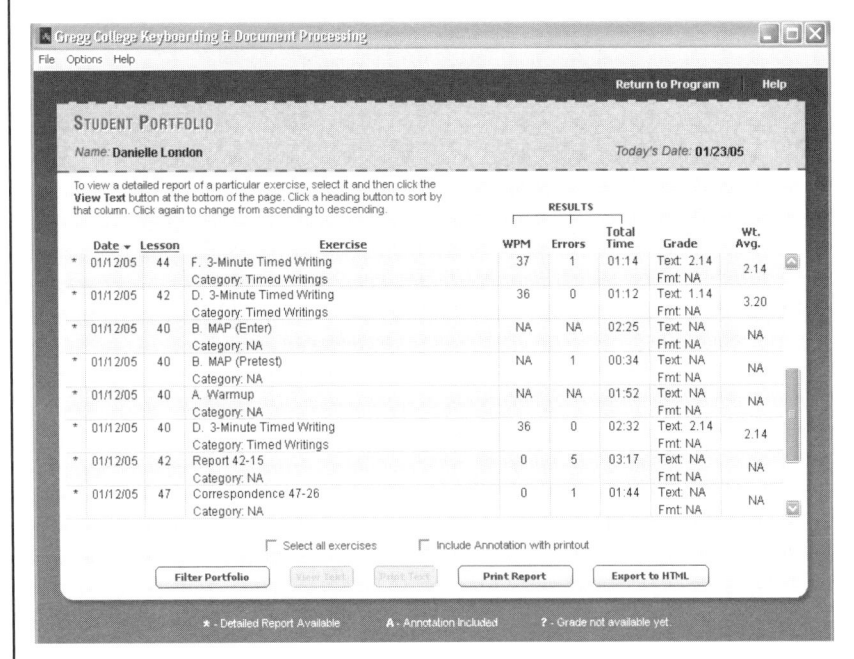

4. There are several options for viewing and printing from the Student Profile:
   - To sort the report by date, lesson number, or exercise name, click on the appropriate column header. The current sort is highlighted, with an arrow indicating ascending order (up arrow) or descending order (down arrow).

20   Student User's Guide for GDP/10 Home Software

- To print a copy of the Student Profile, click **Print Report**.
- To print a copy of the scored text for any exercise, click once on the lines for the desired exercise(s) (they must be preceded by an asterisk in the Date column) and then click **Print Text**.

If your instructor has requested an HTML version of your Student Profile, click **Export to HTML**. When you click the **Export to HTML** button, a *Save as* dialog will display. The dialog will include a default file name (GDPStudentProfile) and the file extension will automatically be set to "HTML files (*.htm, *.html)". Select a location where you want to save the file and click the **Save** button.

Note: It is recommended that a new, unique file name is given to each Export file. To change the file name in the *Save as* dialog box, highlight the default name in the File name field and overwrite it by typing the new file name.

Note | To select an exercise for viewing or printing, that exercise must be preceded by an * in the Date column in the Student Portfolio.

5. To view the text for any exercise (that is, get a Detailed Report), click on the desired exercise line on the Student Portfolio (they must be preceded by an asterisk in the Date column) and click **View Text**. The Detailed Report window (Figure 2-7) displays your text and scores.

Figure 2-7.
Detailed Report Window

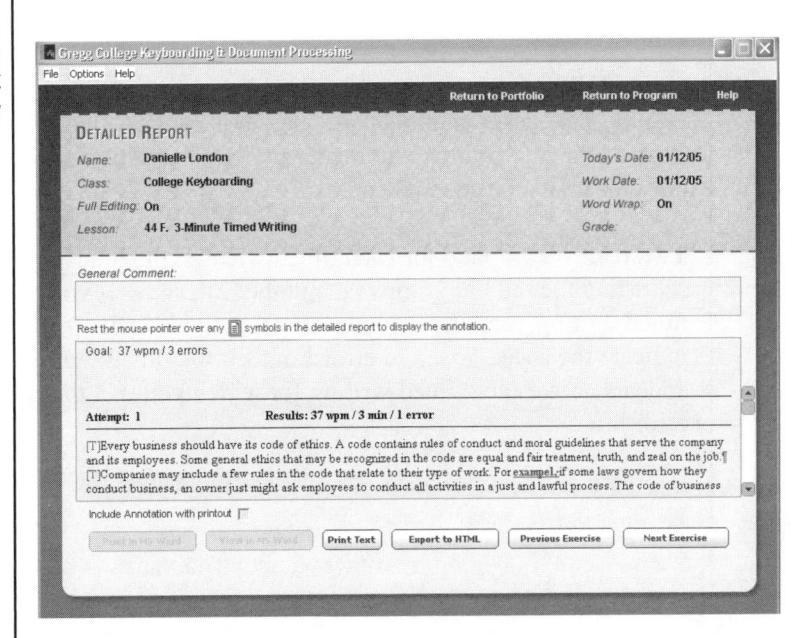

CHAPTER 2 **Using GDP**

- To print the Detailed Report, click **Print Text**.
- If you selected more than one exercise for which to view text, **Next Exercise** and **Previous Exercise** buttons can be used to move among the Detailed Reports.
- Documents appear as unformatted, scored text. To view the formatted document as it appears in Word, click **View in MS Word**. You will be able to make changes to the document, but those changes will not be saved. To return to GDP, select *Return to GDP* on the GDP menu in Word's menu bar.
- To print a formatted version of the document (without viewing it in Word), click **Print in MS Word**.
- When finished viewing the Detailed Report(s), click **Return to Portfolio** to return to the Student Portfolio.

6. To exit the Student Portfolio, click **Return to Program**.

Note: The Detailed Report for any Document Processing exercise displays your Time in MS Word as well as the version of Microsoft Word in use.

2.5.2 Performance Chart

The Performance Chart graphs your progress as you type timed writings. To view this chart, select *Performance Chart* from the File drop-down menu.

The Performance Chart window (Figure 2-8) tracks your best score for each timed writing you completed. The results are graphed in groups of 20 lessons.

The boldface numbers on either side of the chart represent speed, in words per minute. The lesson numbers are listed horizontally under the graph. The timing length appears under the lesson number. The timing length appears only for graphed timed writings.

Two bars are graphed for each timed writing: the blue bar graphs your speed score and the red bar graphs the number of errors. If you made no errors on a timed writing, there is no red bar for that timed writing. Black horizontal lines indicate the speed goal and error limit for the timed writing. A red star appears above each timed writing for which you met the speed goal within the error limit.

Figure 2-8.
Performance Chart

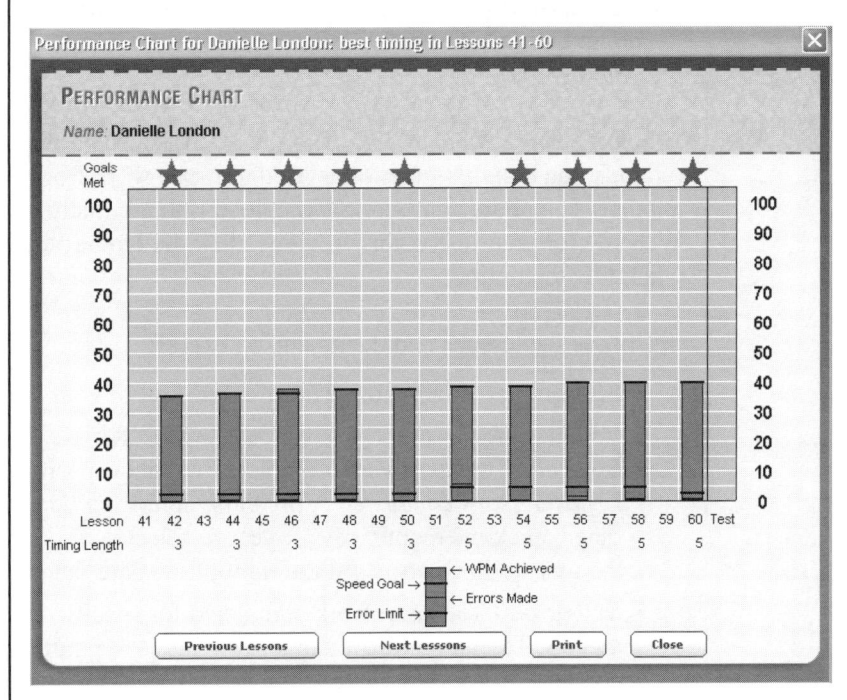

- To print a copy of the Performance Chart for the current part, click **Print**.
- To view the Performance Chart for the previous part, click **Previous Lessons**. To view the Performance Chart for the next part, click **Next Lessons**.
- To close the Performance Chart, click **Close**.

2.6 Importing and Exporting Student Data

GDP's Import/Export feature provides an easy way for you to keep your data files current if you use GDP both on a campus LAN and at home. If you are storing your work on a fixed disk such as a local hard drive—rather than on floppy disks—your instructor can also use this feature to update your data for the gradebook.

2.6.1 Using Import/Export to Transfer Data Files Between Campus and Home

If you use GDP both on campus and at home, your data files must match in both locations. If your data is stored on a floppy disk, you can use the same floppy disk in both locations. If your data is stored on a hard disk, you should use GDP's Import/Export feature to make sure that data files are up-to-date in both locations.

To export work:

1. Select *Export Student Data...* on the File menu. The Export dialog box reminds you that this function is used to move work from one computer to another. To update your work and upload it to the Instructor Management Web site for your instructor's review, click the **Upload** button on the toolbar. Click **OK** to continue.

2. Choose the lessons and documents to export:

    - *All Lessons* - Click *Export all lessons* if all of your work is to be exported.
    - *By Date* - To export work completed within a specific date range, click *Export lessons completed between the following dates*. To select a date range, click the month, day, or year to select it. Type the new date or use the up and down arrows at the right of the date field to change the date.
    - *By Lesson* - To export work completed for specific lessons, click *Export lessons*. To enter a lesson range, type the lesson numbers followed by commas or, for a contiguous range, type the start and end lesson numbers separated by a hyphen. The selected lessons will be highlighted in the lesson number list below. To select lesson numbers from the list, press the **Ctrl** key and click the desired lesson numbers. To select a contiguous range of lessons, press the **Shift** key and click the start and end lessons in the desired range.

    Note: Please be sure to leave the "Include Microsoft Word document files for the selected lessons" checkbox selected if you also want the Word documents to be exported. This will ensure that the document files are available in the Student Portfolio when you import the data into your alternate location.

3. To specify a location where the export file is to be stored, use the default location provided or type the path to indicate a different location or name. To browse for a folder location, click the **Browse** button, select a location from the file directory, and click **OK**.

4. If you are exporting to a floppy disk, put a floppy disk in the floppy disk drive.

5. Click **Export**. Click **Cancel** to close the Export dialog box and return to GDP.

Once the work is exported, it will need to be imported to the desired GDP workstation, for example, to the instructor's workstation or to a home computer.

To import work:

1. Select *Import Student Data...* from the File drop-down menu.
2. In the Open dialog box, select the export file (which has an ".EXP" file name extension) and click **Open**.
3. The exported data is copied to the student data storage location, overwriting existing data if the export includes the same lessons that are in the student's data files.

Note | This use of the Import/Export feature is intended for use in the Home version of GDP when you are storing your data on your home computer's hard disk. If you are using the Home version of GDP and are storing your work on floppy disks, you can simply deliver your data disks to your instructor. If you are using the Distance-Learning option available within GDP, use GDP's Upload feature (see 2.7.3 Sending Distance-Learning Student Data to the Instructor Management Web Site on page 26).

2.7 Using GDP's Web and Distance-Learning Features

2.7.1 E-mailing the Instructor

You can send your instructor e-mail messages from within GDP if the following conditions are met:

- Your e-mail system must be MAPI compliant (for example, Microsoft Outlook and Outlook Express are MAPI-compliant, AOL and CompuServe are not),
- Your e-mail address must be correct in GDP (your e-mail address is in the Personal Information form, which is accessible from the Options drop-down menu), **AND**
- Your instructor's e-mail address must be specified correctly in your settings (see 2.2 Specifying Your Settings on page 11).

To send an e-mail message from within GDP:

1. Click the **E-mail** button on the GDP toolbar.
2. An addressed e-mail message window appears for you to type a message. Type a subject and a message.
3. When ready to send your message, click the **Send** button.

2.7.2 Accessing the Web From GDP

You can access the World Wide Web (Web) if the following settings are specified and valid: the **URL to be accessed when the Web button is clicked in GDP** and the browser. (For more information, see 2.2 Specifying Your Settings on page 11.)

To access the Web from within GDP:

1. Click the **Web** button on the GDP toolbar.
2. GDP launches your browser, establishes an online connection, and opens the Web site specified in your settings.
3. When finished browsing the Web site, you can either close the browser window or switch back to GDP using the Windows task bar.

2.7.3 Sending Distance-Learning Student Data to the Instructor Management Web Site

The Distance-Learning feature within GDP allows you to upload your GDP data files to the Instructor Management Web site and receive back information from your GDP instructors (for example, class announcements and instructor comments on specific GDP exercises). In order for the distance-learning option to work properly, the following conditions must be met:

- Your system must have a default e-mail address. The default e-mail address is the one marked with "(default)" in the Mail settings in Window's Control Panel.

  (GDP uses the system default e-mail address when uploading student data to the Instructor Management Web site.)

- Your instructor's e-mail address must be correct. Your e-mail address in your installation and the e-mail address used by your instructor to register you on the Instructor Management Web site must be identical and correct in your settings. See 2.2 Specifying Your Settings on page 11.

- Your instructor must have registered you on the Instructor Management Web site before you can upload your data.

- The e-mail address your instructor used to register you on the Instructor Management Web site matches the e-mail address in your Personal Information form. (Your e-mail address is in the Personal Information form, which is accessible from the Options menu.)

- You must complete at least one exercise.

At any time while logged on to GDP when using the Distance-Learning option, you can send updated information to the Instructor Management Web site, as follows:

1. Click the **Upload** button on the toolbar to open the Upload dialog box.
2. Choose which files to send to the Instructor Management Web site:
   - To update a complete set of data files, select *Upload all work*.
   - To send only those files that have changed since the last update, select *Upload work completed since your last update*. (This usually takes less time than uploading your full set of data files.)

3. To e-mail updated work, click **Send Work Via E-mail**. This choice sends the student's updated work directly to the instructor at the e-mail address specified in Settings.
4. If the student's e-mail is not functioning properly or is unavailable, The student can use the Student Upload Web site to upload work. Click **Upload Work to Student Upload Web Site**. In the Upload Work dialog box, a location is specified to store the upload file. Once the upload file is stored, click **Store the Upload File**. GDP will try to use a browser to access the Student Upload Web site, located at gdpupload.mhhe.com. This site must be accessed to finish the upload process.

When files are uploaded, GDP establishes an online connection and sends data files in an e-mail to the Instructor Management Web site. This process can take several minutes, depending on the amount of information that needs to be transmitted and the speed of the Internet connection.

2.7.4 Using the Student Website

Overview

If you are a student in a distance-learning class, you can log into the GDP Student Web Site to:

- View the class page created by your instructor
- View your portfolio and annotations from your instructor
- Download your grades and annotations from your instructor so you can import the data into your GDP software

How You are Notified About the Student Web Site

When your instructor adds your e-mail address to a class at the Instructor Management Web Site (IMWS), the IMWS generates an e-mail from your instructor to you. The e-mail tells you the name of the class to which you are registered and invites you to view the Student Web Site (SWS). The e-mail includes a link to the SWS, a password, and directions for logging on to the SWS and changing the password.

NOTE: For security reasons, your GDP software password and SWS password must match. The web site checks the e-mail address and embedded password in each upload file against your e-mail address and password for the SWS. If they match, the upload file is accepted. If they don't match, the software displays a message telling you that the e-mail address and/or password for the upload file do not match those at the SWS. Since as a Home version user you do not log on with a password, you are required to enter a password in the Personal Information dialog that is used for uploading data only. (See 'Changing a Password at the Student Web Site' in this section for more information.)

Logging On to the Student Web Site

The Student Web Site log on page displays when you link to it from your instructor's e-mail or enter the URL for the web site directly in a browser.

The URL for the Student Web Site is: http://gdpstudent.mhhe.com.

Logging On to the Student Web Site for the First Time

If this is your first time logging on to the SWS or you have not yet uploaded student data from GDP:

1. Enter your e-mail address and the password included in the e-mail you received from the IMWS, and click **Log On**.
2. If you are enrolled in more than one GDP Version 10 class, the web site will prompt you to select your class from the list.
3. If your instructor has already created a class page, the class page displays upon successful log on. If your instructor has not yet created a class page, the Portfolio Filter displays.

Subsequent Log Ons to the Student Web Site

Once you complete exercises in the GDP Version 10 software and upload your work to the IMWS, your data will also be available on the SWS. If you are also working on the Campus Version of the software, the uploaded data includes the password you use to log into the GDP software on campus. This password is passed to the Student Web Site and is the password that you subsequently use when you log on to the Student Web Site. This approach allows you to use the same password in the student software and on the Student Web Site.

Entering a Password in the GDP Home Version

Since the Home Version is not password-protected, you must complete the following two fields in the Personal Information dialog in your GDP Home software:

- Password to upload data
- Retype password

When you click the **Upload** button in the GDP software, the software will check this field for your e-mail address and password. If the e-mail address and password are detected, the upload process will continue. If the password is not found, the software displays the following message:

> Please enter a password for uploading data in the "Password to upload data" and the "Retype password" fields on the Personal Information dialog.

NOTE: The GDP Campus Version includes an instructor option for turning off password protection. If your instructor deselects the "Log on password required" checkbox, the "Password to upload data" and "Retype password" fields display on the Personal Information dialog in the Campus Version, as well.

Changing a Password at the Student Web Site

Before you upload data from GDP, you need to change your password on the Student Web Site to match your password in the GDP software. To change a password, you should follow these steps:

1. Launch the Student Web Site located at http://gdpstudent.mhhe.com.
2. Enter your e-mail address and click **Change Password**.
3. Enter the password in the e-mail from the IMWS (or current password if you have previously changed it).
4. Enter your GDP password in the "Your new password" and "Retype new password" fields.
5. Click **Save** to save the changes and return to the Log On screen. You can now log on with the new password.

Requesting a Forgotten Password

If you forget your password, you can request it by following these steps:

1. Launch the Student Web Site located at http://gdpstudent.mhhe.com.
2. Click the **Forgot Password?** link on the Log On page.
3. Enter your e-mail address in the space provided and click **Submit**.
4. The SWS will send an e-mail to you with your password.

Accessing the Class Page

If your instructor has created a class page for your class, the class page will display after you log on to the Student Web Site. (**Note:** If you are enrolled in more than one GDP Version 10 class, you will first have to select a class before the class page is displayed.)

The class page can include tabs for the following information:
- Course Outline
- Syllabus
- Handouts
- Contact Information
- Links

The information displayed on the class page depends on the sections of the class page that your instructor enables when s/he creates the class page.

You can also access the other areas of the Student Web Site from the tool bar at the top of the screen, including:
- Student Portfolio
- Download Grades
- Student Upload
- Help

Displaying the Student Portfolio on the Student Web Site

You can access your student portfolio on the Student Web Site, complete with grades and annotations your instructor has added. To display your portfolio, you should follow these steps:

1. Launch the Student Web Site located at http://gdpstudent.mhhe.com and log on (see 'Logging On to the Student Web Site' in this section for more information).

2. Click **Student Portfolio** on the tool bar at the top of the screen. The Portfolio Filter displays.

3. Modify the filter options, as needed, and click **View Portfolio**. (**Note:** Select fewer exercises to speed the display of the portfolio.)

4. The Student Portfolio displays.

Displaying a Detailed Report

To display a detailed report:

1. Display your portfolio (See 'Displaying the Student Portfolio on the Student Web Site' above).

2. Select the radio button beside an exercise and click **View Detailed Report**.

3. The Detailed Report for that exercise displays.

    a. If the detailed report is for a document processing exercise, the **View in MS Word** button is active. Click this button to display the exercise in Microsoft Word.

    b. Click **Printer-Friendly Version** to display a printer-friendly version of the report.

    c. Use the **Next Exercise** and **Previous Exercise** buttons to navigate between detailed reports without returning to the Portfolio.

d. General comments from your instructor display in the General Comments field. Annotations are represented by notepad icons in the detailed report text. Rest the mouse pointer over any notepad symbols in the detailed report to display the annotation.

Downloading Grades and Annotations from the Student Web Site

If you are a student in a distance-learning class, you can download your grades and annotations from your instructor from the Student Web Site. When you download your grades, the SWS creates an export of your work, which you can then import into your GDP software. To download your grades, you should follow these steps:

1. Launch the Student Web Site located at http://gdpstudent.mhhe.com and log on.

2. Click **Download Grades** on the toolbar at the top of the screen.

3. Instructions display indicating how to download grades and import them into the GDP software. Click the **Printer-Friendly Version** link at the bottom of the screen to print a copy of the instructions.

4. To download grades:
   a. Click the **Download Grades** button on this screen.
   b. The File Download dialog box that displays is the standard dialog box that displays when you download a file or application from the Internet. Click **Save**.
   c. A Save As... dialog box displays. Select the folder in which you want to save the Export file of your grades, make note of this location, and click **Save**. Do not change the filename.
   d. Once you have downloaded your grades, you will need to import it into your software. In order to import the file, you will need to know the location of the file. For this reason, we recommend that you save the file to your Desktop.
   e. The file will begin to download. The download dialog automatically closes when the download is complete.

5. To import your grades into your GDP software:
   a. Launch GDP as you normally would. Because you are using the Home Version, you do not have to log in.
   b. Select Import Student Data... from the File menu in your GDP software.
   c. Browse to the folder in which you saved the Export file, select the file, and click **Open**. Note: You may need to change the view of the **Open** dialog box to Details so that you can see the file extensions.

d. Once you import your grades, you will be able to view your grades and your instructor's annotations in your GDP software.

2.7.5 Creating an HTML Version of a Student Report

Whether or not your instructor uses GDP Instructor Management (the program or the Web site), your instructor may want to view your work using a Web browser. To create an HTML version of any report in your Portfolio:

1. Open your Portfolio by clicking the **Portfolio** button, specifying report settings in the Portfolio Filter dialog box, and clicking **OK**.
2. Open the report (Student Portfolio or Detailed Report) that your instructor has requested.
3. Click the **Export to HTML** button.
4. Specify a unique file name (preferably with your name embedded) and location in the Save As dialog box.
5. Click **Save**.

Once you create the HTML file, you will need to deliver it to your instructor. If you have e-mail access (within or outside of GDP), you can send your instructor an e-mail with the HTML file attached. Otherwise, you can save the HTML file on a floppy disk and hand deliver to your instructor.

2.8 Lesson Features

Bilingual Instruction Screens
All instruction screens in GDP are available in English or Spanish (Español). By default, English is used. To switch to Spanish-language instruction screens, click the **Español** button at the bottom of the screen (in Spanish mode, the button changes to **English**; click this button to return to English instructions). Note that menus, help, and toolbars appear in English only. If there is no **Español** button at the bottom of the instruction screen, then your instructor has opted to make the Spanish text unavailable for your class. Please speak with your instructor if you need to view the Spanish text.

Technique Tips
Technique tips appear randomly in GDP to give you quick pointers on keyboarding. Technique tips appear as an animated text banner at the top of the screen.

Speed/Accuracy Goals

All timings include speed and accuracy goals. When you work on Pretest/Practice/Posttest exercises, your Pretest results will be used to determine whether you will use a speed or accuracy routine for the Practice component of the exercise.

Word Wrap

Some exercises are keyed in Word Wrap On mode, which means that you press the **Enter** key at the end of paragraphs only. Other exercises are to be done in Word Wrap Off mode, which means that you press the **Enter** key at the end of every line. An icon will appear on the toolbar to let you know whether Word Wrap is on or off.

Student Portfolio

All of your work in GDP is stored on a floppy disk or in a data directory on a local drive or a network server. You can view your work —scores and text—by accessing your portfolio from the File drop-down menu or from the toolbar.

Printing

The reports in your portfolio can be printed. You can print your scores in your Student Portfolio as well as your scored text for any exercise.

Scoring

Much of the work you complete in this program will be scored. The program will report your words per minute (wpm) speed and the number of errors you make, as well as achievement of speed and accuracy goals.

One-Space/Two-Space Option

GDP offers the option of typing one space or two spaces after punctuation: periods (at ends of sentences only), question marks, exclamation points, and colons. This option is set on a class-wide level by your instructor, and affects all scored activities, including document processing exercises. Check with your instructor, as typing one space after punctuation when the setting is for two spaces (and vice-versa) will result in scoring errors.

2.9 Types of Exercises in GDP

The exercises in GDP parallel those in the textbook. The software can time, score, repeat an exercise, diagnose (and recommend corrective practice), deliver instruction, and provide directions for the exercises. The major types of exercises are described briefly in this section.

2.9.1 Warmups

Each lesson begins with a Warmup activity (with the exception of Lesson 1), consisting of drills to loosen the fingers. Warmups reinforce learned alphabet, number and symbol keys.

Warmup activities are recorded but not scored. They are listed as completed in the Student Portfolio, and your typed text is available in the Detailed Report.

The Warmup screen consists of a large typing area. Type the Warmup from copy displayed in your textbook. Begin typing when you are ready. Type the Warmup text two times. Click **Next** to continue.

If the Warmup is not typed twice, a GDP message will advise you that the exercise is not completed. Check with your instructor to determine whether you should complete the exercise or proceed to the next activity. Click **Continue with this exercise** to complete the Warmup. Click **Proceed to the next exercise** if you choose to move on to the lesson exercise that follows the Warmup.

2.9.2 New Key Drills

New Key drills introduce you to new keyboard characters. As you sequence through the instruction screens, GDP tells you which finger to use for each new key and provides a multimedia demonstration of the correct keyboarding for the character. As you progress through the exercise, you will type several lock-stepped sequences of the new keys, which require you to type the correct key before continuing. Once the lock-stepped lines are completed, you advance to scored New Key drill lines. Both the lock-stepped and the scored text results can be reviewed in your Student Portfolio.

The New Key drill screen displays the text that is to be typed above the input area. Textual instructions appear on the left side of the screen, and a keyboard map appears below the input area. Word Wrap is off for the New Key drills.

2.9.3 Other Drills

Drills other than new key exercises generally focus on either speed or accuracy.

Accuracy Pattern

Each group of practice lines is typed twice:

```
jamb  lamb  limb  limp  lump  bump  pump  jump
pals  pale  sale  same  sane  vane  cane  cape
cure  core  cove  wove  move  more  mare  maze

jamb  lamb  limb  limp  lump  bump  pump  jump
pals  pale  sale  same  sane  vane  cane  cape
cure  core  cove  wove  move  more  mare  maze
```

Speed Pattern

Each practice line is typed twice before proceeding to the next line:
```
jamb  lamb  limb  limp  lump  bump  pump  jump
jamb  lamb  limb  limp  lump  bump  pump  jump

pals  pale  sale  same  sane  vane  cane  cape
pals  pale  sale  same  sane  vane  cane  cape

cure  core  cove  wove  move  more  mare  maze
cure  core  cove  wove  move  more  mare  maze
```

2.9.4 Timed writings

There are several types of timed writings in GDP, including 12-second speed sprints and 1- to 5-minute timed writings in lesson exercises (accessible from the Lessons menu) plus additional Open, Custom, and Supplementary timed writings (accessible from the Timed writings and Skillbuilding menus only). All types of timed writings work essentially the same:

1. Select the timing from the lesson exercise folder on the Lessons menu or from one of the timed writings folders on the Timed Writings or Skillbuilding menu. In some cases, you are allowed to choose the timing duration.

2. After reading the introductory/instruction screens, turn to the appropriate passage in the textbook and begin typing when you are ready. (For Custom Timed Writings, you must have printed text because Custom Timed Writings are not included in the textbook. Any text can be used for Open Timed Writings; Open Timed Writings are scored for speed only.)

3. Type the copy and, if finished typing the passage before time is up, press **Enter** and begin typing the passage again. Depending on your Full Editing in Timed Writings setting (see 2.2 Specifying Your Settings on page 11), the mouse and standard editing keys may or may not be enabled for editing. Note: The screen timer begins with your first keystroke.

> *Note:* For timed writings that allow you to restart during the first 15 seconds, a beep indicates when the restart period is over. For 3- and 5-minute timed writings, a beep signals when 30 seconds remain. For all timed writings, a beep signals when time is up.

4. When time is up, the copy is scored for both speed and accuracy (except for Open Timed Writings, which are scored for speed only). Your scores will display at the top of the screen.
5. Review the scored copy to pinpoint errors.
6. If desired, you can repeat the timed writing.

> *Note:* For information on the formula used to calculate speed or the way errors are marked in scored copy, see 3.4 Scoring and Error Marking on page 48.

2.9.5 Pretest/Practice/Posttest

Many lessons include a Pretest, Practice, and Posttest three-step routine that identifies speed and accuracy needs and measures improvement. The Pretest/Practice/Posttest activities can be accessed from the Lesson menu and from the Skillbuilding menu.

The Pretest is a preliminary 1-minute, scored timed writing that targets a specific typing technique and is used to determine your initial skill level. Practices are unscored drills that reinforce the skill tested. The Posttest is a repeat of the Pretest. Your goal is to improve your Pretest score when you take the Posttest. Results of your Pretests and Posttests, as well as your typed text, are available in your Student Portfolio.

2.9.6 Document Processing

Documents in the Textbook

GDP links to Word 2000, 2002, or 2003 for document processing exercises. That link is specified in your Settings under the Options drop-down menu.

To produce a document in the textbook, select the document from the Lessons menu. The MS Word Document Options dialog box displays your options for the file to be used for the exercise: choose an option, and GDP links to Word.

Unless otherwise instructed, you should use Word's default settings. Type the document and proofread and spell-check it.

When finished working on the document, exit Word by selecting *Return to GDP* on the GDP menu. A dialog box asks if you want to save the file; you must click **Yes** in order for the document to be saved. If this is a scored exercise, the next dialog box asks if you want the document scored. If the document is incomplete, you should click **No**. If it is complete, clicking **Yes** will score the document and give you an opportunity to review the scored text.

Documents are scored for keystrokes only, not for formatting. Make sure to print a copy of the final document so that your instructor can score it for formatting. If you print the document within Word (before returning to GDP), exercise time on task accumulates while the document is printing, and the document prints without a header (your name, class, and date information). Another printing method, which includes a header and does not add time to the exercise, is to print the document from your Portfolio. To do so, access your Portfolio (from the File drop-down menu or the toolbar), select the document from the Student Portfolio, click **View Text**, and then click **Print in MS Word**.

MS Word Document Options Dialog Box

GDP launches the MS Word Document Options dialog when the **Next** button is clicked from a document processing instruction screen. The document opened automatically has the correct file name when GDP launches it. Do not change the file name unless instructed to do so in your text, or scoring errors may result.

The MS Word Document Options dialog uses the following buttons to open a named document in Word. A disabled (gray) button indicates that those options are not currently available for this activity.

> **Create (document file name)** -- Click **Create** to open a blank, named document.
> Note: The Edit button will be active if you have already worked on this document. Clicking **Create** will delete your previous effort on this exercise and open a blank, named document.
>
> **Edit (document file name)** -- Click the **Edit** button to open and revise a file you have already typed.
>
> **Open (document file name) to create (document file name)** -- Some document processing activities involve editing files typed in other exercises. Clicking this button opens a copy of the specified "Open" file from another exercise and creates (renames) it as the current exercise file name. Your original file (the "Open" file) is not altered.

GDP-Word Interface

When the **Create**, **Edit**, or **Open** buttons are clicked on the MS Word Document Options dialog, GDP launches Word. GDP's Word interface adds the *GDP* drop-down menu to Word's toolbar (to the right of Help).

The GDP menu offers these choices:

> **Return to GDP** -- Click **Return to GDP** when you are ready to score your document, or when you are ready to exit Word without scoring your document and return to GDP. When this option is clicked, Word closes and you return to the lesson that you were working on when you accessed Word.
>
> **Reference Manual** -- The Reference Manual is a separate help system that offers examples of formatted documents, as well as format instructions. If you would like formatting help while you work on a document, click **Reference Manual**.
>
> **Hide Proofreading Viewer** -- This option displays only if you enabled the Proofreading Viewer in your settings from the *Options* drop-down menu. The Proofreading Viewer launches a Read-Only version of scored text, and is available only when you use the **Edit** button (in the MS Word Document Options dialog) to revise a previously scored document. Click **Hide Proofreading Viewer** if you do not want to see a Read-Only version of your scored text.

Use Word's Help system if you have questions about Word functionality. Use the Reference Manual if you want to review examples of formatted documents.

Documents Not in the Textbook

To create documents NOT in the textbook, you can link toms Word by selecting *Go To Word Processor* from the File drop-down menu.

When you create documents this way, you will have to create a name for and save the document within Word. It is recommended that you use a separate data disk for documents not included in the textbook.

For more information, see 2.4.1 Linking to Word Outside of an Exercise on page 18.

2.9.7 Language Arts

These exercises are designed to help you improve language skills for business. Typically, a language arts exercise introduces a rule, illustrates its use by giving examples, then pretests your knowledge by asking you to apply the rule in a particular passage. If you make one or more errors on the pretest, GDP takes you through a tutorial that re-introduces the rule and gives illustrations, then presents a series of sentences to edit or a series of multiple-choice questions to answer. Language arts exercises can be accessed through the Lessons menus or through the Language Arts menu.

2.9.8 Diagnostic Practice

Diagnostic Practices are used to evaluate your weaknesses on keys and then provide exercises to help you maintain an expected WPM and error limit. These exercises are timed and scored and include a Pretest/Practice/Posttest sequence. GDP performs a diagnostic analysis on errors to indicate weak or error-prone fingers and prescribe additional typing drills, printed in the textbook reference section, based on the type and number of errors diagnosed.

2.9.9 Progressive Practice

Progressive Practice exercises are a series of 30-second timings that will help you increase both speed and accuracy. Progressive Practice: Alphabet exercises concentrate on keying all of the letters of the alphabet, while Progressive Practice: Numbers focus on keying numerical expressions and words. The timings range from 16 to 104 wpm (words per minute).

A 1-minute entry timing is taken to establish your beginning speed goal. The error limit for the 1-minute timing is three or fewer errors. Once the entry timing is scored, GDP will present a Progressive Practice paragraph that is 2 wpm faster than your most recently achieved goal (each passage increases incrementally in speed by 2 wpm). Your goal is to key the passage within 30 seconds with no errors. When you have achieved that goal, GDP will promote you to the next passage so that you can increase your speed and accuracy skills. GDP sets a daily maximum of six attempts per Progressive Practice exercise type.

Once your speed for the Progressive Practice has been established, a GDP message dialog displays when Progressive Practice is chosen from a menu. The message reminds you that you will begin at the speed of your last achieved goal. Progressive Practices can be accessed from either a lesson menu or from the Skillbuilding menu.

2.9.10 Paced Practice

One of the best ways to develop speed and control errors is through the use of paced exercises. The Paced Practice paragraphs in GDP are written to contain an exact number of words to be typed within two minutes. Your goal is to complete each paragraph within two minutes with no more than two errors. When you achieve your speed and accuracy goals, GDP progresses you to the next, more difficult, paragraph. Because each paragraph is longer than the previous one, you are forced to push yourself to the next higher speed. To help pace yourself, the paragraph contains quarter-minute markers.

Paced Practices builds speed and accuracy by using individualized goals and immediate feedback. This exercise (accessed from the Skillbuilding menu) consists of a series of two-minute timed writings for speeds ranging from 16 to 96 wpm (words per minute). You will type timed passages with red goal markers at 15-second intervals. A 1-minute entry timing that establishes your base speed is taken the first time Paced Practice is attempted. Paced Practice routines incorporate both speed and accuracy goals. Your results can be seen in both the Student Portfolio and the Detailed Report. GDP allots you a maximum of six Paced Practice attempts in one day.

2.9.11 Sustained Practice

Sustained Practices consist of four paragraphs. Begin the activity by opening your textbook to the Sustained Practice and typing the *first* Sustained Practice paragraph; you take a 1-minute timed writing on the first paragraph. You are expected to complete the paragraph with three or fewer errors to establish your base speed. If you have more than three errors, you repeat the paragraph until it is completed within the error goal. Once your base speed has been established, you take up to four one-minute timed writings on the remaining three paragraphs. As soon as you equal or exceed the base speed within the error limit (three errors) on one paragraph, the software advances you to the next, slightly more difficult paragraph. To complete the first attempt, type the *second* Sustained Practice paragraph in your textbook. To advance to the third paragraph in your textbook, you must type the second paragraph in one minute with three or fewer errors. Sustained Practice exercises are accessible from both the Lessons and Skillbuilding menus.

2.9.12 Technique Practice

There are two basic types of Technique Practices: Keys and Concentration. Technique Practices for keys (including the Backspace, Colon, Enter, Hyphen, Question Mark, Shift, Shift/Caps Lock, Space Bar, and Tab Keys) are designed to help you consciously practice the efficient, touch-typed reach for each key. Concentration Technique Practice is designed to help you keep your eyes on the copy, not on the keyboard. These practices are unscored, untimed, and similar to warmups. Technique Practices are accessed from either the Lessons menu or from the Skillbuilding menu. Text typed for Technique Practices can be reviewed in the Student Portfolio.

2.9.13 Proofreading and Spelling

Proofreading activities allow you to practice your proofreading skills by making corrections to incorrectly keyed passages. You are instructed to edit the passage on screen to correct any keyboarding or formatting errors. The Spelling activity provides you with the opportunity to practice typing words correctly, as well as to edit incorrectly spelled words. Both types of activities are scored.

Documents designated as Proofreading Checks in the textbook serve as a check of your proofreading skill. Your goal is to have zero typographical errors when GDP first scores the document. You can find this information in the document heading under Attempt.

2.9.14 Numeric Keypad

The numeric keypad exercises, which are accessible from the Skillbuilding menu only, teach you how to use the numeric keypad and build skills in typing numbers. There are three sections of numeric keypad exercises:

- **Introduction** exercises teach the keys on the numeric keypad. They are very similar to new key drills on the standard keyboard.
- **Pretest/practice/posttest** sequences resemble other pretest/practice/posttest sequences, except that you type numbers in right-justified columns rather than text in a blank input screen.
- **Practice** exercises are additional, scored exercises that focus on particular kinds of numbers (e.g., long decimal numbers).

The timing and scoring of numeric keypad exercises differs from those of text-based exercises. Time in numeric keypad exercises is recorded as the number of seconds it takes you to complete the exercise (e.g., S 193 means that you took 193 seconds to complete the exercise). Speed in numeric keypad exercises is reported in digits per minute (e.g., 101 DPM).

> *Note* On screen, numbers with four or more digits appear with commas to make reading easier. You should not type the comma or scoring errors will occur.

2.9.15 MAP (Misstroke Analysis and Prescription)

MAP is a special activity that identifies keystroking problems and prescribes remedial exercises to help you fix those problems. This activity is not found in the textbook and is accessible from the MAP and Skillbuilding menus.

To work on the MAP activity, you first take a pretest and have the pretest scored. The MAP program analyzes your pretest, shows a detailed breakdown of pretest results, and recommends up to four different prescriptive drills that should help you avoid making similar errors in the future. (If you made more than four different types of errors, MAP shows the top four problems that need addressing.) You can then work on the prescriptive drills.

2.9.16 Tennis Game

The tennis game is an interactive game designed to help you improve speed, accuracy, and concentration on the keyboard. The tennis game is accessible from the Games and Skillbuilding menus. Results from completed matches are saved by GDP and appear in your Portfolio.

Before playing the tennis game, you set up the game using the Tennis Game Options screen. On this screen, you specify a Skill Level (from 1 to 5 – the skill level determines the speed of play, with 5 being the fastest speed), Number of Sets (1 or 3, with each set consisting of six games), Sound (on or off), Demonstration Mode (you select this option to see the Tennis Game operate by itself), and Select the Game Keys (Select Learned Keys, All Keys, by Fingers, by Hand, by Row, or individually selected – selected keys are highlighted in green).

Playing the Tennis Game

To begin playing the game, click the **Next** arrow on the Tennis Options screen. The Tennis Game screen opens. Two players appear on the play screen: your player is in the left court and your opponent is in the right court. The scoreboard appears at the top of the screen. To begin the game and serve the ball, press **Enter**. The ball is served to your opponent's court. When your opponent returns the serve, a keyboard character appears on screen in a white box covering part of the net. The goal is for you to type that character as quickly as possible.

- If you type the correct character before the ball crosses the net, your player wins the point.
- If you type the correct character after the ball crosses the net but before the ball reaches your player, no point is scored and the rally continues.
- If you type the wrong character or type the correct character but after the ball reaches your player, the opponent wins the point.

After each point, you press **Enter** to serve for the next point. At the end of a game, the scoreboard is updated and the next game begins. At the end of the match (i.e., after either 1 or 3 sets), the winner is announced, your scores are recorded in the Student Portfolio, and the program asks if you want a rematch.

Scoring follows standard tennis rules. A game is won by the first person to win 4 points (15, 30, 40, game), but must be won by at least two points. The score for a game tied at 40 to 40 is called "deuce," and the score for a player who has one point more than the other player (above 40) is called "advantage." A set is won by the first player to win 6 games, but must be won by at least two games. At any time during the match, you can review the rules of the game by clicking the **Rules** button in the bottom right-hand corner of the play screen.

At any time during the game, you can exit by pressing **Esc** or clicking an active toolbar button. If the match is incomplete, GDP does not save the results.

2.9.17 Pace Car Game

One of the best ways to develop speed and control errors is through the use of paced exercises. The Pace Car game uses the same paragraphs as Paced Practice. The Pace Car activity is an interactive game that uses a race car game to help you build speed and accuracy. This game is accessible from the Games menu and from the Skillbuilding menu. Results from completed games are saved by GDP and appear in your Portfolio.

The game can be played in either Paced or Sprint mode. In Paced mode, the paragraphs are written to contain an exact number of words to be typed within two minutes. Your goal is to complete each paragraph within two minutes with no more than one error (The screen shows a pace car just ahead of your car, and the object is to keep up with, but not overtake, the pace car.). In Sprint mode, the screen shows cars that are faster and slower than your car, and the object is to type as quickly and as accurately as possible in order to pass the cars ahead of you. When you achieve your speed and accuracy goals, GDP progresses you to the next, more difficult, paragraph. Because each paragraph is longer than the previous one, you are forced to push yourself to the next higher speed.

Playing the Pace Car Game

Before playing the game for the first time, you will take a 1-minute entry timing to determine your beginning speed. Type the paragraph. If you finish before time is up, press **Enter** and start typing the paragraph a second time. When time is up, the game begins. (If your entry timing has too many errors, GDP will have you retake the entry timing so that a more appropriate beginning speed can be used for the game.) When playing the game in Paced mode, you try to keep up with, but not overtake, the pace car. If you type too quickly, you will collide with the pace car and be penalized. When playing the game in Sprint mode, you type the text as quickly and as accurately as possible in order to pass cars ahead of your car. If you finish before time is up in either version of the pace car game, press **Enter** and start retyping the paragraph.

When time is up, your text is scored and you are given the opportunity to review your scored text. At any time during the game, you can exit by pressing **Esc** or clicking an active toolbar button. If you do not finish the game, GDP does not save your results.

2.9.18 Tests

The timed writing tests and the document processing tests for each part of the textbook are accessible from the Lessons menu after the last lesson in a part (group of 20 lessons). The part tests are included in your textbook. If you are taking an alternate part test, be sure to get the text from your instructor. The easiest way to access a test is to click the *Tests Only* link on the Lessons menu. Click the down arrow next to the test name field to open the Test drop-down menu. Click on a test to open its menu.

Tests are available for Parts 2 through 6. When you are ready to take a test, notify your instructor to be sure you have the correct material needed for the test.

The results of the timed writing tests will be recorded in your Portfolio and the copy will be treated like any other completed exercise. Document processing tests are scored for keystrokes only. Be sure to print a copy of these documents so that your instructor can check formatting manually.

Chapter 3 — Reference Guide

3.1 GDP Drop-Down Menus

Drop-down menus can be accessed from the menu bar running across the top of the GDP screen.

3.1.1 File Menu

Portfolio...	Use *Portfolio...* to view or print a report showing your scores on completed GDP exercises as well as scored text for any exercise. The report can be restricted by date range, lesson number, or exercise type.
Performance Chart...	Use *Performance Chart...* to view or print a graph showing your speed and accuracy on all timed writings in a part (group of 20 lessons).*
Import Student Data...	This feature is used to import data from one GDP location to another to allow for working on GDP in multiple locations.*
Export Student Data...	This feature is used to create an export file of your data, which can then be imported into GDP on another workstation (for example, if you work on GDP in more than one location.)*
Go To Word Processor	Use *Go To Word Processor* to link to Microsoft Word 2000, 2002, or 2003 to work on documents that are not included in the textbook or print copies of completed documents without accessing those documents through the Lessons menu.
E-mail Instructor...	Use *E-mail Instructor...* to create and send an e-mail message to your instructor.
Delete Files	Use *Delete Files* to delete your text for selected lessons and exercise types.*
Exit GDP	Use *Exit GDP* to exit the program.*

*If this feature is inactive on your menu, press **Escape** or click the Lessons icon to return to the Lessons menu.

Note	When *Delete Files* is used, just your scored text is deleted. Scores are maintained in your Portfolio, but the asterisk preceding the date in the Student Profile (indicating that a Detailed Report is available) is removed.

3.1.2 Options Menu

Personal Information...	Use *Personal Information* to enter information such as your initials, a byline, e-mail address, and password for distance learning features. GDP opens the Personal Information form when you need to add or change information.
Settings...	Use *Settings...* to specify browser, word processing, and certain other settings for using GDP.

3.1.3 Help Menu

Program Overview	Use *Program Overview* for a quick text-only introduction to GDP.
Reference Manual	Use *Reference Manual* for detailed instructions on formatting the various types of documents produced in GDP.
Tutorial	Use *Tutorial* to take a short multimedia tour of the GDP program and learn how it works.
MAP Slide Show	Use *MAP Slide Show* to directly access the multi-media tutorial that explains GDP's Misstroke Analysis and Prescription program (This tutorial is also accessible via the **View MAP Slide Show** button on the MAP introduction screen.).
Help	Use *Help* to view the contents tab for Help topics.
Live Update	Use *Live Update* to see if any new updates are available for GDP (Note: You will be notified automatically if this is checked off within your settings.).
About...	Use *About...* to determine which version of the program is being used. This information is useful when calling customer support.

3.2 GDP Toolbar

The toolbar is a row of buttons running across the top of the GDP screen across the Navigation Menu. Use the toolbar for quick access to frequently used features and on-screen guidance. When you rest the mouse pointer over a button on the toolbar, a Tooltip shows the name of the button and the keyboard shortcut, if there is one. See 3.3 Keyboard Shortcuts).

Upload — Use this button, which is active in all GDP 10th Editions versions, to send your data files to the Instructor Management Web site.

E-mail — Use this button to create and send an e-mail message to your instructor.

Web — Use this button to access your campus Web site, if a URL is specified in your settings.

Portfolio — Use this button to access your reports.

Reference Manual — Use this button for help with formatting the various types of documents included in GDP.

Help — Use this button to get information about how GDP works.

3.3 Keyboard Shortcuts

Sometimes it is easier to use a keyboard shortcut rather than to remove your hand from the keyboard to activate the mouse. Here are the keyboard shortcuts in GDP:

Alt	**Menu bar** Activates the menu bar.
Alt+↗	**Next** Moves to the next screen in an exercise.
Alt+→	**Previous** Moves back to the previous screen in an exercise.
Ctrl+A	**Language Arts menu** Opens the Language Arts menu.
Ctrl+G	**Games menu** Opens the Games menu.
Ctrl+L	**Lessons menu** Opens the Lessons menu.

Ctrl+M	**MAP program**	Opens the MAP program.
Ctrl+P	**Portfolio**	Provides access to student reports.
Ctrl+R	**Restart timed writing**	Allows the student to restart most timed writings within the first 15 seconds.
Ctrl+S	**Skillbuilding menu**	Opens the Skillbuilding menu.
Ctrl+Shft+M	**Reference Manual**	Provides formatting guidelines for various types of documents.
Ctrl+T	**Timed Writings menu**	Opens the Timed Writings menu.
Ctrl+X	**Exit**	Exits the program. Not active within an exercise (press **Esc** to cancel the exercise first).
Esc	**Previous Menu**	Cancels an exercise. If a scored exercise, the report is marked canceled.
F1	**Help**	Opens Help.

3.4 Scoring and Error Marking

3.4.1 Error Marking

Errors in scored copy are marked as follows:

- <u>Underlined red</u>: all incorrect words.
- <green in angle brackets>: all omitted words, tabs (designated as <[T]>), and hard returns (designated as <¶>).
- {Blue in braces}: incorrectly inserted words, tabs (designated as {[T]}), and hard returns (designated as {¶}).

Examples

Incorrect word	You **cane** go.
Omitted word	You <**can**>go
Inserted word	You {**perhaps**}can go
Inserted Tab	{[T]}You can go.
Omitted tab	<[T]>You can go.
Inserted hard return	You can go.{¶}
Omitted hard return	You can go.<¶>

3.4.2 One Space/Two-Space Option

GDP offers the option of typing one space or two spaces after punctuation: periods (at ends of sentences only), question marks, exclamation points, and colons. This option is set on a class-wide level by your instructor, and affects all scored activities, including document processing exercises. Check with your instructor, as typing one space after punctuation when the setting is for two spaces (and vice-versa) will result in scoring errors. The default in your settings allows for one space between sentences.

3.4.3 Error Scores

The most widely used rules for determining the error score on a timed writing are the International Typewriting Contest Rules. According to these rules, every actual word that differs from the original source copy counts as 1 error. The determination of errors by GDP is based on these rules.

3.4.4 Speed (WPM) Calculation

In all but numeric keypad exercises, GDP calculates, displays, and records your speed as wpm—that is, as words per minute. A word equals 5 keystrokes (letters, spaces, tabs, hard returns, etc.). Like all other scores, each wpm score is based on the copy in the book: incorrectly added strokes are not counted; similarly, incorrectly omitted strokes are not subtracted.

The words-per-minute (wpm) speed is based on the following formulas.

- 12-second timings: Each letter or space counts as 1 wpm.
- 30-second timings: Every 5 keystrokes (letters, spaces, tabs, and hard returns)
  count as 2 wpm.
- Minute timings: The total number of 5-letter words is divided by the number of minutes in the timing.

$$25 \text{ words} \div 1 \text{ minute} = 25 \text{ wpm}$$
$$50 \text{ words} \div 2 \text{ minute} = 25 \text{ wpm}$$
$$75 \text{ words} \div 3 \text{ minute} = 25 \text{ wpm}$$
$$125 \text{ words} \div 5 \text{ minute} = 25 \text{ wpm}$$

Note | Speed in numeric keypad exercises is reported in seconds, corresponding to the number of seconds it takes you to complete the exercise. For example, S 193 indicates that it took you 193 seconds to complete the exercise.

Chapter 4 — Troubleshooting

If you have any questions or problems as you install GDP or work with your data files, first make sure that your system meets the requirements outlined in 1.2 System Requirements on page 1 and that you followed the exact procedure outlined in 1.4

Installing GDP on page 3. Next, check this troubleshooting guide. If you experience a problem not covered here or not remedied by following a suggestion listed here, record exactly at what point in the program the problem occurred and a description of what happened when you encountered the problem. Then call McGraw-Hill/Irwin's technical support group at **1-800-331-5094** (8 A.M.–5 P.M. CST).

4.1 Installation and Start-Up

Problem: When installing GDP, the Select Destination Location dialog box indicates that the drive does not have sufficient free space.

> *Explanation:* GDP requires approximately 175 MB of free hard-disk space, which the selected drive does not have.
>
> *Suggestion:* If you have another hard disk drive with at least 175 MB of free space, select that other drive and click **OK** to continue the GDP installation. Otherwise, press **Esc** to cancel the installation, then free up at least 175 MB of space and run the GDP installation again.

Problem: When starting the program, a dialog box prompts you to insert a blank data disk.

> *Explanation 1:* GDP has been configured to store student work on a floppy disk, and the program was started without a floppy disk in the floppy drive.
>
> *Suggestion:* Insert a floppy disk (a blank disk if you have not yet worked with GDP or your data disk if you have already done some work in GDP) in the floppy drive.

	If you do not want to store your data on floppy disks, re-install GDP and specify a different student data location.
Explanation 2:	The floppy disk is unreadable.
Suggestion:	Put a new, formatted floppy disk in the floppy drive.

Problem: When starting the program, a dialog box displays an "E003 Path not found" error message.

Explanation: GDP cannot find the data directory you specified for the student data location when you installed GDP.

Suggestion: Make sure that the shortcut for the GDP program includes the full and correct path to your data files. Use Windows Explorer to verify that your data files and directories have not been moved or deleted.

Problem: Launching the program from the GDP program directory results in an error.

Explanation: The GDP program needs to know the student data location when it launches. This information is built into the program icon (shortcut) in the Irwin Keyboarding program group.

Suggestion: Always start GDP from the Start menu, selecting *Programs, Irwin Keyboarding,* and then the GDP program icon for the configuration you have installed (i.e., *GDP Home*).

4.2 Document Processing and Scoring

Problem: For document processing exercises, GDP fails to start the word processor.

Explanation: The Microsoft Word 2000, 2002, or 2003 location specified on your settings is incorrect or is the location for a different version of the word processor.

	Suggestion:	Select *Settings...* from the Options drop-down menu to access your settings. Then verify the full path to your installation of Microsoft Word 2000, 2002, or 2003.
Problem:		The GDP/Return to GDP menu option in Microsoft Word 2000, 2002, or 2003 does not work.
	Explanation:	Templates that are added to the startup group for Word when a Hewlett Packard printer is installed can be the cause of this problem. Hewlett Packard adds a file so that the printer can interface with HP's By Design program.
	Suggestion:	Locate the file called bs2000.dot, bs2002.dot, or bs2003.dot, and move it from its default location to the Templates directory.
Problem:		A document or exercise does not get scored.
	Explanation:	The exercise is not supposed to be scored. Practice documents, warmups, new key presentations, as well as certain practices and skillbuilding and document processing exercises are not scored.
	Suggestion:	If you want to score documents manually, print copies of your documents from within Word. If you want to score other unscored exercises manually, print copies of the completed exercises from your Portfolio as follows: click the **Portfolio** button on the toolbar, specify Portfolio options, click **OK** to view the Student Portfolio, select the exercise(s) you want printed, and click **Print Text**.
Problem:		Scored copy contains numerous "<¶>" or "{¶}" marks.
	Explanation:	You did not follow the word wrap setting indicated in the exercise header at the top of the screen. A "<¶>" occurs in scored copy where word wrap is off and you fail to press **Enter** at the end of the line. A "{¶}" occurs in scored copy where word wrap is on and you mistakenly press **Enter** at the end of the line.
	Suggestion:	Retype the exercise following the word wrap setting in the exercise header.

4.3 Sound

Problem: No sound plays at the end of timed writings or when the restart period is over in a timed writing.

Explanation: GDP uses the Default Sound to signal the end of a timed writing and the end of the restart period. Your computer either has <none> (no audible sound) assigned to the Default Sound, or it has speakers attached to the computer but not turned on.

Suggestion: First, check to make sure that the Default Sound in your Windows Sounds control panel is assigned an audible sound such as ding, chimes, or chord. (If you are not familiar with the Sounds control panel, refer to the User's Guide for your operating system.) Also make sure that your speakers (if any are attached to your computer) are turned on and work.

4.4 E-mail/Web

Problem: The **E-mail** button does not work on the GDP toolbar.

Explanation 1: Your system may not be configured with MAPI. When sending e-mail, GDP uses MAPI and the system's default e-mail address.

Suggestion: Make sure your computer uses a MAPI-compliant e-mail system and that a default e-mail address is set up. Otherwise, use e-mail outside of GDP for sending and receiving e-mail messages.

Explanation 2: Either your e-mail address or the instructor's e-mail address is missing or incorrect in your settings.

Suggestion: Access GDP, then access *Settings...* from the Options drop-down menu, and enter the correct information for both your and your instructor's e-mail addresses.

Problem:	The **Web** button does not work on the GDP toolbar.	
Explanation:	The correct URL for your campus Web site is not specified in your settings.	
Suggestion:	Access GDP, then access *Settings...* from the Options drop-down menu, and enter the correct URL for your campus Web site	

4.5 HELP and Reference Manual

Problem: Clicking on the **Help** button or the **Reference Manual** button launches America Online (AOL).

Explanation: Both the GDP Help file and the GDP Reference Manual are composed as HTML Help files. When you launch an HTML Help file, it opens in the system's default browser. If AOL is your default Internet Service Provider (ISP), it also serves as your default browser. Therefore, opening the HTML Help file or Reference Manual will also start up AOL

Suggestion: The first time you click on **Help** or **Reference Manual**, AOL will launch, in addition to the Help or Reference Manual file. Please note that you do not need to log-on to AOL in order to use the H elp or Reference Manual system. Minimize AOL to your taskbar instead of exiting from the program. The next time you click on **Help** or **Reference Manual**, the file will display without also displaying AOL.

4.6 Distance-Learning/Instructor Management Web Site

Problem: When using the distance-learning feature, you are not able to upload your data to the Instructor Management Web site via e-mail.

Explanation 1: Your system may not be configured with MAPI. GDP uses MAPI and the system's default e-mail address to upload data to the Instructor

Management Web site. E-mail systems such as Microsoft Outlook are MAPI-compliant. AOL and CompuServe have their own e-mail systems, which are not MAPI-compliant.

Suggestion: The preferred method is to send the data via the Student Upload Web Site. Click **Upload** in the top toolbar and select Upload Work to Student Upload Web Site. Otherwise, set up a MAPI-compliant e-mail system on your computer. If you continue to use GDP on a computer with a non-MAPI e-mail system, you can export your work and, using your own e-mail system, send the export file as an e-mail attachment to the Instructor Management Web site.

Explanation 2: Your e-mail system or Internet connection is down or the transmission is interrupted.

Suggestion: Verify that your e-mail system and Internet connection are working properly outside of GDP. For example, you can send an e-mail message to yourself.

Explanation 3: Your instructor has not yet registered you on the Instructor Management Web site.

Suggestion: Ask your instructor to register you on the Instructor Management Web site.

Explanation 4: Your e-mail address does not match what your instructor entered as your e-mail address on the Instructor Management Web site.

Suggestion: Access GDP and select *Settings...* from the Options drop-down menu. Verify that your e-mail address in the Settings dialog box is correct, and tell your instructor what the correct address is. Also verify with your instructor that the McGraw-Hill's Instructor Management Web site's email address in the Settings dialog box is the correct e-mail address for the Instructor Management Web site. Make necessary changes in the Settings dialog box. If your e-mail address is wrong on the Instructor Management Web site, your instructor can correct it there.

Explanation 5: Your password does not match the password on the Student Web Site.

Suggestion: Once your instructor has registered you to a class, you will receive an e-mail with a password in order to access the Student Web Site. Using the e-mailed password, you must first log-on to the Student Web Site and change the password to match your password within the GDP software. To edit your password within GDP, access the GDP software and select *Personal Information...* from the Options drop-down menu. Edit the 'Password to upload data' field and then retype your password in the appropriate field.

Problem: You receive an e-mail stating that the GDP data was successfully received by the Instructor Management Web site, but your data does not appear when the instructor tries to view it at the Web site or within your Student Portfolio on the Student Web Site.

Explanation: The e-mail address and password that identify you at the Instructor Management Web site and Student Web Site are the address and password stored in your Personal Information, which are not necessarily the address and password at the workstation you're using to send data to the site.

Suggestion: Make sure that your e-mail address and password in *Personal Information...* (accessible from the Options drop-down menu) are the same as the e-mail address and password your instructor has for you at the Instructor Management Web site. In addition, verify that your passwords match in the GDP software and the Student Web Site.

4.7 Data Storage Limits

Problem: A message indicates that the data disk is full.

Explanation: You are about to exceed the available disk space and need to free disk space before continuing.

Suggestion: When this message appears, click **OK** to close the message dialog box. Exit GDP and make a copy of the full data disk, if you wish. Then restart GDP, and select *Delete Files* from the File drop-down menu. In the Delete Files dialog box, select the lesson(s) and exercise type(s) to delete and click **OK**. In the Confirm dialog box, click **Yes** or **Yes to All** to delete the selected files. When you delete files, you delete text (Detailed Reports) only. Scores for exercises with deleted text are retained in the Student Portfolio.

Problem: A message indicates that the Student Portfolio file is full.

Explanation: The maximum number of exercises that can be listed on a Student Portfolio is 1,000. When the Student Portfolio exceeds 1,000 exercises, the program automatically overwrites exercises starting with the oldest first. When this happens, you will not be able to access old exercises that are overwritten in the Student Portfolio.

Suggestion: Make a copy of the data disk (or data directory), to have in case you want to access old exercises that will not be accessible when GDP is used in the future. Then continue using GDP.

Index

A
About... (Help menu), 46
Accessing the Web, 25
Alt, 47
Alt+left arrow, 47
Alt+right arrow, 47
AOL, 25, 54

B
Backing up student data files, 6
Browser, 12

C
CompuServe, 25, 55
Ctrl+A, 47
Ctrl+G, 47
Ctrl+L, 47
Ctrl+M, 48
Ctrl+P, 48
Ctrl+R, 48
Ctrl+S, 48
Ctrl+Shft+M, 48
Ctrl+T, 48
Ctrl+X, 48
Custom Timed Writings, 17, 35

D
Delete Files, 19, 45, 57
Detailed Report, 9, 19–22, 30
Diagnostic Practice, 8, 39
Distance learning, 8, 9, 13, 25–27, 46, 54
Document processing, 36, 44, 51
Drop-down menus, 16, 45

E
E-mail, 9, 12, 13, 25–29, 45, 47, 53–58
E-mail Instructor..., 25, 45
Error marking, 48
Esc key, 15, 43, 44, 48, 50
Exercise screens, 15, 16
Exit GDP, 15, 45
Export Student Data..., 45
Export to HTML, 21, 32
Exporting student data, 23

F
F1, 48
File menu, 45
Floppy disks, 2, 5, 7, 9, 23, 32, 50
Full Editing settings, 13

G
Games menu, 18, 47
GDP configurations, 3
Go to Word Processor, 18, 38, 45

H
Help button, 46
Help menu, 46
Home Distance-Learning version, 4
HTML, 21, 32, 54

I
Import/Export feature, 23
Importing student data, 23
Installation problems, 50
Installing GDP, 3–6
Instructor Management Web site, 9, 11, 15, 26, 47, 54
Instructor's e-mail address, 12, 25
Internet, 27, 31, 54

K
Keyboard shortcuts, 47

L
Language arts exercises, 17, 39
Language Arts menu, 17, 47
Lessons menu, 14, 17, 47
License Agreement dialog box, 4
Linking to Word outside of an exercise, 18
Logging on, 9, 28
Log-on screen, 11

M
MAPI, 25, 53–55
Menu bar, 16, 47
Menus, 45
Microsoft Outlook, 25, 55
Misstroke Analysis and Prescription, 17, 41, 46

N

Navigation menu, 16
Next button, 17
New key drills, 34
Numeric keypad exercises, 41

O

Open timed writings, 17, 36
Options menu, 46
Overview, 8, 46

P

Pace car game, 18, 43
Performance Chart, 22
Performance Chart..., 45
Personal Information..., 46
Portfolio, 18–22
Portfolio button, 47
Portfolio..., 45
Pretest/Practice/Posttest, 36
Previous button, 17
Printing student work, 18
Problems, 50–57
Program Overview, 8, 46
Progressive Practice, 39
Proofreading, 13, 38, 41

R

Reference Manual, 9, 38, 46, 48, 54
Reference Manual button, 46
Required materials, 2
Requirements, 1

S

Scoring, 33, 48, 51
Select Destination Location dialog box, 4, 50
Select Student Data Location dialog box, 5
Settings, 7, 11–12, 25, 32, 46, 51
Settings dialog box, 12
Settings..., 11, 46, 52
Shortcuts, 47
Skillbuilding menu, 17
Sound, 53
Speed calculation, 49
Spelling, 41
Status bar, 16
Student data storage location, 5
Student materials, 2
Student's e-mail address, 12
Student Portfolio, 9, 18–24, 30–32, 33
Sustained Practice, 40
System requirements, 1

T

Technique Practice, 40
Tennis game, 42–43
Tests, 44
Timed writings, 8, 13, 17, 35–36, 48Ed writings
Timed Writings menu, 17
Title bar, 16
Toolbar, 16, 47
Troubleshooting, 50–57
Tutorial, 11, 17, 46

U

Upload button, 26, 47
Updating student data on the Instructor Management Web site, 15, 23, 24, 26

V

Viewing and printing student work, 18

W

Warm-ups, 34
Web, 25, 26
Web browser, 12
Web button, 47
Word 2000, 2002 or 2003, 1, 8, 12, 18, 22, 31, 37, 51, 52
Word processor, 12, 18, 45
Word wrap, 33, 52
Working on lesson exercises, 14–18

Z

Zip disks, 2, 5

NOTES